ALAN MOORE: CONVERSATIONS

Conversations with Comic Artists   M. Thomas Inge, General Editor

Alan Moore: Conversations

Edited by Eric L. Berlatsky

University Press of Mississippi   Jackson

www.upress.state.ms.us

The University Press of Mississippi is a member of the Association of
American University Presses.

First printing 2012
∞
Library of Congress Cataloging-in-Publication Data

Moore, Alan, 1953–
Alan Moore : conversations / edited by Eric L. Berlatsky.
    p. cm. — (Conversations with comic artists)
Includes index.
ISBN 978-1-61703-158-8 (cloth : alk. paper) — ISBN 978-1-61703-159-5 (pbk. : alk. paper)
— ISBN 978-1-61703-160-1 (ebook) 1. Moore, Alan, 1953–—Interviews. I. Berlatsky, Eric L.,
1972– II. Title.
PN6737.M66Z46 2012
741.5'942—dc22
[B]   2011009838

British Library Cataloging-in-Publication Data available

CONTENTS

INTRODUCTION

Alan Moore's privileged position in the history of comics is certain. It is also complex and contradictory. He is, perhaps, still best known for *Watchmen* (1986–87), though his prodigious output since has reduced that epoch-making series to just one of his many accomplishments in the field. *Watchmen* itself is a contradictory text, a superhero story about the dangers of heroism, a Cold War tale that also eerily predicts the events and aftermath of 9/11, a meditation on the philosophy of time that presents the reader with two seemingly mutually exclusive temporalities, sequential and simultaneous. It is a series that was originally published in the United States, takes place there, and comments on its status as a Cold War superpower, but is written and drawn by two Englishmen. Created for one of the "big two" corporate comics companies, whose copyrighted characters and work-for-hire contracts often allow little room for creative freedom, it is written by one of the most iconoclastic, rebellious, and freethinking figures in the medium. These tensions and ambivalences helped make *Watchmen* that great rarity, a text that is both widely popular and critically lauded. Its selection as one of *Time* magazine's "100 Best English-Language Novels since 1923," merely cemented the broad consensus about the book's quality and importance. Along with Art Spiegelman's Pulitzer-winning *Maus* and Frank Miller's *Batman: The Dark Knight Returns*, both also published in 1986, the book has been frequently credited with kickstarting the newfound perception that comics were "not just for kids anymore" and would henceforth be taken seriously. While comics may have taken several steps backward before reaching its current position, wherein sequential juxtaposed images are all but assumed to be a valid and interesting aesthetic medium, and even a commercial draw, *Watchmen* certainly played a significant role in this cultural transformation.

For Moore, however, the contradictions and complexities go well beyond his most popular and fêted creation. Known as the single most important figure to shift the balance of power and influence in mainstream comics away from the artist and towards the writer, he began his career as a little-known and most often pseudonymous "cartoonist," responsible for both the words and images in his weekly funny-animal newspaper strip, *Maxwell the Magic Cat* (under the name "Jill de Ray") and a weekly half-page feature in *Sounds*, a national alternative music magazine (under the name "Curt Vile"). These strips find Moore primarily as a humorist, architect of wryly dark and off-kilter gags (*Maxwell*) and a series of giddy, trippy parodies of the mystery and science fiction genres (*Roscoe Moscow* and *The Stars My Degradation*, respectively). The inventive, if occasionally cramped, use of page space in the two *Sounds* strips prefigured Moore's innovative breakdowns in his later work, despite the fact that by then, he was no longer his own artist and was directing layouts in legendarily elaborate full scripts.

In contrast to these humble beginnings, his worldwide renown was built on the brief period during which he was writing superheroes for DC Comics, from 1983 to 1989. During that time, DC published *Watchmen*, *V for Vendetta* (begun for *Warrior* magazine in England), *Batman: The Killing Joke*, almost four years worth of the monthly horror/superhero series, *Swamp Thing*, and a variety of smaller projects. Before coming to DC, Moore wrote superheroes for Marvel UK (*Captain Britain*) and *Warrior* (*Marvelman*) in England. Indeed, at one point during 1982–83, he and Alan Davis (illustrator of both strips) had a monopoly on superhero comics created in England. From this, it might seem that Moore was inevitably married to the long-underwear adventure stories that dominated the industry since the 1960s. In fact, however, Moore's relationship to superheroes was always an ambivalent affair. While *Captain Britain* (and *Swamp Thing*) functioned within the boundaries of superhero genre tropes, if intelligently and intricately so, both *Marvelman* (called *Miracleman* in the U.S.) and *Watchmen* took the genre apart from the inside. Moore's restlessness with superheroes could be seen elsewhere, as well. It came forth in a feminist essay about the poor treatment of women in mainstream superhero comics, in an "affectionate character assassination" of Marvel boss Stan Lee (both essays in *Daredevils*, a 1983 Marvel UK comics magazine), and in his unwillingness to be confined to that genre, despite its market dominance.

In the admittedly more flexible British market, Moore wrote straight science fiction (*Future Shocks*, *Skizz*, *Dr. Who*, and *Star Wars* shorts), feminist space opera (*Halo Jones*), sci-fi comedy (*D.R. and Quinch*), horror-comedy (*The Bojeffries Saga*), and dystopian noir (*V for Vendetta*) in addition to *Maxwell* and the *Sounds* strips. On the other side of the Atlantic, his mainstream superhero work was spliced with horror, noir, and science fiction, while he kept a hand in smaller press adventure comics and the occasional creator-owned "alternative" foray. His much-publicized departure from DC in 1988–89, and his short-lived abandonment of superheroes was then less a sudden career about-face than it was a conscious choice to emphasize certain elements of his trajectory over others, sacrificing a measure of economic security for creative freedom when it seemed these two strands were no longer reconcilable. The conflict between economic solvency and creative liberation did not spring suddenly on Moore in the late eighties, however. Rather, it had continually been present in his working life for nearly the entirety of the previous decade. A proud member of the Northampton working class, Moore was heavily influenced in his comics-reading youth both by the Stan Lee/Jack Kirby Marvel Age and by the underground comix of Robert Crumb and his contemporaries. While Mort Weisinger–era *Superman* was an admitted moral exemplar for the young Moore, among his creative idols were the iconoclastic writer, William Burroughs, and the avant-garde musician/composer, Brian Eno. Faced with economic hardship quite often in his youth, especially in the aftermath of his expulsion from secondary school for dealing acid, Moore was continually faced with the choice of money or creative freedom. He tended to choose both.

In the early part of the eighties, Moore split his time writing between the corporate UK sci-fi weekly magazine, *2000 AD*, and Dez Skinn's newly founded *Warrior* magazine, which offered the possibility of creator-owned strips. While Moore's participation in *Warrior* derived partially from dissatisfaction in the ways creators were treated in the corporate environment of *2000 AD*, the subsequent jump from *Warrior* to DC was precipitated, at least somewhat, by dissatisfaction with the economic rewards that *Warrior* finally yielded. Indeed, Moore was willing to sign away his rights in *V for Vendetta* for the remuneration offered by DC. So, while Moore's move to DC was never a wholesale move to "large" corporate comics, his later departure was also never a complete abandonment of superheroes or the steady income they offered.

The conflict between profitable superhero genre work and "serious" creator-owned material continued through the nineties, despite Moore's rejection of both Marvel and DC. With the emergence of Image Comics as a third "major" superhero publisher, Moore was able to finance his longer, more complicated projects by writing *1963* and *Spawn* (for Image), *WildC.A.T.s* (for Wildstorm), *Supreme* (for a variety of publishers), and related titles. The real work of the decade, though, was on the creator-owned side of the ledger with *Big Numbers*, *From Hell*, and *Lost Girls*. *Big Numbers* (with Bill Sienkiewicz) was perhaps the most ambitious project, focusing on the arrival of a U.S.-style shopping mall in a thinly veiled replica of Moore's native Northampton, but the book became an economic sinkhole, forcing Moore to abandon his recently established independent publishing venture, Mad Love. *From Hell*, a metafictive retelling of the Jack-the-Ripper murders and aftermath, took nearly ten years to complete and shuttled from publisher to serial publisher, as did *Lost Girls*, a lengthy pornography starring Alice (from Wonderland), Dorothy (from Oz) and Wendy (from *Peter Pan*). The latter volume took sixteen years to see its way to final publication.

The delay of the full-length book versions of *From Hell* and *Lost Girls* until 1999 and 2006 respectively made most of the nineties seem like a comparatively creative fallow period for Moore, at least for those not following the small presses' inconsistent serialization of these works. The two giant volumes are testimony, however, to Moore's pursuit of independent and creative projects outside of the superhero mainstream. *From Hell*'s focus on magic, masonry, and murder in grisly anatomical detail and scratchy black and white Eddie Campbell pencils signaled a rejection of the mainstream's preoccupation with four-color superheroics regardless of how "grim and gritty" they became in *Watchmen*'s aftermath. *Lost Girls*' explicit depiction and examination of the conflicting natures of sex and violence (in lush Melinda Gebbie inks and colored pencils) did the same, if in a decidedly different direction. For that reason, it was certainly surprising when Moore returned to monthly superhero comics almost full time, indirectly for DC no less, with his line of "America's Best Comics" (ABC) in 1999. It was, perhaps, less shocking when he "retired" from mainstream comics again in 2005, once more over corporate interference and misuse of his creative properties.

More recently, Moore's focus has been on his performance art and music (always a part of his repertoire), his Northampton "underground" magazine, *Dodgem Logic*, and his as-yet-incomplete second novel, *Jerusalem*. This final (?) turn away from corporate comics has also been a turn away from and against film (after disastrous Hollywood adaptations of several of his works) and even a turn away from the comics medium itself, with only very occasional installments of *The League of Extraordinary Gentlemen* (originally linked to ABC but owned by Moore and Kevin O'Neill) and 2010's Lovecraftian miniseries, *Neonomicon*, to sustain his comics followers. The struggle between independence and creativity on one hand and the economic rewards of corporate hire seems to have been won, at this date, by the former, although such a victory would likely not have been possible without investment in the latter.

While this dichotomy in Moore's working life sheds significant light on the nature of each individual project, it too is not the end of the contradictions and paradoxes an overview of his career yields. Also important, for instance, is Moore's simultaneous fascination with contemporary science and mathematics and his seemingly contradictory 1993 conversion to "magic." Declaring himself a wizard/magician on his fortieth birthday, Moore began (by his own claim) communing with other-dimensional beings, usually under the influence of some mind-altering substance. While *Watchmen* engaged with Einsteinian and quantum physics, and *Big Numbers* explored the significance of fractal mathematics and chaos theory, Moore's turn to magic, the kabbalah, Aleister Crowley, and his own notion of neoplatonic "Idea Space" would seem to be a turn toward the irrational. In fact, however, the "magic" Moore most avidly preaches is the power of the human imagination, particularly through art and writing. If Moore communicates with beings from "another dimension," he quite often admits that these beings may well come from his own mind, just as the snake god he worships is actually a hand puppet. Moore's public performance as a mystical madman, then, seems to have more to do with the celebration of human creativity than it does with a leap into insanity, although the line between the two is sometimes blurry. Either way, to suggest that Moore moves from "science to magic" over the course of his career proves to be fallacious.

The early *Swamp Thing* is already invested in mystical/magical ideas (providing the initial spark for DC's entire line of magical and horror titles with the Vertigo line, despite Moore's objections) and seems like a direct, if more entertaining, precursor to the didactic magic textbook provided in *Promethea*. Likewise, the scientific and mathematical trappings of the early *Halo Jones*, *Watchmen*, and *Big Numbers* (all written before the "conversion") are reflected in the "science-heroes" of Moore's latter-day ABC universe, particularly Jack B. Quick (from *Tomorrow Stories*) and Tom Strong, whose stories present cutting-edge scientific and science fiction notions in a playful register. If anything, Moore's preoccupation with both science *and* magic seems to be a search for some kind of order in the universe (or a longing for such order), some pattern that may be found in fractal expressions of chaos theory, or of human consciousness as illustrated through magical ritual and understood through a kabbalistic mapping of symbolic terrain. Moore's claim, reprinted in this book, that he likes to "balance the mad howling diabolism with a dose of scientific reality" indicates his own consciousness of the seemingly contradictory nature of his fascination with both Reason and Imagination, and his intent to foreground and navigate those contradictions.

Some of the conflicts and discrepancies in Moore's thinking are less consciously sculpted, however. In the 2009 interview with Alex Musson included here, Moore expresses his disdain for genre distinctions, blaming them on a hypothetical "spotty clerk at W. H. Smith's." In so claiming, Moore stakes his claim that "art is art" and that there is no reason to separate the great writer/artists of fantasy, science fiction, or mystery from those of "realistic" art and literature. Moore's feelings about this have changed and adjusted over the years, however. After his first departure from DC, for instance, Moore, in a series of interviews with Gary Groth in *The Comics Journal*, declared his intentions to abandon superhero and other genre fiction altogether, asserting the very distinctions he would later deny. In these interviews, he notes that certain social, political, and philosophical ideas could not be expressed adequately within the confines of genres that dictated the nature of plots and characters to such a degree. If he wished to launch a critique of violence and power, as he was soon to do in *Lost Girls*, he notes that it would be impossible to do so in the superhero genre, which requires a punch-up at least once every twenty pages or so. *Big Numbers* was to be Moore's *magnum opus* in non-genre comics writing and his early-nineties interviews with Groth stake a significant claim for the devaluing of genre work in favor of more "realistic" comics. While Moore is careful not to dismiss genre out of hand, he does insist that "there are things I want to say that cannot be said within genre," and that the notion of genre writing is itself a "reductionist approach to the world" (Groth, "Big Words, pt. 2," 81–82). With the collapse of *Big Numbers* and Mad Love, however, Moore was soon back to genre work, sometimes with little attempt to transcend the genre (*Spawn*), sometimes with a clear effort to redefine or exceed genre's constraints (*From Hell, Lost Girls*), and sometimes with an attempt to reinvigorate moribund genres (The ABC line of comics). At the same time, Moore was writing and publishing his first novel, *Voice of the Fire*, which mixed genre elements and a focus on the history of Northampton. Regardless, Moore quickly abandoned the critique of genre that he aired with Groth during the *Big Numbers* days. These days, Moore insists that valuable work can be done in genre or outside of it, and that it is the external division of one category from another that is the problem, not the creative work itself. Indeed, Moore is quick to praise and discuss both writers of "high art" (like James Joyce) and masters of genre fiction (like Mervyn Peake, Jack Trevor Story, H. P. Lovecraft, and Michael Moorcock).

Moore's abiding interest in gender, feminism, and "queer" sexualities might also be read as contradictory in ways that may well be linked to his intermittent discomfort with genre. While the rounded portrayal of complex and strong-willed heroines like Halo Jones, Abby Cable (in *Swamp Thing*), and Laurie Juspeczyk (in *Watchmen*) reflect Moore's concerns in his early feminist essay in *Daredevils*, the superhero genre all but requires Laurie, for instance, to wear transparent and revealing underwear as her exploitative "uniform."

Likewise, for some feminists, Sally Jupiter's willingness to forgive her rapist in *Watchmen*, or Moore's capacity to play rape for laughs in *The League of Extraordinary Gentlemen* may read disturbingly as a male power fantasy, and not a particularly enlightened one. Likewise, while Moore's respect for and championing of alternative and queer sexualities is pervasive in his work (e. g. *Swamp Thing, Lost Girls, Top Ten, Watchmen, Promethea, League*, and "The Mirror of Love"), sometimes the portrayal of such sexualities comes uncomfortably close to reproducing patriarchal culture's exploitation of women as sex objects. The predominantly lesbian sex available in *Lost Girls*, for instance, may be read simultaneously as an affirmation of the value and humanity of both women and queer sexualities and as the kind of exploitative "girl on girl" action that appears in typical pornography, and which primarily appeals to the male gaze.

There is little doubt that Moore would have (lengthy and detailed) rejoinders to any such objections to his work. Indeed, pointing to these possible contradictions is not meant to accuse Moore of duplicity or incoherence, but to point to the value and usefulness of a collection of interviews that span Moore's career over a thirty-year period. In printing interviews from 1981 to 2009 in the same place, it becomes possible to see both Moore's consistently radical politics (and interest in anarchism), and his increasing and ever changing focus on sexual liberation and expression. It likewise becomes possible to see Moore's developing means of collaborative expression within the comics medium, his shifting attitude towards film, his increasing concentration on performance art and prose at the expense of his comics work, his changing attitude toward and relationship with other creators, and his initial enthusiasm toward, and then disillusionment with, the comics industry. Moore has never been shy about sharing his opinions, allowing for elaboration upon all of the issues discussed briefly above, and it is fascinating to see just how much those opinions remain consistent and where Moore has adjusted his views over the years.

Likewise, it is interesting to note how substantially Moore's interviewing persona has changed. While Moore has been accused of "reluctance to be interviewed" (Whitson 3), in fact, that rarely has been the case. While Moore was cheerfully willing to be interrogated early in his career for the purposes of publicity, or merely for the opportunity to chat with friends, fans, and peers about his work, he later became an adept manager of his public conversations, using them more purposefully to disseminate his views and construct his image. The interviews, in short, become another medium of performance. In a 2006 article about Moore and William Blake, Roger Whitson discusses

Moore's cultivation of a "celebrity fantasy," a public image of iconoclasm shared with his fans. Annalisa Di Liddo's recent critical study of Moore similarly focuses on his work, regardless of medium, as "performance." While the earliest Moore interviews find him cheerfully and humorously declaring comics writing "easy," voicing his as-yet-unrealized desire to revive Marvelman (even going so far as to close the interview with Marvelman's magic word), and mocking *X-Men* scribe Chris Claremont mercilessly, his later forays are much less informal, used to disseminate information about magic and kabbalah, on one hand, and to carry on a public relations war with DC Comics, on the other. While Warner Brothers has a publicity machine to manage the reception of its film versions of *V for Vendetta* and *Watchmen*, for instance, Moore only has his own minimal celebrity to express his dissenting opinion, and that same celebrity ensures that he can be interviewed when he wishes.

The series of interviews Moore gave about *Lost Girls* is an example of his savvy use of the form (and is represented in this book by Chris Mautner's 2006 conversation). Moore clearly knew that the contents of *Lost Girls* was potentially controversial, and he was willing to give interviews to nearly all comers, peppering the Internet with a preemptive defense of the book, proclaiming its intent as a piece of art *and* as pornography (self-consciously refusing the distinction between the two), articulating its antiwar politics, and patiently explicating its formal qualities. Never unwilling to discuss his work in detail, Moore used the available media (especially the Internet, despite his claims of relative ignorance of the new technology) to provide a counter to any accusations of obscenity. Reading (or watching, or hearing) Moore interviews, both early and late, one cannot help but be impressed with his agile mind, sense of humor, and wide range of reading and thinking. Despite these continuities, however, it becomes evident how the purposes of his public conversations have shifted. Rather than attempting to publicize his work and become "known," Moore now can use an already established reputation to bring particular ideas and thoughts to the fore, whether they be about magic, sexuality, politics, or the currently depressing state of DC and/or Marvel comics. Over the last couple of years, he has been even more circumspect, choosing his interlocutors more carefully and/or keeping the conversations centered on topics of his choosing. It is, perhaps, then, not a surprise (although it was a disappointment) that he declined to be interviewed for this book, despite his magnanimity in allowing older material to be republished.

The other dramatic shift from the early interviews to the late is in the length of the conversations, or at least the publications. Again, this seems to be linked to two developments. First, with Moore's increased and increasing popularity and celebrity, magazines, journals, and fanzines were more likely to cede more column inches to the inclusion of Moore's verbiage. With the explosion of *Watchmen* onto the scene, Martin Skidmore was willing to devote space for a twenty-thousand-word roundtable interview in his UK fanzine, *The Fantasy Advertiser*. This extraordinary length became more the norm than the exception once the Internet grew in ubiquity and popularity. Websites are not, of course, constrained by space in the ways traditional print publications had been. Combining this shifting media with Moore's famed volubility led to a surfeit of lengthy and provocative interviews. Even before the web's media dominance, however, lengthy conversations were fairly commonplace. Perhaps the longest was Dave Sim's thirty-six-thousand-word "Correspondence From Hell," conducted by fax and printed in the pages of Sim's independent comic, *Cerebus*, in 1997. This free-flowing discussion is still the most revelatory about Moore's conversion to magic, and the relation of said conversion to *From Hell*, but its prohibitive length made it impossible to reprint again here, despite Sim's willingness. Gary Groth's three-part "Big Words" for the *Comics Journal* may be its only real competitor for both length and interest, focusing on *Big Numbers*, but also covering Moore's career to that point. Less focused are two book-length interviews conducted by Bill Baker, and another by George Khoury. Khoury's is the most thorough on matters of Moore's childhood and its impact on his comics writing career.

Selecting interviews for this book, then, was complicated by issues of space. Rather than choosing a series of career-retrospectives, I focused on conversations that specifically address the creative work being done at the time of the interview. In most cases, and especially in Moore's early years, I include entire interviews that are interesting for what they reveal about Moore's creative process, philosophy, and politics, and especially those that seem valuable for the enjoyment and interpretation of each work. The same principle of selection holds true for the later interviews, although increasingly there, because of length, I had to resort to some use of excerpts. Only the first half of Daniel Whiston's epic twenty-six-thousand-word 2002 interview, "The Craft," is included, and Jess Nevins's conversation about the second volume of *The League of Extraordinary Gentleman* is represented only by a substantial excerpt. Some of the included interviews have been (and may currently be) intermittently available on the Internet, or, in Nevins's case, in book form, but others are rare and difficult to locate in their original print versions, having initially been published in limited-print-run fanzines or industry periodicals. Any repetition in the book is due to an effort to maintain continuity, completeness, and clarity in each interview. Excerpts are always of consecutive chunks of conversations so as to retain the relevant context in any exchange. While Moore's gargantuan productivity made it possible for some conversations to have virtually no overlap with others, the chronologically overlapping release of projects like *Lost Girls*, *From Hell*, and the ABC titles led to several conversations that focused on one project, while touching on others. An effort was made to cover, in some fashion, all of Moore's most important work. Even so, there is very little discussion of fascinating projects like *Halo Jones* and *The Bojeffries Saga* due to constraints of space and available material. As in any book of this kind, there are regrets about what had to be excluded. For me, the most important interviews not included because of length, or because permissions were denied, are Groth's, Sim's, Skidmore's (which also included Dave Gibbons, Steve Whitaker, and Fiona Jerome), and Eddie Campbell's 2002 interview in *Egomania* (reprinted in the *Disease of Language* book), principally devoted to Moore's performance pieces. Adi Tantimedh's discussion of *Lost Girls* with both Moore and Melinda Gebbie is also very provocative. I encourage those interested in Moore to pursue those interviews (listed in the bibliography below) to supplement those collected here.

ACKNOWLEDGMENTS

First thanks must obviously go to Alan Moore, with whom I have never spoken or communicated, but not for lack of trying. If anyone is reading this book, it is obviously because of his or her interest in Mr. Moore and his colossal and fascinating artistic output. My own role is merely that of a collector and editor, and I can only hope that I have given Moore and his readers justice in the choosing and editing of interviews. Mr. Moore also has my thanks for allowing the project to go forward, even when he had no real interest in participating directly and for granting permission to use images and interviews for which he held some copyright.

In terms of people I actually have contact with, I must first thank my wife, Jennie, who no doubt thought my adolescent comics obsession would pass shortly after we first met in 1988 (at the height of Alan Moore's fame and popularity). She has, nevertheless, stuck by me both through my drifting away from such youthful frivolities and through my recent return to them, this time dressed up as "serious work." Thanks also to my daughters, Katie and Julia, who indulge my tendency to be as childish as they are, if not more so. My brother, Noah, probably also deserves some credit (or blame) for my renewed interest in comics. My parents, no doubt, wonder where they went wrong, but they are kind enough not to say so.

Direct contributions to this project have been made by a wide variety of people, most of whom I have never met in person, but who have burned the email wires with me, helping me gather obscure and rare Moore interviews and copyright permissions for them. Foremost among those Moore obsessives who deserve thanks are Padraig Ó Méalóid and (the pseudonymous) "Loopy Joe." Ó Méalóid's collection of Moore rarities and ephemera on his LiveJournal (http://glycon.livejournal.com) proved an invaluable resource and was the direct source for the first interview included in this book. He also put me in touch with the exceedingly gentlemanly David Lloyd, was kind enough to answer a variety of questions about Moore's writings and interviews, and sent me a variety of electronic copies. Ó Méalóid's interviews with Moore on the Forbidden Planet Blog Log are also great resources for those interested in Moore's recent works. Alan Moore could not ask for a better advocate and fan. I found the mysterious "Loopy Joe" on the *4 Color Heroes* website, and his personal collection of rare Moore writings and interviews was equally helpful to me. It is through Loopy that I was able to obtain a copy of the rare *Hellfire* interview included here. Without Ó Méalóid and Loopy, the book would definitively not exist. I would also like to thank Annalisa Di Liddo, who, early on, sent me a list of the interviews she had acquired and used for her critical study of Moore. The list included both conversations from *Comics Interview* that found a home here. I found Di Liddo on the Comics Scholars Listserv, whose members, especially Mike Rhode, proved exceedingly helpful to me in tracking down materials and individuals. Thanks also to Danny Fingeroth for helping me to locate David Anthony Kraft (who deserves thanks for not dismissing me out of hand when I accidentally mistook him for someone else).

Obviously, the book could not exist without the permission to use material by all of the copyright holders, both for interviews and for images, and I thank them all, *en masse*. Additional thanks are due to David Lloyd who provided me with some information missing from the scan I had and to David Roach, who sent me some additional material of which I had no previous knowledge. Matthew De Abaitua and Daniel Whiston were also kind enough to answer some questions about the original publications of their interviews. I would also like to thank Guy Lawley, Christopher Sharrett, and Chris Mautner, none of whom apparently held the copyrights for their interviews, but who were enthusiastic about the project regardless and helpful in answering all of my questions. Jess Nevins, Andrew Musson, Tasha Robinson, and Daniel Whiston were all kind enough to allow me to use excerpts of their interviews, alleviating some of the space crunch. I would also like to thank several people who granted permissions (or were at some point willing to do so) for interviews that had to be excluded for reasons of space. Both Bill Baker and Martin Skidmore, in particular, were perfect gentlemen and pleasant conversationalists over email. Dave Sim was kind enough to take time out of his day to give me a call and cryptically agree to the use of his interview (although he insisted it was not necessary that he do so). Adi Tantimedh was particularly dedicated in his pursuit of the inclusion of his "Finding the Lost Girls" interview, and, in the end, Jonah Weiland of Comic Book Resources was also amenable. In all cases, I regret not being able to include their conversations. Although Eddie Campbell ultimately turned down my request to reprint his interview, I thank him for responding so kindly, promptly, and politely to my request. I would also like to mention Steve Whitaker, whose 1984 interview is included here. Mr. Whitaker passed away in 2008, and I never communicated with him in any way about these interviews, or anything else. Still, Guy Lawley's heartfelt remembrances of Mr. Whitaker made me wish that I had been able to do so. Chris Staros of Top Shelf Comix also deserves some special thanks for conveying my various requests for a personal interview (and for the use of older material) to Alan Moore. I undoubtedly took up far too much of Mr. Staros's time attempting to gain an audience with Moore. It is through no fault of his that I failed to do so. In addition, Walter Biggins and the University Press of Mississippi deserve thanks for giving me the autonomy to complete the project and for shepherding it through to its conclusion.

I would also like to thank Florida Atlantic University, and particularly Andrew Furman, Wenying Xu, and Johnnie Stover for allowing me to teach courses in comics, when, truth to tell, I was hired to do something else, and had no formal training in the field. Thanks also are due to Jessica Pitts for her invaluable help with the index. Final thanks go to members of my graduate course in Comics and Graphic Novels and my undergraduate American Comics and Graphic Novels. Teaching those courses allowed me to give serious academic thought to Alan Moore and other comics creators, eventually leading directly to this project, and perhaps future ones. In particular, Charles Herzek noticed that I had a Superman watch and told me that I should teach a course in comics. I politely told him that owning a watch had little connection to serious academic endeavor, but it turns out that I was wrong.

EB

Works Cited or Referenced

Baker, Bill. *Alan Moore's Exit Interview*. Milford, CT: Airwave Publishing, 2007.

———. *Alan Moore: On His Work and Career*. New York: The Rosen Publishing Group, 2005, 2008. (Previously published as *Alan Moore Spells It Out*).

Campbell, Eddie. "Alan Moore Interviewed by Eddie Campbell." *A Disease of Language*. London: Knockabout-Palmano Bennett, 2005. 111–40. Originally published in *Egomania* 2 (2002).

Di Liddo, Annalisa. *Alan Moore: Comics As Performance, Fiction as Scalpel*. Jackson, MS: University Press of Mississippi, 2009.

Groth, Gary. "Alan Moore Interview [Big Words, pt. 1]." *Comics Journal* 138 (October 1990): 56–95.

———. "Alan Moore: Big Words [pt. 2]." *Comics Journal* 139 (December 1990): 78–109.

———. "Alan Moore: Last Big Words [pt. 3]." *Comics Journal* 140 (February 1991): 72–85.

Khoury, George. *The Extraordinary Works of Alan Moore: Indispensable Edition*. Raleigh, NC: TwoMorrows Publishing, 2008.

Moore, Alan. "Stan Lee: Blinded by the Hype." *Daredevils* #3–4 (March–April 1983).

———. "Sexism in Comics: Invisible Girls and Phantom Ladies, pt. 1." *Daredevils* #4 (April 1983): 18–20.

———. "Sexism in Comics: Invisible Girls and Phantom Ladies, pt. 2." *Daredevils* #5 (May 1983): 18–20.

———. "Sexism in Comics: Invisible Girls and Phantom Ladies, pt. 3." *Daredevils* #6 (June 1983): 15–18.

Sim, Dave, and Alan Moore. "Correspondence From Hell (4 parts)." *Cerebus* 217–20, 1997. 38 pages. Reprinted in *Alan Moore: Portrait of An Extraordinary Gentleman*, eds. Gary Millidge and smoky man. Leigh-on-Sea, England: Abiogenesis Press, 2003. 307–45.

Skidmore, Martin, Steve Whitaker, Fiona Jerome, and Peter Hogan. "Interview with Alan Moore and Dave Gibbons." *Fantasy Advertiser* 100 (March 1988): 20 pages. http://www.johncoulthart.com/feuilleton/2006/06/24/watchmen/. Posted online June 24, 2006. Accessed December 7, 2010.

Tantimedh, Adi. "Finding the Lost Girls with Alan Moore and Melinda Gebbie (3 parts)." *Comic Book Resources*. April 15, May 26, May 29, 2006. http://www.comicbookresources.com/?page=article&id=7151. Accessed June 22, 2009. 23 pp.

Whitson, Roger. "Paneling Parallax: The Fearful Symmetry of William Blake and Alan Moore." *Imagetext* 3.2 (2006): 24 paragraphs. http://www.english.ufl.edu/imagetext/archives/ v3_2/whitson/. Accessed December 7, 2010.

CHRONOLOGY

1953   Alan Moore is born November 18 in St. Edmond's Hospital in Northampton, England, to Ernest Moore, a brewery worker, and Sylvia Doreen, a printer. Moore grows up in the area known as "The Boroughs." The family home includes younger brother, Michael, and maternal grandmother, Clara. Moore resides in Northampton for his entire life.

1958–63   Moore attends Spring Lane Primary School and begins checking books out of the library and reading "omnivorously" (Khoury 16). He also begins buying and reading comics from a market stall, both British comic strips like *Topper* and *Beezer* and American imports like *Flash*, *Blackhawk*, and *Fantastic Four*.

1964–65   Moore passes his "eleven-plus" exams, making him eligible to attend the more "middle-class" Northampton Grammar School. Moore enters his new school as no longer among the strongest students and soon loses interest in academic success.

1966–69   Moore begins to get involved with British comic fandom, becoming lifelong friends with Steve Moore (no relation). He attends the second British comics convention.

1970   The Moore family is forced to move to another part of town when the local council declares their neighborhood a "clearance area." Use of psychedelic drugs and hippie rebellion becomes a central part of Moore's life, and he is expelled from secondary school for dealing LSD. According to Moore, the headmaster subsequently made it impossible for him to gain admission to other schools by spreading the word about his infractions. Moore also begins participating in the Northampton Arts Lab and contributes poetry and illustrations for Arts Lab–affiliated handmade publications, *Embryo* and *Fitz Rovel*. He also writes a two-page essay about *The Shadow* for a fanzine called *Seminar*. He works a variety of odd jobs, including as a tanner and as a toilet cleaner.

1971–74   Moore meets his first wife, Phyllis, and they move in together. They marry in 1974 and Moore works for a subcontractor of the local gas board.

1974–77   Moore's strip, *Anon E. Mouse* periodically appears in *ANON* (The Alternative Newspaper of Northampton). Moore decides to quit his job and devote himself to cartooning full time.

1978   Moore's daughter, Leah, is born on February 4.

1978–79   Moore's earliest published comic strips (written and drawn by Moore) appear in *The Back-Street Bugle* (an Oxford-based publication) and *Dark Star*, a fanzine/newspaper. In March 1979, Moore, under the pseudonym "Curt Vile," begins publishing the half-page *Roscoe Moscow, in, "Who Killed Rock n' Roll"* in *Sounds*, a national music weekly. In August, *Maxwell the Magic Cat* begins to appear in *The Northants Post*, under the pseudonym Jill de Ray. Moore uses the pseudonyms so that he can continue to collect unemployment and help support his family.

1980–83   Alan and Phyllis Moore's second daughter, Amber, is born. Moore turns his attention primarily to writing, as he considers himself too slow to continue drawing his own strips. He submits a "Judge Dredd" script to *2000 AD* editor Alan Grant with the help of Steve Moore and is soon submitting and publishing short scripts for Marvel UK (for *Dr. Who Weekly* and *Monthly* and *Star Wars: The Empire Strikes Back Monthly*) and *2000 AD*. *Warrior Magazine* begins in 1982 and Moore starts writing longer stories in installments for all three publishers. These include the E.T.-style *Skizz* (1983 with Jim Baikie) and the humorous science fiction, *D.R. and Quinch* (1983–85 with Alan Davis) for *2000 AD*. His biggest Marvel UK project is *Captain Britain* (with Alan Davis), appearing in a series of magazines (*Marvel Super-Heroes Magazine*, *Daredevils*, and *The Mighty World of Marvel*). Moore also writes a series of *Nightraven* prose stories and critical essays for these publications. *Warrior* includes *V for Vendetta*, *Marvelman*, and *The Bojeffries Saga* (with David Lloyd, Garry Leach and Alan Davis, and Steve Parkhouse, respectively). Moore and his band, the Sinister Ducks, release the single "March of the Sinister Ducks," b/w "Old Gangsters Never Die" in 1983. Moore uses the pseudonym Translucia Baboon for the recording.

1984   *Saga of the Swamp Thing* (with Steve Bissette and John Totleben) for DC Comics in the U.S. and *The Ballad of Halo Jones* (with Ian Gibson) for *2000 AD* begin to appear.

1985   In addition to *Swamp Thing*, Moore writes a variety of shorts for DC, including "For the Man Who Has Everything," in *Superman Annual* #11 (with Dave Gibbons). He also writes a backup feature in Howard Chaykin's *American Flagg* and other shorts. *Warrior* folds and *Miracleman* (formerly *Marvelman*) begins to appear in the U.S., now in color, for Eclipse Comics.

1986   *Watchmen* (with Dave Gibbons) appears for DC, along with the two-part "Whatever Happened to the Man of Tomorrow" Superman story (with Curt Swan). Moore ends his run on *The Ballad of Halo Jones* for *2000 AD*, marking the end of his affiliation with the magazine. Moore cites poor treatment and exploitation by *2000 AD*'s publishers and Titan Books (who collected various *2000 AD* strips) for his decision to end the series, despite its being unfinished. Moore also stops *Maxwell the Magic Cat*, citing a *Northants Post* anti-gay editorial. "In Pictopia" (with Don Simpson) is published in *Anything Goes* #2 by Fantagraphics.

1987   Moore completes both *Watchmen* and his run on *Swamp Thing*. A variety of short stories and independent publications appear, including *Real War Stories* #1 and the prose fantasy story, "A Hypothetical Lizard," in *Liavek: Wizard's Row*.

1988   *Batman: The Killing Joke* (with Brian Bolland) and the colorized continuation/completion of *V for Vendetta* appear for DC. Moore leaves DC and founds Mad Love Publishing with his wife Phyllis and their mutual girlfriend, Deborah Delano. Moore falls out with DC over copyright and creative rights to the properties he co-created (especially *Watchmen* and *V for Vendetta*), a proposed ratings system for adult-oriented comics, and fair payment for *Watchmen*-related merchandise. *AARGH!* (Artists Against Rampant Government Homophobia) becomes the first Mad Love publication in response to anti-gay legislation, "Clause 28," in the UK. Moore's contribution is "The Mirror of Love," a poem about gay love with art by Steve Bissette and Rick Veitch. Moore's screenplay to Malcolm McLaren's unfilmed *Fashion Beast* is published. *From Hell* (with Eddie Campbell) is begun in the pages of Steve Bissette's horror anthology, *Taboo*. Moore and Dave Gibbons win a Hugo Award for *Watchmen*, the first (and last) comics project to win the award.

1989–90   *From Hell* continues and *Lost Girls* (with Melinda Gebbie) is begun in *Taboo*. "Shadowplay: The Secret Team," Moore's history/exposé of CIA activities is published by Eclipse (with Bill Sienkiewicz) in

Brought to Light. "Lust," a short story with art by Mike Matthews, appears in *Seven Deadly Sins*. The first two issues of *Big Numbers* (with Bill Sienkiewicz) are published by Mad Love before the publishing venture and Moore's marriage collapse. Phyllis and Deborah Delano move out with Moore's daughters. *Big Numbers* is never completed.

1991   *From Hell* begins publication as a ten-issue maxiseries (also reprinting the *Taboo* material). Moore's poem, "The Children's Hour" appears in *Now We Are Sick: An Anthology of Nasty Verse*.

1992   *The Complete Bojeffries Saga* appears for Tundra Press, including five new Bojeffries stories (with Steve Parkhouse).

1993–94 Moore's graphic novel, *A Small Killing*, is published by Dark Horse (with Oscar Zarate). On his fortieth birthday, Moore declares himself a practicing wizard/magician. A paranormal experience in January of the following year confirms the decision, and his first magical "working," "The Moon and Serpent Grand Egyptian Theatre of Marvels" is performed. *Spawn* #8, Moore's first superhero contribution for Image appears (with Todd McFarlane), along with *1963*, a parody of 1960s Marvel Comics (with Steve Bissette and Rick Veitch), and a *Spawn*-related *Violator* miniseries (with Bart Sears and Greg Capullo). Moore's song lyrics are published in *Negative Burn*.

1995   The first volume of (the never completed) *From Hell: The Compleat Scripts* appears. Moore's prose stories, "The Courtyard" and "Light of Thy Countenance" appear in *The Starry Wisdom: A Tribute to H. P. Lovecraft* and *Forbidden Acts*, respectively. Moore performs "The Birth Caul," after his mother's recent death. The performance takes place in Newcastle, on Moore's forty-second birthday, with David J and Tim Perkins. Moore continues to write *Spawn*-related miniseries for Image and begins his eighteen-month stint on the superhero team book, *WildC.A.T.s*. *Lost Girls* is picked up by Kitchen Sink Press.

1996   *Voice of the Fire*, Moore's first novel, is published. It is composed of a series of thematically linked short stories set in historical Northampton. Moore writes a *Spawn/WildC.A.T.s* miniseries and begins his work on *Supreme* (with Chris Sprouse), for Image.

1997   Moore's epic interview with Dave Sim appears in the pages of *Cerebus* #217–220. Moore and his magical associates perform "The Highbury Working," in London. Wildstorm's *Judgment Day* and *Voodoo* supplement the ongoing *Supreme* and *WildC.A.T.s*.

1998 "Dance of the Gull Catchers," an epilogue to *From Hell* is published by Kitchen Sink, along with some stories featuring Will Eisner's Spirit in *The Spirit: The New Adventures* (with Dave Gibbons).

1999 *From Hell* is finally published in a single volume by Eddie Campbell Comics. *Supreme: The Return* appears for Awesome Entertainment, but Moore principally turns his attention to the America's Best Comics (ABC) books, published by Wildstorm. DC Comics purchases Wildstorm, indirectly rehiring Moore. The ABC titles that begin in 1999 are *The League of Extraordinary Gentlemen* (with Kevin O'Neill), *Tom Strong* (with Chris Sprouse), *Promethea* (with J. H. Williams III), *Top Ten* (with Gene Ha and Zander Cannon), and *Tomorrow Stories*, an anthology. Eddie Campbell publishes his adaptation of "The Birth Caul." Moore also provides the basic script for *The Worm*, a collaborative project, promoted as "the world's longest comic strip." "Snakes and Ladders" is performed at Red Lion Square in London.

2000–2001 Eddie Campbell's adaptation of "Snakes and Ladders" is published. The *From Hell* film is released. "Angel Passage," a magical tribute to William Blake, is performed.

2002 The second volume of *The League of Extraordinary Gentlemen* is published, along with the anthology series, *Tom Strong's Terrific Tales*, and other ongoing ABC titles. "This Is Information" (with Melinda Gebbie) is published as part of *9-11: Artists Respond*.

2003 *Alan Moore's Writing for Comics* reprints some early articles regarding Moore's methods and writing philosophies. George Khoury's *The Extraordinary Works of Alan Moore* is published, including a lengthy interview and reprints of rare material. *Smax*, an ABC miniseries featuring a *Top Ten* character, is also published (with Zander Cannon). The *League of Extraordinary Gentlemen* film is released, as is a documentary film, *The Mindscape of Alan Moore*. The *League* film is the first of a series of Moore film adaptations to become controversial, as Moore has to defend himself (and 20th Century Fox) from frivolous accusations of plagiarism.

2004 Moore's gay rights poem, *The Mirror of Love*, is republished by Top Shelf, with photographs and art by José Villarrubia.

2005 *Watchmen* is named one of *Time* magazine's "Top 100 English-Language Novels since 1923." Moore co-writes the *Albion* miniseries with his daughter Leah, and her husband, John Reppion (art by Shane Oakley). Moore's *Top Ten: The 49ers* graphic novel (with Gene Ha) also appears.

2006   A three-volume complete collection of *Lost Girls* (with Melinda Gebbie) finally appears from Top Shelf/Knockabout. *A Disease of Language* collects Eddie Campbell's *Birth Caul* and *Snakes and Ladders* adaptations, along with a lengthy interview with Moore about his performance pieces. Moore's nonfiction prose piece about Steve Moore, "Unearthing," appears in the Iain Sinclair edited collection, *London: City of Disappearances.* The *V for Vendetta* film is released, prompting prolonged conflict between Moore and Warner Brothers, after Warners claims that Moore is enthusiastic about the film. Moore demands that his name be removed from the project and begins extricating himself from his remaining commitments to DC/Warner Brothers.

2007   Moore marries his *Lost Girls* collaborator, Melinda Gebbie. *The League of Extraordinary Gentlemen: Black Dossier* is published by ABC/Wildstorm/DC, marking the end of Moore's affiliation with those imprints. Moore lends his voice to an episode of *The Simpsons* starring famous comics creators.

2009–10   The one-volume edition of *Lost Girls* is released from Top Shelf, along with the first installment of *The League of Extraordinary Gentlemen, Vol. 3: Century.* *25,000 Years of Erotic Freedom* is published. It is a brief prose treatise on art and eroticism based on a 2006 article in Jay Babcock's *Arthur* magazine, "Bog Venus vs. Nazi Cock-Ring." *Dodgem Logic,* Moore's self-published "underground magazine," begins publication. The *Watchmen* film is released. *Neonomicon* (with Jacen Burrows) and the multimedia version of "Unearthing" also appear. The former is a comics sequel to the prose story, "The Courtyard." The latter includes photography by Mitch Jenkins, a musical soundtrack, and Moore's reading of his 2006 story.

ALAN MOORE: CONVERSATIONS

From the Writer's Viewpoint

DAVID LLOYD / 1981

SSI (*Society of Strip Illustration*) *Newsletter* 40 (May 1981): 10–20. Reprinted by permission of David Lloyd and Alan Moore (via Chris Staros of Top Shelf Productions).

This interview was conducted by David Lloyd, Moore's collaborator on the later *V for Vendetta*, (although he is unnamed in the text) and consists of a series of questions posed to a variety of British comic strip writers of the day. The writers replied by mail, and Lloyd then cut and pasted their replies into the newsletter (in the days before the desktop computer). I have only reproduced Lloyd's questions and Moore's responses below. A scan of the entirety of the interview (including the other responses) can be found at Padraig Ó Méaóloid's "livejournal" of Alan Moore ephemera: http://glycon.livejournal.com/2709.html. This is, from what I have been able to ascertain, the first "published" Alan Moore interview. Due to the method of composition, there were quite a number of typing irregularities, typographical, grammatical, and spelling errors in the newsletter version. Most have been corrected or regularized silently, except for those where the original intent was difficult to ascertain. These are retained in their original form and marked with "[sic]." EB

There was a lot of sense in Dennis Hooper's contribution to the March newsletter in which he bemoans the plight of the writer in strips.

Until recently I had little real contact with the writers of scripts I was commissioned to work from. I'd hazard a guess that most of us on the illustration side of the business have little contact with writers and, consequently, we're still largely unaware of their views and feelings in regard to their craft.

In order to try and gain some insight into the views of writers and find out what opinions, feelings, etc. they have in common, I compiled a questionnaire and sent it to five of the most respected and reputable strip writers in British comics—namely: Angus Allan, Pat Mills, Steve Moore, Alan Moore, Steve Parkhouse.

(Note: An expanded version of Pat Mills' answers can be found in the next edition of *BEM*.)

Q1.) Do you find it relatively "easy" to write strip scripts? If you do, was it ever "hard" to write scripts? If you find it "hard" now, was it ever "easy"?

am: I find writing comics to be staggeringly easy. Naturally, this is not to say that situations don't rise occasionally where one just stares at a blank piece of Croxley Script and over-fills the ashtray. Continuity problems, tricky transition sequences, and stuff like that. But even in these infrequent circumstances, extricating yourself is more a problem of *craft* than graft.

On an average day, working at a fairly leisurely pace I can turn out a complete five-page script. On a tough day I can turn out a couple and still be finished by the early evening. This enables me to wrap up a whole job, start to finish, while I'm still feeling relatively fresh-faced and enthusiastic.

Q2.) Are you, on the whole, satisfied with the way artists translate your ideas? If you have any, give examples of good and bad experiences relating to this. (Embarrass the hell out of whoever you like—Life is *far* too serious to be taken seriously . . .)

am: By and large, I've been very lucky as far as the artists chosen to work on my scripts are concerned. It doesn't really bother me unduly that such and such an artist might have decided to do a number of frames differently to the way I'd specified in the script. As far as I'm concerned the only important consideration is whether the artist enjoyed the script and had fun translating it into pictures. If this is the case, then nine times out of ten you'll get a good story roll off the other end of the conveyor belt . . . irrespective of whether it tallies with every trivial detail that I've put into the script. An example of jobs that have pleased or displeased me artwise . . . a good example of someone doing everything according to me specifications and turning in a crack-hot job as a result would be the way John Stokes handled my "Stardeath" story in *Dr. Who Monthly*. Everything I'd asked for was in there, no matter how ridiculous or time-consuming, and as an additional bonus lots of little details had been squeezed into the backgrounds which contributed greatly to the old-fashioned space opera atmosphere that I'd been aiming for.

As far as jobs that have *displeased* me go, then I must reluctantly admit to being less than ecstatic about the way a gent named Walter Howarth handled the story which finally emerged in this year's 2000 *AD Summer Special* under the title of "Southern Comfort." Sure, there were other factors involved, and I don't want to be too hard on a guy who obviously had enough problems already. I just thought I'd mention it because it helps to talk about these things, helps us to understand the essential frailty of human existence and to be prepared for the inevitable tragedy that waits just around the corner.

Q3.) Do you find your work satisfying—or would you (do you) prefer to write for other mediums, e.g. short stories, T.V.? (Disregard obvious financial advantages involved when answering this.)

am: I love my work, although having previously been employed in cleaning toilets, this is perhaps less than surprising. And while one day I'd certainly like to have a crack at writing novels, short stories, T.V. and film scripts, stage plays, kiddie porn, and all the rest of the stuff, at this point I can't see comics as ever becoming anything less than my principle area of concern. Without condemning individuals for what, after all, is their own decision, I must admit to being a little disturbed at the current trend of comics being used as a way-stage to fine art, with the creative people hanging around in comics long enough to gain a cult reputation before retreating to some sumptuously decorated studio and turning out self-indulgent portfolios at twenty quid a throw. It seems to me that there is still some sort of creative stigma attached to working in comics, and that too many of the people in the medium regard themselves as failed novelists, film producers, or fine artists. Whereas, to me, the medium is possibly one of the most exciting and underdeveloped areas in the whole cultural spectrum. There's a lot of virgin ground yet to be broken and a hell of a lot of things that haven't been attempted. If I wasn't infatuated with the medium, I wouldn't be working in it. After all, whatever the economic situation, this country will always need toilet cleaners.

Q4.) Do you think you get a sufficient cut of the financial cake as a writer of strips?

am: I think I'm adequately paid. Actually, just between you and me, I'm grossly overpaid. Like I say, I can turn out a four- or five-page script in a single day and get a return of somewhere between sixty and ninety quid for my efforts. On top of this, I get to buy ludicrous amounts of comics each month.

Q5.) Would you like to collaborate with artists as a matter of routine?

am: Yeah, I'd like very much to collaborate with artists as a matter of course. Failing that, though, it'd be nice just to know for certain which artist your strip was going to.

The advantages of such a collaboration are fairly obvious . . . you get a chance to iron out problems before they arise and to make sure that you're both working in the same direction. You can discuss the minor but important points of characterization and sort out the stickier patches of storytelling a lot more easily if it's just a matter of picking up the phone. Also, this allows the artist a little more input into the actual story . . . after all, much of my job [sic]

Q6.) Name your favorite writing job (series or one-off) and give reasons for choosing it.

am: My favourite writing job was a story called "Southern Comfort." Steve McManus, in an ingenious attempt to curb the flow of shimmering and lucid metaphor that I use to give the humblest caption box a certain poetry and élan, asked me to do a two-part story without captions. I dunno about anybody else, but I really enjoy tackling structural problems like that. In fact, up to a certain point, I think that the more severe the restrictions and limitations, then the greater the creative effort needed to overcome them and the better the eventual result. Anyway, in this instance I put a lot of sweat into the writing and to my great delight, at the end I found that I'd engineered a superb Swiss-precision piece of Graphic Narrative, a real Rolls-Royce piece of storytelling. Of course, the eventual result was as chronicled in my answer to question two. I'm sorry to keep going on about it, and I'd hate anyone to think that I was bitter. After all, into each life a little rain must fall, eh?

"Bax the Burner," on which I was lucky enough to have the services of sickeningly talented boy-genius Steve Dillon, remains another firm favourite.

The storytelling was nothing special or innovative, but I was pleased inasmuch as the story was the only one in which I've hung the plot around a strong emotional content and not had the whole thing come off as being incredibly trite and sentimental. "Oh Bax . . . who *cares* that you're a homicidal mutant pyromaniac? Love is never having to say you're sorry."

Q7.) What ambitions do you have for "strips" as a whole?

am: There's such a lot of things I'd like to see happen to comics over the next few years that it's difficult knowing where to start.

I'd like to see less dependence upon the existing big comic companies. I'd like to see artists and writers working off their own bat to open up space for comic strips in magazines which might not have considered them before. Secondly, I hope that kid's comics in the eighties will realise what decade they're in and stop turning out stuff with an intellectual and moral level rooted somewhere in the early fifties. Stories concerning the daring escapades of plucky Nobby Eichmann, Killer Commando decimating the buck-toothed Japs with

From "Bax the Burner," by Alan Moore and Steve Dillon from *2000 AD Annual*, 1982. Reprinted in the U.S. in *Sam Slade: Robohunter* #6, page 18, March 1987. Copyright © 2010 Rebellion A/S. All rights reserved. www.2000ADonline.com, used by permission.

his cheeky cockney humor and his chattering stengun don't have a lot of immediate relevance to kids whose only exposure to war is the horrible morally grey mess that we've got in Northern Ireland.

I'd like to see an erosion of the barrier between "boys" and "girls" comics. I'd like to see the sweaty, bull-necked masculine stereotype and the whimpering girly counterpart pushed one inch at a time through a Kenwood Chef. I'd like to see, and this is pure whimsy, a return to the old-fashioned little studio set-ups like [Will] Eisner/[Jerry] Iger had in the thirties and forties. This would give the artists and writers a greater autonomy, since they'd be selling stuff to the companies as a sort of package deal. It would give them a stronger [share of] the merchandising royalties. And I should imagine that some editors might be quite pleased to save time in commissioning one complete job rather than hassling 'round trying to commission two or three separate people.

I'd like to see an adult comic that didn't predominately feature huge tits, spilled intestines, or the sort of brain-damaged, acid-casualty gibbering that *Heavy Metal* is so fond of.

My greatest personal hope is that someone will revive *Marvelman*, and I'll get to write it. KIMOTA!

Garry Leach and Alan Moore

DAVID ROACH, ANDREW JONES, SIMON JOWETT, AND GREG HILL / 1983

Hellfire 1 (1983): 15–20. Reprinted by permission of David Roach.

This interview was conducted at the 1983 Cymrucon by David Roach, Andrew Jones, Simon Jowett and Greg Hill. It is printed with the full permission of Alan and Garry—so sue them, not us! The eagle-eyed amongst you may notice a cameo appearance by Dez Skinn.

Hellfire: How do you go about producing a comic story?

Alan Moore: Well, you come up with your plot ideas first. Say we talk about *Warrior* and a series like *V for Vendetta*—what I did first was to sit down and work out the entire world, all the stuff that I'm never going to use in the strip, that you never need to know, but I've got to know it. You've got to have the whole world in your head so that you can get the texture of it. So I started working out this world from the premise that Margaret Thatcher was going to lose the 1982 elections. Then I worked out that Michael Foot gets in. You know, science fiction! [Laughter] Well he gets rid of the cruise missiles in this country. In 1988, World War III breaks out and a lot of the world gets badly screwed up, but because Britain's no longer a nuclear target, it doesn't actually get hit by any bombs. However, the weather is altered forever due to all these calories of heat which are poured into the upper atmosphere, resulting in the Thames Barrier breaking and a lot of England being under water, and then in 1992, after a couple of years of riots, chaos, hunger, dysentery, plague, and all that, the Right Wing groups—who are the only ones with any real organization—get together and take over.

So once I've worked out the politics of the situation, how the government works and all the details like that, I can start thinking about the actual plotlines for individual episodes, making sure that the plot hangs together nicely with a good beginning, middle, and end, not necessarily in that order, as long as they're in there somewhere.

Then I break it down into as many panels as is required. For a six-page *V* story, that'll probably be about forty-two panels, because Dave Lloyd gets a lot of panels onto a page; whereas if I'm doing *Marvelman*, where you've got panels with people knocking down walls and stuff like that, then it's about five or six panels a page.

It's like a film where you've got to take out the forty-two best frames which tell the story. Then you've got to go though all the panels and get the dialogue worked out, which is incredibly difficult!

What you've got to do to get dialogue right is to eavesdrop on public transport. For example, Harold Pinter, his stuff sounds incredibly strange because it's so much like real life. I remember sitting upstairs on a bus with two families sitting behind me, and one person is saying,

"Now do you know, I like a bit of salad."

And another one says, "That's funny, I like salad, now my wife—you can't stand salad, can you?"

And she says, "Well . . . I like tomato."

And he says, "Oh, I like tomato. Now, it's funny, I know you can't stand tomato."

And another one says, "Oh, but my wife likes tomato. Now cucumber, that's a different thing altogether. Now I like cucumber."

"Oh really, I'm not so partial to cucumber . . ."

[Laughter]

Well this went on for about half an hour. This is how real human beings talk. You know what I mean. It's HORRIBLE! I'm depressed for weeks afterwards, but fortunately not everybody talks like that.

Garry Leach: Some people talk like you!

Alan: Yeah, some people talk like me, but you've got to try and catch this sort of speech pattern, and everyone's got a different one. You've got to listen to people and store it all up in your head so that you can make dialogue sound natural. That's really important, because I think that in comics writing, much of the dialogue is incredibly stilted. I mean, they all talk in code! It's all sort of, "What th' . . . ," and nobody actually says that in real life. The walls burst open and an 'orrible scaly monstrosity, dripping acid, bursts through, and everyone says, "What the . . . " [Laughter]. So okay, once you've got your dialogue down, the flow of the captions has got to be right. You've got to have it so that once they've read the first word, they'll want to read the second and so on. You sort of grab them by the throat at the beginning of the story, drag them all the way through, and deposit them at the end. They should never stop reading. If they do, it's not their fault, it's yours. It's your job as a writer to sort of bully them through it. Actually, what I've just said probably applies to any form of writing, not just comic writing. Where comics are different is that you've got all these pictures as well. So, as a writer, I've got to work out the literary structure of the story and also the way it will look in pictures.

For example, what sort of angle are you going to use? If you're trying to make someone look helpless and vulnerable or set someone up for being killed and get the suspense going, you've got to have a high angle shot looking down on them, so that they're little tiny figures. If you want them to look powerful like Marvelman, you have a shot looking up at them so that they're looking down—just basic elementary visual psychology—know what I mean?

Hellfire: Like Gil Kane's "up the nose" shots.

Garry: Let's not get too carried away! [Laughter]

Alan: You learn a lot of things like that from films and looking at some of the books on films: *Alfred Hitchcock* by Truffaut, which says, "That's why he did this. That's why he did that. That's why he set up that scene like that," and this stuff helps to teach you how to use pictures to tell a story and how to create mood and atmosphere, without which the story and dialogue would be really flat. So, when I go through and write the scripts, it'll say:

PANEL ONE: A chatty description of the panel so the artist knows what to draw.

Then it'll say:

BOX: Put a little caption here.

And then for the two men talking, you'd have:

FIRST MAN: Blah blah blah blah, blah
SECOND MAN: Blah, blah, blah
PANEL TWO: etc.

Now, obviously, Garry's a better artist than I am, and so you've got to trust his opinions on how the story should be told. I mean, all I turn out are these 'orrible ratty bits of smudged paper with coffee rings on 'em. They're not a work of art in themselves. It's not until Garry, or whoever, has finished the artwork that you've actually got something complete. I'm only ever doing half a piece of art. Garry's only ever doing half a piece of art. It's when they go together that it starts moving.

So, perhaps Garry can tell you about what happens when he actually gets the script and has to draw the thing.

Garry: Well—getting the script for the first time is always a bit of a shock, 'cos basically it makes no sense at all. You read it four or five times and still haven't got the point of the story. If you're lucky, you can leave it floating around in your head for about a month, and at the end of that month, you've got a better idea because you've had the time to think about it. A comic is like a film in that the pacing has got to be right. A lot of the comics tend to go for an action angle, so that with Marvel you get fifteen pages of fight with just a few pages of dialogue before it. Ideally, you should pace the story better than that, and that's the trickiest bit of all. You've got to get the right feel and balance to the story, and the style is also important. I try to vary my style a bit 'cos the wrong style can ruin a story completely. For example, *Ronin* drawn in Don Heck style might not be the best comic you've ever seen, or *The Spirit* done in Jack Kirby's style would never have worked. That's always something to take into consideration. A lot of the time, the editors don't give the story to the person who should be drawing it, which is why a lot of comics are pretty forgettable.

It's a difficult process, and I've tried lots of different methods over the years that I've been working. One of them on *Marvelman* was to get Alan's typed pages and to string them out like something that's come out of a tickertape machine, marking off where all the pages were going to be so that I could see where I was at any point in the story. It was one massive long manuscript—not that it made any difference to the story, of course.

Hellfire: What do you think of the Marvel idea where the artist works from a plot synopsis?

Garry: It's horrible, because basically the artist is like the director of photography of a film, and if you've got someone who's inept, incompetent, and doesn't know about basic emotions, then the comic is ridiculous.

Alan: If the artist has just got a plot that says, "Daredevil talks to so-and-so on this page and at the end, so-and-so will come in," then from that, the artist won't know what expression to put on the mouth. So if he draws a chap grinning, and then Chris Claremont comes along and gives a huge balloon to it saying, "My wife and family have just died . . . "

Hellfire: " . . . Part of me is relieved, but part of me is torn in anguish." [Laughter]

Alan: Yeah, if he does that, then the artist is gonna look really silly. It's not his fault, but if he knows what the dialogue will be to start with, then it helps, doesn't it?

Garry: As Alan says, it's really important, because good writing doesn't necessarily mean crowding the panels out with word balloons. To have a go at Chris Claremont again—he doesn't really trust his artist, so what you get is a caption at the top of the panel, which immediately slows the pace down. Because he doesn't trust the artist to give him what he wants, you end up with two sets of information. With *V for Vendetta*, you don't have a caption at all, because Alan trusts Dave to tell the story. You don't need that caption with Dave.

Alan: And you don't need thought balloons either. Quite frankly, as a writer, I think the age of the thought balloon is over. You don't get thought balloons in real life telling you whether someone is going to steal your wallet or invite you home for lunch. What you've got to do to make an opinion of them is to observe the way they talk and the things they do, and after a while, you'll think, "Yeah—he's a nice bloke," or, "I hate him."

You don't have thought balloons in films, and you can still follow the story perfectly well. A lot of the writers use the thought balloons to explain all their characters' pretty feeble motivations. In the middle of a fight, there's this big slab of metaphysics above their heads. You don't think when you're in a fight, apart from "AARGH! BURN! DESTROY!" You certainly don't start thinking the deep and inner thoughts of Immanuel Kant or anything like that. You don't run through a sort of philosophical tract, especially when someone's trying hard to bend a steel girder 'round your head, believe me.

Garry: I always remember a great one from the *X-Men*, where Storm gets blown up, and all these explosions have gone off. There's all this white energy blazing round her, and she's got this bloody great balloon hovering above her trying to get the intensity of the moment across. That's really bad writing. They're making it easy for themselves and difficult for the artist.

Alan: Let's really kick Chris Claremont here! There was one particular issue, which was supposed to be really dramatic. It was where the Phoenix (the only good character he ever created) died (and he's been bringing her back ever since). Well, at the end of the story, he suddenly realized that he'd hardly explained any of the plot and how it all fitted together. It needed a lot of explanation, and he only had three panels left. So what he did was to have the lead character—the boyfriend of the woman (who had just died/committed suicide nobly-but-tragically)—stand there thinking: "Oh Jean! Now I realize that you must have blah blah blah . . . . . . and then blah blah . . . . ," all the way up to the last panel where he's sinking to his knees with emotion, but of course he *has* to sink to his knees because the top of the panel is just full of text in this massive balloon. [Laughter] And that's bad writing.

Garry: Obviously, things like the emotion in the story could have been done with just a silent panel, and if the artist's good enough, he could just get an expression on the face that just tells you everything you need to know about that story and what the writer intended, if it works well.

That's why the Marvel type of plotting doesn't work. It just gives you a story that doesn't carry the tension that it could do.

Alan: And no one reads all that stuff anyway; you skim through 'cos you get so bored with the first balloon that you think, "I'll skip the next two," and you can usually follow the story quite well. You can cut out every second balloon because they're not necessary.

Garry: Just as every panel should be there for a purpose and should have a definite meaning, so should every balloon and caption.

Hellfire: What do you think of Marvel characterization?

Alan: The thing with characterization is that it's important, but it's largely done wrong. When I started reading comics with Superman and Batman, they had no characterization whatsoever. They were utter blanks, but because they were utter blanks, you had a little room to project things onto them. Even though Batman was no creature of the night by any stretch of the imagination (he was a bit of an oaf who ran about in tights), you could imagine that he was a creature of the night. I'm sure that's where a lot of this "creature of the night" Batman image comes from. Everyone projected it onto him; there was nothing in the stories to suggest that.

Now what happened when Marvel came along in the sixties was that they thought, "Let's be realistic and give them human characters. We'll let them have one characteristic." They made Spider-Man neurotic, so that whereas Superman goes about being incredibly powerful and beating up villains, Spider-Man goes around being incredibly powerful, beating up villains, and then feeling guilty about it afterwards.

That's characterization the Marvel way. They're neurotic. They worry a lot. If they haven't got anything mentally wrong with them like that, something physically wrong with them will do—perhaps a bad leg, or dodgy kidneys, or something like that. To Marvel, that's characterization.

Getting back to Chris Claremont again, just for a moment. His thing with characterization is that he makes all his X-Men foreign. One's a Russian. One's a German. Russian! They're incredibly Russian. They sort of sit there and let you know how Russian they are by thinking:

"How I long for my Ukrainian homeland. How I miss my poor dead brother, Thiodore."

And then:

"How I miss the happy camaraderie of the bread queues and the surprise purges."

Garry: "And the tractors and the vodka." [Laughter]

Alan: Yeah, I'm sure that no Russians talk or think of things like that. And because the writers don't know much Russian or German, they have them saying "Da" occasionally instead of "Yes," and then perhaps everyone will think, "Russian!!"

Hellfire: The only Russian that Claremont knows is what he learned off *The Man from U.N.C.L.E.*

Alan: Right! And that's it. That's what they have instead of characterization. They must be crippled, neurotic, or foreign, and they don't bother to get anywhere near the complexity of human character. No one has just one character. It depends on what day it is and who you're talking to. When you're talking to your mum, it's a lot different from when you're talking in a pub. You become a different character; you change.

In comics, it's very much one-dimensional characterization. The level of writing in the industry is really at a low level.

Hellfire: Do you think it would be possible to do a character in comics whose complexity as a character matches that of a real person?

Alan: I think so, yeah. I mean, why not? It's possible to suggest that if you wrote a good enough story and if the artist's good enough. As Garry says, you can get a lot into the look in an eye or the way a person is standing. You know—the body language and posture and stuff like that. I'm sure that you could do a character who is every bit as believable as one in a book or in a film. I don't see why not; it's just that it hasn't been done terribly noticeably so far. There are some great expectations of course, like the characters in Will Eisner's stories. Okay, the stories are usually very short, so he has to introduce the characters quickly, and they're very broad characterizations, but he does create terribly fascinating characters, in a few pages, that you'll remember for the rest of your life. Like the one about Gerhard Schnobble, who's the bloke who can fly. He falls out of a window as a kid, and he flies, but he doesn't want to tell anyone. It's not like Marvel comics 'cos he's a tiny bloke with a really sad little face, and he's a real little jerk.

Then one day, he's had enough, and the world will know that Gerhard Schnobble can fly; and he's got this look of determination on his little face. So he goes up to this skyscraper and takes the lift to the roof. Now, the Spirit—who's not really in the story at all—is having a gun battle with some villains, but Gerhard Schnobble doesn't pay any attention to this because all he can think about is flying. He just goes up to the roof thinking, "They'll look up and they'll see me, Gerhard Schnobble!" He looks down, and they haven't noticed him, so he just leaps into space, and he flies. He's happily doing this graceful curve, when he gets this stray bullet through him. He falls and lands in the gutter with his hat following him down. Nobody notices. Not one person realizes that he has flown. That's the end of the story, and it's heartbreaking.

Eisner gets so much character into the way he draws the guy. You know his entire life story from the way he stands. So yeah, I think that you can create good characters in comics. Not the writer, but the writer *and* the artist.

Dez Skinn: Like in *American Flagg!*

Alan: Yeah. In the first issue, [Howard] Chaykin introduces about 15 different characters, and you don't have any trouble identifying them in the second issue.

Hellfire: How much do editors interfere with your work?

Garry: That depends where you work.

Alan: Yeah, at IPC . . .

Garry: IPC are terrible.

Alan: In some cases, they will interfere because they want to be seen to be doing a job. It doesn't matter whether the stuff's good enough already or whether they're making it worse by changing it. I hate having anything of mine changed. I can't help it. It's a personality flaw, but at IPC they'll think, "Oh, I'm not really working unless there's a lot of blue pencil on the script."

Garry: This really does happen all the time at IPC.

Alan: So, they'll take out a line here, they'll take out a box there and stuff like that, but at other places they won't touch the script at all. They'll just let it go through.

Dez: At IPC, you get to be an editor by being there long enough. You don't have to have any particular talent at IPC to become an editor. You just start out as an office boy, and you'll find that in ten years you're an editor just because you stayed there while most people with any sense have left because, hopefully, they can do better things on the outside.

Garry: There's one thing I remember from over at IPC, which was excruciatingly embarrassing for me. There was this *Mach One* story for some special. It had this big-business type villain and to make him seem worse than he was—'cos there were no actual props or anything—, I had this clue that he smoked. So when he was talking to Mach One, I had him flicking his cigar around and blowing smoke rings into the air and stuff like that. Well, it just so happened that at that point in time, IPC had decided that smoking in comics was a bad influence. The first thing I knew about it was when I saw my artwork in print, and there was this guy sitting there holding his fingers next to his mouth. And in another panel, he was blowing a kiss in the air for no apparent reason. What had happened was that they'd touched out all the artwork so that this guy is doing inexplicable things, and it just looks terrible.

Alan: I've seen them take out the cigar but leave the smoke in, and it looks as if someone is standing there with their head on fire. Suddenly, in the middle of the story, BANG—spontaneous combustion. [Laughter]

Garry: Sometimes it is justifiable, 'cos when one person is doing the story, you carry everything in your head, and you know exactly where you are and exactly what it is you are doing. But what is immediately apparent to you might be totally incomprehensible to someone else, and it does take an outsider to say, "Hey, this is wrong—you should spend two panels more there, telling the story," or, "Maybe the guy should be standing forward so that you can see his face."

Alan: I think it's the arbitrariness that sometimes gets to be very depressing. In the last part of *Skizz*, which was the horrible *E.T.* rip-off that I did in *2000 AD*, you've got this cuddly little alien that everybody likes who's having a really bad time on Earth, 'cos everyone's been beating on him, 'cos he's little (that's the plot, so you needn't read it), but anyway, he's going with his alien friends back to space and is saying goodbye to this girl who has looked after him. It's been running for twenty-one episodes, and obviously there's some sort of emotional bond. I just wanted them to look at each other, then he reaches forward, and they just kiss each other, and then he's gone. There's no words at all, just a three-panel silent sequence was all I wanted to do. When I actually picked up the comic and read it, I just wanted to burst into tears, not because it was emotional, but because they'd put all these balloons in saying: "No words, Skizz. Just . . . farewell." I mean, can you imagine that a big strapping, working-class lad like myself would write dialogue like that!? What really rankled me was that my name was on the script. People were going to believe that I wrote, "No words, Skizz. Just farewell." They're gonna beat me up in the street. There's no point to those little arbitrary changes at all. It would have worked perfectly well without the balloons.

Garry: When I was doing a *Future Shock* over at IPC, at that time they were doing minimal dialogue with large pictures—lots of action everywhere and very little to read. Anyway, some bright spark on the board of directors says, "Look at this, we're not getting value for money—not enough word balloons on the page. We want changes and we want 'em fast." So this little hotshot goes blistering down to the *2000 AD* office. Well, I'd just done this *Future Shock* with about six words per balloon. Lots of nice open spaces everywhere, lots of characters trundling 'round. Now they've been told to rewrite that

Skizz, page 95, by Alan Moore and Jim Baikie. Originally published in *2000 AD* #330, August, 1983. Copyright © 2010 Rebellion A/S. All rights reserved. www.2000ADonline.com, used by permission.

script. They do not like it. So what happens is that every square inch of that page that doesn't have a figure on it is covered with word balloons. They'd been told to do it, and so they successfully filled up every square inch that hadn't been utilized to its full.

Alan: And it wasn't necessary.

Garry: Exactly, with captions like that . . .

Alan: It didn't make the story better.

Garry: They could have shoved all the artwork to the end for all the sense it made. That's what you get for working with big corporations. That's why we're all doing *Warrior*.

Hellfire: How about DC?

Alan: DC have been very nice with me; they're not changing anything. I don't know, perhaps it depends on the writer or the artist. It's stupid, but there is a personality thing in comics 'cos it's such a small field, it's ridiculous. I'm not gonna get recognized in Tesco's. You can be a minor celebrity at conventions, which is nice, but it's such a small field that there is this status thing whereby some people don't get messed around with because they've got big names, or whatever—or perhaps just long names like John Tartaglione. [Laughter]

Hellfire: It would appear that not only do you write the stories for yourself, but you get very involved with what happens to these characters . . .

Alan: If you write a story that you don't personally find exciting, then nobody else is gonna get excited about it. If you've written a story that you wouldn't laugh at, then no one else is going to find it funny. You've got to make sure that the story has the effect that you mean it to have. If you want to get a laugh, then make it funny.

This also applies to the art. If you want to do a frightening picture, then make sure that it does its job and that it does frighten you. For example, the last panel of *Marvelman* in issue #3, where Kid Marvelman gets pushed off a building and just stands on air with lightning behind him. What I said was I wanted him looking like the angel of death. I wanted it to look really terrifying. Of course, that's really easy to write. It only takes me five seconds to write that, and then I can go and have a cup of tea and a lie down. Now, I think that last panel is heartstopping. I mean, it really is good. It's frightening. You get an idea of the power and madness that's really graphic there.

Now, what Garry had to do to get into that was to spend the whole day working himself into a peak of vicious psychotic frenzy. He had to think *evil* all day.

Garry: I wanted to go out onto the streets and burn babies with cigarettes.

Alan: Yeah! That's it! Mean! Mean! Mean!

It's like method acting, I suppose. I do it with scripting. For writing *Swamp Thing*, I wanted to have a bath of mud and sludge so that I could lie in it for three days, and then I could write it. You have to get inside the characters as much as if you were an actor. You don't start writing or drawing from the outside. You start writing or drawing from the inside, if you see what I mean.

Garry: See, what was really worrying about that was that both Alan and me started identifying with Kid Marvelman.

Alan: We thought he was great, yeah.

Garry: Forget Marvelman! Kid Marvelman was the boy.

Dez: But it's always the villains, isn't it?

Alan: The villains are always much more interesting than the heroes.

Dez: They can do more. The heroes are so namby-pamby because they have to be the good guys. The villains are so over the top, it's wonderful.

Alan: I prefer to make my heroes more ambiguous so that they have got some nasty edges. People who are so good—there aren't very many of them. You don't meet them, and they're not very interesting when you do.

You have to go into your work very intensely. This is a shaming sort of admission, and I hope you won't laugh 'cos it'd hurt, but when I'm writing some of the *V* stories sometimes, and it's really tragic, I'm sitting there—a grown man—and there's tears rolling down my face. I've got myself into the position where I'm incredibly uptight, and that's terribly neurotic. If people saw me, I'd be slapped away.

Hellfire: Jack Lemmon said the same thing when he was on *The South Bank Show*.

Alan: Did he?

Hellfire: He was saying that when he was doing *Save the Tiger*, he was driving down the road, and he suddenly realized that he was feeling very strongly for his character in the film, and that because his character was getting mentally unhinged, he was getting very worked up about it.

Alan: Yeah, you've got to—and that'll communicate. Okay, your audience probably won't burst into tears, but they'll feel some emotion. It'll put itself over in some way. You really have to put yourself through the wringer a bit if you want to turn out a really good story.

If you want to frighten the reader, then it's got to be something that scares you. You've got to get some sort of intensity in there, and I think that applies to the art as well.

Garry: Yes, it does, but with a lot of artists, you can see that they are merely performing a function. They're not interested in the story. One artist in whom this is incredibly apparent to me is Steve Ditko. He used to love his stuff during the sixties, but you can tell by looking at his artwork now that he isn't interested in what he's drawing. It's functional and only works on that level.

Alan: One thing with artists, with Alan Davis for example, I once saw him design a character. It was a woman, and he was drawing her. He was sketching and saying, "I think she'll have a build like some of those older Russian athletes, and that means that her torso is pushed up and the rib-cage is really thick, and there'll be a little extra muscle there, and that means she'll probably stand like this, and she'll have really long legs." He was working it all out anatomically, and at the end, when he'd got this character, he was inside the character from the bone outwards. He now draws the character inside out. The same goes for Garry, for Dave Lloyd. It's not good enough to just draw something with two arms, two legs, and a head, even if it's perfectly drawn. It's got to be alive. You've got to know who you're drawing and who you're writing and make them real. To do that, you've really got to get right inside them.

Garry: One of the biggest laughs of all time is the *Marvel Way of Drawing Comics* book. There's this great section in there which should be framed, mounted, and put on every wall in the country. Basically, it says: "This is a superhero's face. This is a wrong superhero face—the chin is receding. This is a wrong superhero face—the chin is coming out." What they fail to see is that it's a superhero face, okay, but it's the face of Captain America, Reed Richards, Peter Parker. All they've done is change the hairstyle. Now, the thing that makes people human is the fact that their noses *do* chip out at the end. Their chins *do* recede. What makes characters are things like that—recognizable qualities.

People always ask me why I used Paul Newman as the model for Marvelman. The thing is, if I'd done the standard Garry Leach face for it, when anybody took over the strip, they'd replace it with their own standard face. It's one of the major faults over at Marvel and DC that every [artist] has a standard hero face, and they put that face on every character they draw. They just change the hairstyle.

Alan: I said in an article that if you shave the heads of all Jack Kirby's women, their own mothers just couldn't tell 'em apart 'cos they are identical. Women's faces aren't allowed to have lines on them. Because of the way comics have grown up, a line on a women's face makes her look old or ugly. She's got to be totally plastic and smooth—as few lines as possible—perhaps a bit of cheekbone if you're John Byrne. Long eyelashes, little tiny mouth, stuff like that. They've got no character. They are totally interchangeable.

Marvelman's face has changed since Alan Davis took over. Alan started off by broadly following on from Garry, but Alan saw the character as slightly different. If you want to know who he's facially based on now, it's a page 3 girl from the *Sun*. What Alan wanted to do, and I went along with it, is that all these terribly masculine heroes, as Garry says, they all look the same, and all the ones with blond hair are identical, and you can't tell them apart. What Alan wanted to do was to get a certain asexuality into Marvelman because he's really pretty, and we thought it would be nice to give him a woman's face and get that standard of beauty there. You've got to have an angle, like Garry says, it's not good enough to have standard hero, standard heroine, standard villain.

Hellfire: Garry, when you started drawing Mickey Moran, he looked a lot like Marvelman. What do you think of Alan Davis's version of the character, which looks much more middle-aged?

Garry: I wouldn't have drawn him as old as that, but that's just a personal thing. Maybe it's because I come from a more classical school where the heroes have to have more classical features. I respect what Alan's done with the character. It's just something that I wouldn't have done, personally.

Alan: Obviously, I wrote the scripts with Garry in mind, and Garry's got a very strong vision of the character, but it wouldn't be fair to Alan to expect him to follow Garry's vision of the character. Alan's got his own ideas, and what Alan thought was interesting about the character was the difference between Mike Moran and Marvelman. Talking about Garry's vision of the character (this wasn't a criticism or anything, it was just an opinion), he was saying that out of Garry's Mike Moran and Marvelman, "I wouldn't mind being Mike Moran either." He thought that Mike Moran looked pretty good as well as Marvelman, and he tried to emphasize the difference between the two by making Marvelman more like an asexual god figure and Mike Moran more like a fat, middle-aged slob. So you've got the string vest stuff and the stomach hanging over, and he's got breasts, and Moran looks like most of us feel when we get up in the morning. It's just a different version of the character really.

Hellfire: It's just that there's so much difference between the first issue and the current ones that I thought that maybe it's part of the script or something.

Garry: The character looks like he's visibly deteriorating.

Alan: That's one thing in it, that it's obviously being a much greater strain on him in terms of the story, and the more it goes on, the more Mick Moran is going to deteriorate. The stuff that's happening to him isn't gonna do him any good—not at that age.

Garry: People can deteriorate over the space of a couple of weeks.

Alan: Look at any American President! Jimmy Carter, just before he got in, looked really nice. You look at him two months later and the eyes are hanging down. Richard Nixon—it was like something from the Quartermass experiment, wasn't it? In four years, he turned into something unbelievable. The sort of thing you expect to find under your sink unit. [Laughter] It does happen.

I don't want to explain it too logically and say, "Oh, we planned all that," because we didn't. It's just the difference between two artists and the way they see the characters. If it's too jarring, then we apologize, but it's just the way that Alan wanted to take the character. In some ways, it brought out a different aspect of the character that I was writing. Garry brought out one aspect, and Alan brought out another.

Garry: I think it was interesting to see the fact that the character continuity did continue after the change. We spent a long time considering, should Alan continue straight away. Then we decided that I would ink a couple of episodes so that it would slide slowly into Alan's style, and there wouldn't be this vast sudden difference.

Alan: There are differences, obviously. People have written in saying, "Alan hasn't got anywhere near Garry's command of Letratone," which is not really fair. Yeah, Garry's a master with Letratone.

Garry: Thank you.

Alan: That's alright. I wouldn't say it if I didn't mean it.

Garry: Scout's honour?

Alan: Yeah. Garry really knows how to use it. I think he probably knows more about design and that sort of stuff than Alan does.

Garry: I don't know. You want to see what he's doing lately.

Alan: It's pretty good, yeah, but the thing Alan's tried to do is to drop out the Letratone. Like, for example, Dave Lloyd never uses it. He doesn't like it. He'd rather use line. That makes a strong visual difference to a strip. It's just one of those things, I guess.

Hellfire: In the latest *Warrior*, someone writes in and says that too much of the art is slick and soulless. They cite Garry's work as an example. He says that David Lloyd's work has got real emotion to it. What do you think of that, and do you try to change your art to appeal to a certain type of audience?

Garry: I don't change my art much. I do have a definite style of drawing, but I do try to change my art to fit in with the story I'm illustrating. The thing is that most artists have one style, and it's very rare that they can change hats. Rich Buckler does it. You've got the [Jack] Kirby Buckler, the [Neal] Adams Buckler, and the [Gil] Kane Buckler that he's doing at the moment. Most artists have one style. Any change occurs because your thinking is changing. When I started out, I was very interested in people like Gil Kane, but recently I've come to appreciate people like Alex Toth more, who does really minimal line work. I suppose if I ever get 'round to it, I'll start dropping a lot of line out of my work, and you will see a cleaner image.

What was in that letter was just a personal opinion put forward. You cannot really say, "This is good comic artwork. The rest isn't." It's impossible because you're dealing with such a vast audience. If it was true, then say one or two comics would sell, because nobody would like the rest of the artwork. That's why there is such diversity—because everybody's tastes differ.

Alan: One thing that was in that letter: He was taking people like [Georges] Rouault and the primitives—[Henri] Rousseau, people like that—and saying that they are getting expression and feeling into their artwork. There's no doubt about it, you look at a piece of Van Gogh's artwork and you can see the feeling and the passion there. But it's whatever is fashionable at the moment; like occasionally intellectual art is in the ascendant and everyone thinking, "This is what we want," clean photographic images, intellectual content. That's fine, but he cited David Hockney as another person who is soulless. Now I like David Hockney's stuff. I think it's great. Maxfield Parrish, another clean, perfect artist—it's not soulless. It's just concerned with something cerebral rather than something emotional. When the intellectual artists are at the top, you'll get people like Rousseau coming in and everyone will say, "You can't draw," and he'll have a pretty bad time of getting his work established.

At the moment, there is quite a strong feeling, in certain parts, for strong emotional artwork. I like it as well, but it's silly to say that artwork which is not emotional is not good art, because it's just an opinion.

The standard moron's comment about art is, "I don't know about art, but I know what I like," but it is absolutely true, and there is nothing more you can say about art. That's the end. That's the final word. It does just come down to an opinion.

Alan Moore

GUY LAWLEY AND STEVE WHITAKER / 1984

Comics Interview 12 (1984): 9–27. © Fictioneer Books, Ltd. Reprinted by permission of Guy Lawley and David Anthony Kraft, publisher, Fictioneer Books, Ltd., #1 Screamer Mountain, Box 1241, Clayton, GA 30525.

Since the 1979 publication of Alan Moore's first strip in a nationally distributed paper—the hilarious *Roscoe Moscow*, which he wrote and drew under the pseudonym "Curt Vile"—he has become not only one of the most respected comics scripters in Britain, but also the most prolific—working for *Warrior, 2000 AD*, and Marvel UK simultaneously, as well as writing and drawing a weekly five-panel strip for a local newspaper. He has also been a rock journalist and an occasional member of the rarely seen Sinister Ducks, a wonderfully eccentric band which includes David J from Bauhaus. David and Alan have just recorded, "This Vicious Cabaret"—which appeared in strip form in *Warrior* #12—for release as a single.

With the addition of DC's *Saga of the Swamp Thing* to his workload, 1984 finds Alan busier than ever. Nonetheless, on a wintery day in the English Midlands town of Northampton, we received a warm welcome from Alan, his wife Phyllis, and their lively daughters, Leah, age six, and Amber, three.

The conversation which follows revealed Alan's talent to be based on a wide range of influences, a deep-seated integrity, and a wicked sense of humor, all shot through with a rich vein of honest humility.

GUY LAWLEY: You grew up in Northampton?

ALAN MOORE: If you can call it growing up, yeah.

STEVE WHITAKER: And you read comics as a kid?

ALAN: Comics, when I was growing up, were part of a working class tradition. Mothers gave them to their kids to pacify them. Instead of a Valium, it would be a copy of *The Topper* or *The Beezer.*

STEVE: As opposed to the posh boys' comics like *The Eagle* or *Boys World*?

ALAN: We knew our places in those days, Steve. We didn't want to rise above our station! I think the first American comic I picked up was an early *Flash*. I was just enchanted by the idea of the superhero, as I was before that by science fiction, magic, fantasy, children's versions of the Greek myths, the Arthurian legends—anything that wasn't real. Then you get The Flash—the idea of someone being able to move that fast, the costume coming out of the ring! After that, I just bought anything I could find . . . *Blackhawk*, all the Mort Weisinger stuff—the Superman family, the kryptonite; that was an infatuation. Then came *The Fantastic Four* and I became a Marvel zombie, which was an enjoyable thing to be up 'til about 1968.

STEVE: The year it all splintered apart . . .

ALAN: To a degree it was a matter of Marvel losing its integrity. That's a pretty sweeping statement, but in my eyes at the time, that's how it was. Frankly, the DC characters had been dull for a number of years, but Superman is still Superman. He's got that integrity and I don't think anything could disrupt it.

STEVE: Were you active in fandom?

ALAN: I had a minor involvement in fandom from age fourteen to seventeen. When I was about sixteen or seventeen I got involved with Northampton Arts Lab, where you'd get together with some people, hire a room, put out a magazine, do performances. I learned a lot about timing dialogue in comics from acting, and I learned how to use words really effectively from poetry. There's a poem by Brian Patten called, "Where Are You Now, Batman?" It has a haunting line about, "Blackhawk has gone off to commit suicide in the hangers of innocence." It made you think, "Ah! If only they'd look at those characters with a bit of poetry in the comics themselves!" I think that's where my attitude came from.

GUY: When you started doing strips, you were drawing as well as writing?

ALAN: Yeah. The first one of any import was for an Oxford underground paper called the *Back-Street Bugle*. In the mid-'70s I was working for a pipefitting company, getting really depressed at the idea of working in an office for the rest of my life. Then Phyllis and I got married, and I thought if I didn't pack in work now, I soon wouldn't have the nerve to. So I went on welfare for a while, but I was thinking, "It's about time I was making some money out of cartooning." For a long time nothing happened, then I sent *Sounds*, a weekly music paper, two episodes of *Roscoe Moscow*, about this deranged alcoholic detective lost in a fantasy Raymond Chandler world. It was blatantly stolen from Art Spiegelman's *Ace Hole*. I was bringing in a lot of influence from *Arcade*, which is probably the best comic in the history of the universe! *Sounds* sent me a telegram, 'cause I wasn't on the 'phone system. There was Phyllis with our poor starving baby in her arms, and I got this telegram saying "Liked *Roscoe*. Stop." It was like something out of the movies, you know.

So I was doing *Roscoe* once a week. It wasn't very good 'cause I can't draw, but I suppose by my slogging away at the stippling, it acquired a certain demented energy. It did teach me storytelling—each week, being faced with a regularly defined white space to tell a certain amount of story in. Then I got *Maxwell the Magic Cat* in the *Northants Post*, a local weekly newspaper. Because it was going on the Children's Page, I said I'd do it under the name of "Jill De Ray."

GUY: Wasn't that the name of some demented French nobleman?

ALAN: Gilles De Rais was a child murderer—probably the biggest child murderer in history! [Laughter.]

STEVE: It's moved off the Children's Page now.

ALAN: Yeah, that was their decision. It seems to have quite a cult following. I'm still doing it. God knows why! But I realized I couldn't make a living out of drawing . . . I was too slow. I knew Steve Moore, who was doing a lot of scripting. He was doing *Future Shocks*, the SF shorts in *2000 AD*. So, I did a sample script, a *Judge Dredd* story, and showed it to Steve. He corrected the obvious deficiencies for me, and I submitted it to Alan Grant at *2000 AD*. He was great. He spent a lot of his own time encouraging budding scriptwriters. I started doing *Future Shocks* for him.

At the same time Marvel UK's *Doctor Who* comic accepted a *Cybermen* back-up strip I did. That was my first work with David Lloyd. After that I did one about some plastic monsters—you know what *Dr. Who* is like—

STEVE: They're all plastic! [Laughter].

GUY: How did you come to work for *Warrior*?

ALAN: I'd just joined the Society of Strip Illustrators. I was interviewed for the *SSI Journal*, and they asked me what I wanted for the future. And I said that apart from fame, wealth, weapons, and a good five-cent cigar, I wanted someone to revive *Marvelman*. Since I was about twelve, I'd had this brilliant idea for reviving the character. At the same time, Dez Skinn was doing little comic strips to advertise toothpaste, stuff like that, and Dez phoned me up in 1981, one day, and said, "Would you like to do a treatment for *Marvelman*?" So, I worked out the continuity up to 1985. Garry Leach drew it.

GUY: You set the series very much in the real world, with the exception of the alien technology which comes from the outside . . .

ALAN: And then put this superhero in a silly, skintight costume in the middle of London.

GUY: The whole strip becomes, to some extent, a comment on superheroes . . .

ALAN: *Marvelman* steps back from the superhero, examining it from one step away—commenting on the obvious clichés and the absurdities of comics. I want to have all the superhero icons there: the fortress of solitude, the secret identity, the powers, the origin story . . . and yes, there *is* going to be a Marveldog! You take all these clichés, twist them one degree to the right and you've got something that's totally fresh. The idea of the secret identity has become a major plotline in *Marvelman*. It's not just a gimmick.

STEVE: There isn't the usual wish-fulfillment element in *Marvelman*. You don't make the superhero identity something which is desirable.

ALAN: It's frightening, what anybody that powerful would do to people around them psychologically. Look at Marvelman. He's not a human being. I can see him gradually developing a complete contempt for human beings. Everyone would look so crude compared to him. I'd like to explore this idea at DC—what Superman has done to the Earth by his very presence. No matter how hard people struggled, no matter what advances they made, what personal bests they achieved, they'd be nothing compared to Superman or Marvelman. I also think the superhero is an incredibly poignant figure.

GUY: The experiment which created Marvelman was "Project Zarathustra," which brings in the idea of the Übermensch, Nietzsche's twisted vision of the superior man.

ALAN: Yeah, that's the origin of the superman concept, and it's a fascist ideal. I mean, humans to a superman would stink. They'd be uncoordinated. Every move Marvelman makes is pure poetry.

STEVE: So why does he make love to his alter ego's human wife?

ALAN: I suppose he has needs like everyone else!

GUY: He's changing, isn't he? Marvelman and his alter ego, Mike Moran, are moving farther apart as the strip develops.

ALAN: We're not going to make a big thing of it—no Dark Marvelman! [Laughter.]

STEVE: Mike Moran is much more accessible than Marvelman . . .

ALAN: He's nicer than Marvelman, who is almost totally unknowable. With Marvelman, the danger is that his heart will turn to stone. His emotions could die. His mind works by different standards and values, whereas Mike is just an ordinary bloke. I'm trying to portray what such a situation would do to a normal bloke, to his life—that human angle on the whole thing.

GUY: Will the strip ever be seen in an American edition, in color? I can fore-see problems with Marvel Comics . . .

ALAN: I dunno. We'll just have to see. I'm not prepared to change his name.

STEVE: 'Round about the same time as *Warrior*, Marvel UK asked you to take on their latest incarnation of *Captain Britain*, which Alan Davis was drawing.

ALAN: After Garry Leach handed *Marvelman*'s pencils—and then the whole thing—over to Alan Davis, it became a real problem. You had the only two

British superhero strips both being done by the same artist and writer. Keeping them different became our main objective, really. It helped having an artist like Alan. He designs a character from the skeleton up. So, they've each got a different body language, posture . . .

STEVE: Captain Britain's your average meathead superhero.

ALAN: Yeah—with all those muscles and the military posture. Whereas Marvelman is slim, graceful—a ballet dancer's body. Marvelman's my optimum superhero, the one I'd do with no restrictions.

STEVE: Captain Britain's more mainstream . . .

ALAN: He's pure Marvel! He's there in the Marvel Universe with a billion other super characters all around him. You can't get that same realism.

STEVE: Was it only two episodes you wrote before you killed him off?

ALAN: Yeah, I tend to kill off characters I take over.

STEVE: It's actually a rebirth situation, breaking the mold, rebuilding the character in your own image.

ALAN: I feel I can't do anything with a character until I've destroyed and rebuilt him from the ground up. Well, anyway, that's what I did with Captain Britain.

GUY: Your other major strip in *Warrior* is *V for Vendetta*.

ALAN: It's one of my favorites. I feel proudest of that strip.

GUY: How did it come about?

ALAN: David Lloyd was drawing *Nightraven*, the thirties pulp-style feature for Marvel UK, and he was fed up with going to the library to look up 1930s references. Dez wanted to continue a *Nightraven* type of strip. I said, "Let's keep that exoticism of setting but in a different time. Let's do it in the future." I worked out the history of the world: World War III in 1988, the aftermath, the fascist takeover of Britain in 1992. I worked out who the main characters would be—with the Fate computer, the Head, the Finger . . . these different government departments . . .

GUY: And the star of the strip, this mysterious anarchist called V who models himself after Guy Fawkes and wages a one-man war on the government.

ALAN: The ambience in *V for Vendetta* is the *real* star of the book. What V does is to take certain twentieth-century preoccupations—like fascism, the bomb, individual liberty—and boil them down to a sort of ground zero, where everything's played out in absolute terms. Also, I was influenced by Harlan Ellison's "The Prowler in the City at the Edge of the World." Jack the Ripper against this sterile future environment. The juxtaposition excited me—a creature of the past in the future. That eventually grew into V, who is an anachronism. He's into old films, all the old culture that's been eradicated. He quotes Shakespeare and Goethe. He is a lavish creature who doesn't fit these bleak backgrounds.

The strip really grew by itself. England was to be ruled by these vicious National Front Nazis, so I could get in a dig at them, and I could get in a fashionable dig at the nuclear thing. I intended it to be a pretty trite piece of propaganda. But it didn't work like that. It came out superficial and hollow. I realized that the only way to treat it honestly was to take the fascist characters and get deeply involved in their mentality. So there's various different types of fascists in it: Finch, the "policeman with the honest soul," who's got reasons for supporting the regime, and Almond the wife beater, the emotional fascist.

STEVE: He's an amazingly well-studied character. He deserved everything he got. That's a marvelous scene, where V kills him.

ALAN: Dave Lloyd and I had a chuckle when he got it. There's no violence, just V's hunched back.

GUY: And the expression on Almond's face!

ALAN: I want people to understand the implication of what V does. He's killed Almond, and you get that kick out of it. You say, "He deserved it!" But in the next episode, you're forced to say, "Yeah, but he was married. What's going to happen to his wife?" So, there's the whole episode with Rosemary Almond, the widow. In most comics, there's no permanence in death. The bodies are whisked away. In *V for Vendetta*, they're still there the next morning. The plot isn't the most important thing in *V for Vendetta*. It's the resonances. The real story's going on in the subtext . . . between the lines.

V for Vendetta, page 77 (partial), by Alan Moore and David Lloyd. Originally published in *Warrior* magazine in the U.K. in 1983. Copyright © 1988–1989 DC Comics. All Rights Reserved, used by permission.

The first book set up the situation, established the characters. In the second book, "The Vicious Cabaret," V's not around very much. Instead, we're getting into the minor characters, like Rosemary Almond. The main story's about Evey, the apparently orphaned girl V sort of adopts in the first book. I'm sure this approach will lose us a lot of friends, but it's what we wanted to do. The second book doesn't work out too well on it's own, in comic-book terms.

STEVE: It's a necessary part of the whole, though.

ALAN: The third book will tie it all together. It's got a definite climax. If you see all three books as one novel, there's nothing wrong with having character studies making up the middle.

GUY: The characters are so well rounded. Adam Susan—the lonely, celibate, head of the government . . .

ALAN: He gives a rational, eloquent defense of fascism, as a necessity for the times, and as a necessity for living. And I want people to think, "Yeah, that is true—*to a degree.*" And yet while the passion of what V says in his TV broadcast in *Warrior* #16 is not as logical as Adam Susan's speech, it's a lot more appealing.

STEVE: He's talking about honesty with yourself.

ALAN: Exactly. I perceive two absolute principles of politics: fascism and anarchy. All the others are just subdivisions. The only question in politics is, "*Should* we be ruled?" That's what's being discussed in *V for Vendetta.* And I don't know the answer.

GUY: Do you think that might be expecting a bit much, hoping to come to a philosophical conclusion like that?

ALAN: I'm not so much interested in coming to a conclusion as in examining the problem thoroughly. I've got a strong dislike of what I've referred to as "The Baby Bird School of Comic-Book Moralizing"—where the writer gets the audience to sit there with their beaks open and feeds them. "Here's what you should think about nuclear war. . . ." We might be good comics writers, but we don't necessarily know anything about morality, human nature, and politics.

STEVE: It has to be left up to the reader to choose.

GUY: *V for Vendetta* seems very inherently British.

ALAN: There are a few people in America who do like it. I thought it might be too British to translate well. Frank Miller liked it, but he had one problem. He didn't know who Guy Fawkes was! But *we* had to put up with those references to Benedict Arnold in *Superboy* without knowing who he was! [Laughter.]

GUY: *The Bojeffries Saga* is your most English strip of all.

ALAN: That's my other favorite. It's as experimental in its way as *V for Vendetta.* Humor in comics, since Harvey Kurtzman's brilliant *Mad*, has become formularized—fast humor, lots of sight gags in every panel. I wanted to get the character stuff back into humor, and the England of the fifties that I can remember—the quirkiness of it all. Steve Parkhouse is the main vision behind the strip.

STEVE: It's an opportunity for you to use all that colloquial, idiomatic language.

ALAN: I love language—slang, jargon, poetry—how silly it can be, and how powerful and evocative.

STEVE: It could be a problem for American readers.

GUY: That's what people said about Monty Python! Alan, are you getting a lot of positive feedback from the States about *Warrior*?

ALAN: *Warrior* is not widely distributed in the USA. It is available and a number of the comics professionals read it, which is what happened with 2000 *AD* and *Judge Dredd*—something which spreads out from the artists and creative people to the fans. The reaction has been favorable. It's been a contributory factor in my getting work in the USA.

GUY: Did you sit down and think how the Swamp Thing related to his world, like with Marvelman and V?

ALAN: The main thing I wanted to understand was the character himself. I wanted a credible scientific explanation for the Swamp Thing. There were some things in the origin that bothered me. His being a plant hadn't been explored in depth.

GUY: Just gimmicks like the hand regrowing . . .

ALAN: [Len] Wein and [Berni] Wrightson had him root once, I think.

GUY: You make whole stories out of these things!

ALAN: They're interesting in their own right. "The Anatomy Lesson" in *Swamp Thing* #21 is my favorite one to date.

GUY: Steve Bissette and John Totleben have a lot of idea input to the strip, don't they?

ALAN: Yeah. One of the most amazing things about *Swamp Thing* is that, totally independently, in two different countries, me and Steve and John have come to an almost identical vision of how the character should be treated. In my first letter to them, I said I felt the reality of the Swamp Thing had been lost. He'd become this guy who was just a certain color, a certain posture. I said, "Let's do some real close-ups where you can see the vines, you can see the leaves, you can see the patches of mold—that texture to him." And Steve and John said, "Great! This is just what we want to do!"

We're doing a Demon plotline, using Jack Kirby's Demon. Most of the plot is Steve's. His wife Nancy works in a home for autistic children, such as the one we're using in the story. And the idea of Kamara—this creature who feeds on fear—being let loose in an environment where these kids live in their own private universes of fear, was Steve's. They sent me these sketches of the Demon, and the look on his face, smoldering with repressed violence, was fantastic!

STEVE: But he's bright and red and yellow all over . . .

ALAN: We're changing that. He's going to be more grim and shadowy. Writing the Demon, I felt this weight on me—the world-view of a creature from hell!

STEVE: So *Swamp Thing* is still essentially a horror book?

ALAN: I call it a horror book. Once I'd got the character sorted out, my main question was, "How am I going to approach a horror book?" That's a field in itself and one I'm really interested in. The Wein and Wrightson *Swamp Thing* was looking back to a 1940s Universal Studios movie vision of horror. As Stephen King said in *Danse Macabre*, the reality set has altered. Take the Val Lewton version of *Cat People*. The scenes in the park are so obviously shot on a sound stage—the lighting's wrong. People expect something different now. And things have changed since the first *Swamp Thing*. EC has, again, come to dominate the horror field.

STEVE: You mean through the Pacific stuff, such as *Twisted Tales*.

ALAN: Yes, it's an EC retread, with some influences from the undergrounds. And Bruce Jones does it really well. He's a good writer. But it's derivative. I want to explore other territory. In 1984, you have to accept that kids have been exposed to special effects in movies much more graphic than anything they'll ever see in comics, despite the supposed special effects advantage that comics have got. They've seen brutal, basic horror of the most visceral kind, and I think that has a numbing effect. Also, I'm very conscious that we're competing for kids' money with video, with films, and with Stephen King books—not with *Tomb of Dracula*, or *Werewolf by Night*, or things like that. The emphasis has to be on what *comics* can offer, compared to the films. Comics are a much more personal experience. It's the dissimilarities between comics and film that interest me more than the similarities.

STEVE: The art in *Swamp Thing* is brilliant. There's nothing like it in comics today.

ALAN: Yeah, it's excellent. There's a wrap-around quality to the art. That bit where Woodrue becomes the whole of the world's vegetation—you're right in there with him. It's a really visceral experience. I want to involve people emotionally that way.

STEVE: Like that bit in issue #22 when Woodrue eats a piece of the *Swamp Thing*'s body that he's just cut off! That's a damned-sight more disturbing than seeing somebody disemboweled.

ALAN: I'm getting a whole motif of eating going on in *Swamp Thing*. I think it can be very disturbing. It's difficult to really frighten people.

STEVE: Is the Comics Code a problem?

ALAN: Not really. They don't like a lot of sex and a lot of violence. But if you don't fixate on sex or violence, that leaves you with a lot of room to do things.

GUY: In common with people like Stephen King and Ramsey Campbell, you're looking 'round to find things in the real world of 1984 that frighten people, things that aren't classic horror themes, aren't you?

ALAN: I'd tell you a contemporary horror story, but I'm going to use it as the Liz and Dennis storyline, and I don't want to give too much away. However, it's something that really happened to a cousin of mine. It's about the destruction of one human being's whole personality by another. That's an example of human evil that, to me, is more frightening than any number of demons

From *Swamp Thing* #34, pages 11–12 (partial), by Alan Moore, Steve Bissette, and John Totleben. Copyright © 1985 by DC Comics. All Rights Reserved, used by permission.

from hell. The investigation of human evil is something that fascinates me. If my stories are *saying* anything, it's that everybody has the capacity for evil. To pretend it's something that only happens to monsters and supervillains is evading the issue.

I want to vary the types of horror. I'm doing a story about the nuclear issue. John Totleben's come up with this character, "Nuke-face." He's a bum who drinks radioactive sludge. His face is this horrible smear. It'll look amazing. The story is going to be called "The Nuke Face Papers." Each section ends with a newspaper clipping, just cut out of the paper, about beaches being closed off because of nuclear waste being found on them, and these incredible mutated sponges growing on drums of nuclear waste in the Pacific.

GUY: It's something Michael Moorcock's done—using newspaper clippings to refer to the ambience of the real world.

ALAN: Lovecraft did it too. It gives the storyline credibility. I wanted to do a story that doesn't smack of the early seventies, that doesn't preach. I think the nuclear issue is the contemporary fear that's entered the mass subconscious, especially since the film *The Day After*. Nearly everyone I know has had nuclear End-of-the-World dreams. Horrors are not werewolves. I like to look around at the real world and find what frightens *me*. That *frisson* of fear . . . the moment when what you assumed was a tomato stalk on the draining board suddenly runs toward your hand! That's what I'm after.

GUY: We've talked about the way you really define your characters and the worlds your strips are set in. Everything's so thoroughly thought out—the way a writer of a novel might think things out. Are you bringing in standards of writing from outside comics?

ALAN: A lot of emphasis has been placed on the cinematic quality of comic-book storytelling. But if you're using words, there's got to be a literary element there, as well. I don't consider myself a very good writer. Maybe I write pretty good comics, but in the broad arena I wouldn't be anything special. Even the best craftsmen in the medium, people I respect immensely—like Will Eisner—would be the equivalent of someone like Damon Runyan, in the literary field—a good, middle-range writer. But there's no reason why comics should not achieve the same effect as the *very best* books. There's nothing inherently inferior about the medium, but it will be held back until scripters are asked to be good writers. There have been a lot of great artists in comics, but the content of the stories just doesn't bear up to close scrutiny, generally speaking.

STEVE: Even with the new generation of writer/artists, the emphasis is on the art. But then, you get something like *Love and Rockets*.

ALAN: Which is brilliant! That's what I'm talking about. That's *writing*! Take the "Sopa de Gran Pena" story. That's like Gabriel García Marquéz or John Steinbeck! I couldn't write like that. Well, maybe one day, but not now. And Eddie Campbell, he's another good one. I admire the acuteness of the observation in his stories.

STEVE: You're talking about comics in terms of their being an art form, aren't you?

ALAN: Yeah, but I don't want to get into justifying comics as art. That's just semantics. It *is* art, but it's not gallery art. It's cheaply available to a large number of people. I love that [Marshall] McLuhanesque ideal. To me, mass reproduction of the Mona Lisa is a bigger phenomenon than the original. My ideal is the *Zap Comix* ideal. Keep every issue in print forever. I don't like the collector mentality.

GUY: I know you feel strongly about the range comic scripters have been drawing on getting narrower and narrower.

ALAN: It's not an original thought of mine. It's been plain to see for years how the medium has suffered from auto-cannibalism. Over the last two decades, the innovation of Stan Lee has been watered down, breeding imitators, and imitators of imitators. It's inbreeding, which leads to sterility. You've got to fertilize the field by drawing on a number of influences from the culture around you. Like, I'm interested in art, and the first story in *Swamp Thing* is based on a Goya engraving, "The Sleep of Reason Produces Monsters."

GUY: You draw on musical influences a lot too. "Another Green World" in *Swamp Thing* is an Eno album title.

ALAN: Brian Eno is one of my biggest influences. He had no respect at all for all that precious mystique of music. He's got a purely mechanical approach to art and craft. He said, in effect, "There are hard scientific principles at work here. If you look at them, you can work out what they are, and you can use them." And he worked out ways to get the creative process going. I've got a box of his "Oblique Strategies," which are oracle cards. You read the phrase or word on the card, and even if it seems meaningless, you have to obey it and try to apply it to your work. It jogs your mind into a new frame of reference, gets the creative juices flowing.

I don't subscribe to the precious attitude toward art, where you sit and wait for the Muse to settle on your brow. You can't just wait for an inspiration—not when you're doing it for a living. I mean, Van Gogh could, but he ended up penniless in a loony bin. If you wait for the Muse to fly in your window, you'll wait for weeks, and she'll be off down the road somewhere screwing around with some fifteen-year-old kid who's just written his first poem about the evils of modern warfare! [Laughter.] You've got to develop a mechanical approach, think about what you're doing, and experiment. For example, you've got a strand of narrative in words and a separate strand in the pictures. What happens if you divorce the two?

STEVE: I've noticed that you let the pictures shoulder a lot of the burden of what is normally left to expository dialogue. But in your stuff, quite often, the words don't really relate to the pictures in anything but an ironic way. They're telling the same story, but . . .

ALAN: . . . from different sides. Yeah, I like to do that. In that episode where V's storming the TV studios in *Warrior* #15, there's no dialogue at all. There's just the sound from the TV monitors—the dialogue from three or four different TV shows—a sitcom, a documentary—and the action on the TV interrelates with what V's doing. So, you get V killing someone accompanied by a bit of canned laughter from the TV. I like that juxtaposition. I don't know why it works, but it does. The connection is somehow made in the reader's own mind.

STEVE: This ties in with something I wanted to ask you about. Coincidence has been abused and overused as a plot device in comics, but you seem to be consciously avoiding it.

ALAN: I'm interested in coincidence as a phenomenon. I do use it, but as a storytelling device. The juxtaposition we were just talking about is synchronicity really. And I use it for scene changing. Much of comics writing comes down to finding interesting ways to change scenes, and I use overlapping dialogue a lot. That relies on the coincidence of what people are saying being relevant to a scene miles away, so the words link the scenes.

STEVE: It binds the story together without affecting the integrity of things.

ALAN'S DAUGHTER: Dinner's nearly up!

ALAN: Are you real men, or do you eat quiche? [Laughter.]

[Alan, Steve, and Guy adjourn to eat an excellent bleu-cheese quiche cooked for us by Phyllis. Alan shows the Japanese comics—the Wolf and Baby-Carriage *books Steve Moore gave him for Christmas (more commonly known in English now as* Lone Wolf and Cub—EB)—*and Steve and Guy remark on how they influenced (Frank Miller's)* Ronin. *This conversation continues as they return to the tape recorder.]*

ALAN: Those Japanese comics have very simple stories, but they're given a lot of weight by the way they're told. Me and Steve Moore like to talk about the difference between our styles. Steve is very action-oriented. He likes to have a lot happening all the time. And it works. But, for me, I like building up situations and characters so that when something does happen, even if it's only a little thing, it has that weight and that power. One of the big problems with comics is they're geared towards the superhero style. And as Paul Neary once said, the superhero is geared toward hyperbole. You start off with the greatest superhero of all time, so he has to fight the greatest villain of all time. Next issue, you need an even greater villain, and so on, until you have a villain who eats planets. And when you're using that character every few months, it becomes *commonplace* for people to eat planets. The more stepped-up it is cosmically, the less effective it becomes.

I'm trying in my own way to put some of the mystique back into super-heroes—the majesty they had for me as a kid. I want to make them less commonplace.

GUY: For example, in *Swamp Thing* #24, the Justice League is not referred to by name, nor are the individual heroes. You call them the "Overpeople," which refers back to what we were saying about *Marvelman* and the Nietzsche connection.

ALAN: I asked Steve and John to draw them with their faces shadowed—make them a bit more mysterious.

STEVE: It's lovely work. Hawkman looks really great for a change.

GUY: Do you send your artist a full script?

ALAN: Yeah, very much so. I make suggestions as to the camera angles, the lighting, the background, the mood, sometimes the color, the posture, and the body language. I try to put everything in there. But I make sure that the artists know that if they've got a better idea, they're free to use it. After all, they've got better visual imaginations than me. I provide them with a spring-board, so if they're facing a blank sheet of paper after a really heavy week-end—their families have been wiped out by Hurricane Tracy or something [laughter]—they've got somewhere to start.

STEVE: You leave a lot of the storytelling up to the artists, don't you?

ALAN: I do put a real burden on them. But now I've learned to gear my stories to an individual artist's strong points. I'd like to make one thing very clear. It annoys me when people talk about "Alan Moore's *V for Vendetta*" or "Alan

Moore's *Marvelman*," and I'm not going to enjoy hearing about "Alan Moore's *Swamp Thing*." I can't claim to be an individual artist in my own right. The end result, the strip you see on the page, is the meeting between me and the artist. That's where the creation is. I've been incredibly lucky with the artists I've worked with.

GUY: Are there any artists you're particularly looking forward to working with—perhaps some of the British artists you haven't collaborated with yet, like [Brian] Bolland, [Michael] McMahon, or [Kevin] O'Neill?

ALAN: They're pretty much at the top of the list. But I'd be interested to work with anyone new, to explore the different strong points of any artist's work. There are only two kinds of artists I wouldn't like to work with. The first kind consists of artists who write better than I do—Eisner, Miller, Eddie Campbell. The second kind would be anyone who thought their art more important than the stories. I don't consider my stories more important than the art. It's got to be equal.

Alan Moore

CHRISTOPHER SHARRETT / 1988

David Kraft's Comics Interview 65 (1988): 5–23. Reprinted by permission of David Anthony Kraft, publisher, Fictioneer Books, Ltd., #1 Screamer Mountain, Box 1241, Clayton, GA 30525.

Another introduction to Alan Moore and his work seems superfluous at this point. With the coverage of *Watchmen* in the *Nation*, *Rolling Stone*, *Spin*, *Village Voice*, *Time*, and *Newsweek*, Moore's centrality to the comic-book renaissance is assured. While the current crop of artists and writers ([Howard] Chaykin, [Frank] Miller, et. al.) gives him some stiff competition, there is little question, especially given the extent to which he is imitated, even at this early phase of his career, that Moore's erudition, his wonderful prose style, and the range of ideas he brings to his work make him important both to comics and to contemporary fiction overall.

The following interview touches on a range of ideas in Moore's masterwork, *Watchmen*, including the implications of hero worship and the political and moral concerns basic to Moore's conception of the superhero in all of his major works to date . . .

CHRISTOPHER SHARRETT: Do you see any irony in the Juvenal quote ("Who Watches the Watchmen?") being used as an epigraph to the Tower Commission Report? *Watchmen* was obviously underway well before the Iran-Contra scandal broke.

ALAN MOORE: It's the supreme and perfect irony, really. The fact that *Watchmen* was set in a parallel world aside, we were of course writing about our world in the 1980s. We found that in order to avoid treading on people's toes in terms of their prejudices, it is easier to sidestep certain emotional reactions people might have by dealing with issues with the aid of comic-book conventions. Rather than, say, mention Ronald Reagan, who for some reason many people seem to like, we used Richard Nixon. Mentioning Reagan within the confines of this story would probably cause a lot of people simply to switch off and not get to the more important ideas we wanted to transmit. We were using a science fiction story as a framework for an examination of problems in our own world. Given this, there were numerous odd coincidences happening all the time as *Watchmen* was being written, but the Tower Commission Report was wonderfully apposite. We got a call from DC congratulating us on the P.R. coup of the decade! [Laughter.] The only thing to surpass it was Reagan suggesting to Gorbachev that, who knows, they might team up to fight the aliens.

CHRIS: I'd like to ask you some questions about the themes of *Watchmen*. It seems that the book is finally about Rorschach and Ozymandias in terms of their centrality to the narrative, and they are rather archetypal figures in their connections to certain types of protagonists in literature. Rorschach seems like this wretched, acted-upon character who figures prominently in modern art from [Georg Büchner's] *Woyzek* to [Alfred Hitchcock's] *Psycho*, while Ozymandias is a more classical hero, a symbol of empire and a person in absolute control of his destiny.

ALAN: You could see them in those terms, particularly with the final confrontation, if you like, although it's not much of a confrontation. The *denouement*, with what happens to Rorschach and what happens to Veidt, might support that interpretation, I suppose. What we were trying to do with *Watchmen* was primarily to avoid a sort of baby-bird school of moralizing where the readers sit with their beaks open as they are force-fed certain predigested morals by the writer. We wanted to avoid the type of adventure fiction where the character who wins all the fights ends up with the white hat and is seen as the hero. Instead, we invented six characters, each of whom has a radically different view of the world. Rorschach has a view which is very black but essentially moral. The Comedian has a view which is also black but essentially amoral. Dr. Manhattan has his own peculiar view of the world, which could also be seen as valid. Indeed, according to some readings of *Watchmen*, it might be possible to construe Adrian Veidt as the hero. What I wanted to do was to give each of the characters, including the ones I politically disagree with—perhaps *especially* the ones I politically disagree with—a depth that would make it feasible that these were real, plausible individuals. I especially wanted to avoid making Rorschach and the Comedian foils for my own moral opinions. I wanted these characters to have the kind of integrity to cause the reader actually to sit down and make some moral decisions. We wanted to present the reader with a variety of worldviews and some hard choices to make.

CHRIS: It does seem, however, that the most important questions center on Veidt/Ozymandias, and that Veidt is a very particular rendering of the super-hero as a symbol of power. Veidt seems to be fascism with a democratic face.

ALAN: Certainly the book is about power, but it's about different manifes-tations of power. Veidt can still be seen as liberal even though he's wiped out half of New York. Veidt is a character who has used the resources of his intellect and will to create a vast material empire which he can use to his own ends. Dr. Manhattan, on the other hand, is a more impersonal power, which hangs over each of us. If he were to wipe us out, it wouldn't be anything per-sonal, which is the general situation we face in the nuclear age. Rorschach is a character with a great deal of personal power. He's obviously impoverished and powerless in terms of normal society, but his integrity gives him power. It was an investigation of the different uses of power and the effects of power. I would say that *Watchmen* was not *about* Ozymandias more than any other character. The moral implications of Veidt's actions are central to the book, and we wanted to sort of underline these implications through the use of the pirate narrative. The pirate narrative pretty accurately mirrors in a meta-phorical sense Ozymandias's passage from a sort of young idealist to a slayer of millions.

CHRIS: Is it fair to say that *Watchmen* is about the foolishness of utopian dreams? As Rorschach remarks, utopias are usually built on a foundation of dead bodies.

ALAN: I think we all entertain dreams of a better world. I don't think I was suggesting that any dream of utopia is wrong. My main concern was to show a world without heroes, without villains, since to my mind these are the two most dangerous fallacies which beset us, both in the relatively unimportant world of fiction and in the more important field of politics. Human instinct seems to categorize the world continually in terms of heroes and villains. I suspect that if we had the power to look inside Hitler's head, into the heads of the greatest monsters in history, you would find heroes. The worst crea-tures no doubt saw themselves as heroes, so the whole category is rather pointless.

CHRIS: I'm fascinated with the idea that Veidt is a Kennedy-style figure rather than a Nixon-style figure. His charisma is part of the equation that makes him dangerous. Frank Miller also touches a bit on the particular dan-gers of Kennedy-style charisma through the Ken Wind character in *Elektra: Assassin*.

ALAN: Yes, it's interesting indeed. Charisma is a dangerous thing, because it's so unquantifiable. People don't seem to have charisma in direct relation to their goodness. Charles Manson had his fair share of charisma. Bernie Goetz was granted charisma on a different level by the media, and as usual it was well beyond that which he actually earned. The charisma of the hero is something that we tend to project upon people to take care of different sorts of needs. We give people the charisma of the hero or the charisma of the villain which ultimately elects them to a kind of demi-godhood where we can no longer judge their actions. It's a dangerous notion. As I've said, I think we must get away from the idea of heroes and villains so that we can see our world made up simply of people, sometimes weak people, sometimes strong people, people working for their misguided ends or whatever. I suppose the central question of *Watchmen* is the question Dr. Manhattan asks of himself on Mars, which is, "Who makes the world?" What I was trying to say in *Watchmen* is that we *all* make the world. It isn't the heroes and villains, the Dr. Manhattans and the Richard Nixons exclusively. It can just as easily be a pudgy, acne-ridden, mentally subnormal kid working for a right-wing newspaper.

CHRIS: Seymour is finally the ordinary common man?
ALAN: He is the ordinary common slob and also the most low-life, worthless, nerdish sort of character in the entire book, who finally has the fate of the world resting in his pudgy fingers. You may have noticed also that we spend a good deal of time with the people on the street. We wanted to spend as much time detailing these characters and making them believable as we did the main characters. We wanted all of these very ordinary human beings, who sometimes speak sensibly but most often don't, who sometimes know what they're doing, but most often don't, to have a place in this vast organic mechanism that we call the world.

CHRIS: One criticism I've heard of *Watchmen* is that its politics become reversed. The book seems very radical, very progressive, but the bleak ending seems to suggest that the only change in the world is the kind effectuated by charismatic leaders.
ALAN: I could see how people could read that into it, but it certainly wasn't what we intended, and I don't think it's the most obvious sort of message the book conveys. In some ways what we were trying to say was quite the opposite. To my point of view, our leaders are, in a sense, riding a wave on a surfboard. They're not in control of the wave, but because they're on top of it, we sometimes get that illusion. The wave is in fact something vast and

unfathomable which has its beginning in the mass unconscious or whatever and works its way out. Perhaps what Veidt did was totally unnecessary. The real point is that power resides with everyone, that we are all responsible. The world is far more complex than our political systems sometimes would have us believe, although of course these powerful individual leaders have a prominent role, but that too must be seen as the responsibility of everyone. The last line of *Watchmen*, "I leave it entirely in your hands," was directed at the reader more than Seymour. The fate of the world is undecided: everyone has responsibility. What the reader does in the next ten minutes is as important as everything Ronald Reagan does.

CHRIS: If I can go back to Veidt for a second, is it reasonable to assume that Veidt's plan fails? I ask this principally because you take the name Ozymandias from Shelley's poem, which is a meditation on the folly of power.

ALAN: I wouldn't want to say what you can assume from the ending. It seemed to me that it would detract from the work if we were to allow the tension to be dissipated by a resolution. What I wanted to do was crank up the tension. I wanted to leave the reader with this ending where even after this spectacular massacre, one doesn't know if the whole thing worked or if another Comedian-like twist of fate and circumstance would have it all amount to nothing and become the ultimate joke. I think some people were disappointed with the ending because they wanted something rock-solid and conclusive. We wanted the reader to make the decisions.

CHRIS: I think the ending is fine as it stands, but you do invite an enormous amount of conjecture.

ALAN: Yeah. I understand this and do it quite a bit meself. I think it's perfectly acceptable. Who knows, maybe Seymour didn't reach for Rorschach's diary but took another piece of crank mail instead. Perhaps the whole thing didn't work. Yes, I think there's a case to be made, particularly given the tone of Shelley's poem, that this dream of utopia might end up as a cracked head in the middle of a wasteland.

CHRIS: If I could touch for a moment on Rorschach, he's the most demented character, but you've obviously given him a poet's soul. He's capable of waxing lyrical.

ALAN: It's a kind of black lyricism, but, yeah, I would agree. Of course, my main inspiration for that character's voice was the notes Son of Sam gave to the police.

CHRIS: I was thinking also of the story of Carl Panzram.
ALAN: Who? I don't believe I know the name.

CHRIS: Carl Panzram was a rather famous mass murderer executed in the 1930s. He read Kant and Schopenhauer in prison, kept a journal, thought of the world as nothing but cruelty and horror. Rorschach's examination by Dr. Long sounds a bit similar to Panzram's examination by Dr. Karl Menninger.
ALAN: That's fascinating. It does sound like Rorschach, doesn't it? It's also the classic serial killer, who seems to have a rather high I.Q. and is usually extremely disaffected. But, no, the influences were Steve Ditko's Mr. A and Son of Sam. Mr. A was this marvelous Ayn Randian character who was utterly merciless with any form of evil and was unable to see any shades of grey in terms of morality. What we did with Rorschach was to take this even further. I used to ask, "What does Mr. A think of when he masturbates?" The problem was that Steve Ditko's character was very much of a moral cipher. I put this character into a physically unpleasant body and combined it with the sort of mad, crack poetry of the Son of Sam notes talking about the cracks in the sidewalk and the blood in the cracks and the ants that fed upon the blood. Rorschach was one of the characters I enjoyed writing most, but the experience was a bit grueling. Issue #6 was a kind of paean to existential despair, and I had to settle meself into that frame of mind, which isn't the nicest place to be.

CHRIS: The figure of Hooded Justice is interesting. He's a central figure in some ways, particularly because he's the first superhero, but we never learn much about him. We're especially in the dark concerning what motivates him.
ALAN: He is a central figure in certain ways, but in writing *Watchmen*, we wanted to approximate real life as closely as one can in a comic book. Just as there are a lot of subliminal little connections among events, there are also actions which have no real relevance to anything. I created a bit of a red herring here. Some readers latched onto the idea that Hooded Justice disappeared without leaving a definitely identifiable body and assumed that he might be the murderer and so forth. But the only story we give you is what's there. There's some material that you can assemble, based on the idea that when the events of the fifties overtook him, Hooded Justice decided to go on the run to protect his identity. The Comedian probably took advantage of the situation, and the bad blood which began with Hooded Justice beating up the Comedian in the trophy room ended with the Comedian putting a bullet in

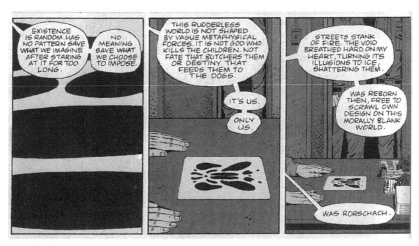

From *Watchmen* #6, page 26 (partial) by Alan Moore and Dave Gibbons. Copyright © 1987 DC Comics. All Rights Reserved, used by permission.

his brain and throwing his body in the river. It was just another miserable, grubby, violent sort of story in the lives of these superheroes. Some were killed, some went bad, some simply disappeared and were never seen again.

CHRIS: The gay motif involving Captain Metropolis and Hooded Justice is interesting. The gay angle was always implicit to superheroes, especially Batman, but never fully explored.

ALAN: There again, I wanted to approximate real life as much as possible, and that meant giving each of the characters a sexual identity, a political identity, and most components one would usually associate with personality. I tried to avoid making each of my characters someone who can be summed up in thirty-five words, which is basically the maxim which has been passed down in the comics industry for ten years. I think it was at Marvel that it was actually graven in stone that the *best* characters can be summed up in thirty-five words. I would hate to think I could be summarized in thirty-five words, and I wouldn't want to go to dinner with anyone who could be. It strikes me that ordinary people have a number of aspects to their personalities. People have sexual dimensions, political dimensions, different emotional dimensions, and given the world of *Watchmen*, it seemed likely that there would be roughly the same percentage of gay people as in our own world, and that certain professions might attract a higher percentage of gays than other professions. It seemed sensible to me that costumed crime fighting might be one of those professions. But it isn't all that important, finally, anymore than it's important that the cab driver is gay. She's a character who happens to be gay. She has a certain personality and her gayness is an aspect of that personality. But at the same time, yes, there is a sexual element to costumed adventuring, and this becomes a subtext to the book. The sexual element takes various forms. It can be argued that Rorschach's energies must surely be displaced sexual energies. In writing him, it was plainly obvious that he never had any relations with anyone at all, and furthermore viewed the entire subject with violent distaste, presumably because of his experience with his mother.

CHRIS: I'd like to ask just a couple of final questions on the characters. Ozymandias appears to be a bit undermotivated considering that we know so much about Rorschach, Nite Owl, Dr. Manhattan, and the others. We learn, for example, that Veidt's parents come to America in 1939 but have to assume the reason why.

ALAN: As you know, we gave one issue to each of the characters, with a different method applied to each character's background. With Rorschach there was a psychoanalytic approach. With Dr. Manhattan, it was a kind of fourth-dimensional approach with reference to the theory of relativity. With Veidt, you'll notice that in his story, as he's recounting his life, he's facing away from us. This distances the whole thing. All we know is what he himself chooses to tell us. Yes, there are blanks, as you suggest. He doesn't choose to go into his feelings. Perhaps this is a person who is extraordinarily bright, who measures himself against other people and decides what to do with his life. He decides he wants to tackle the big things, as it were, and to measure himself against people like Alexander. I recall the story of Julius Caesar being found crying on his thirty-first birthday and asked, "Why are you crying Caesar?" His reply was that by his age Alexander ruled most of the world. It struck me that this might apply to Veidt in that he couldn't bear the thought of anyone ever being better than him.

CHRIS: It's nice the way that Veidt, as a modern Caesar, is able to saturate the world with his presence through his position as a corporate head. His name is on everything from jogging shoes to cologne. The corporate capitalist as Caesar.

ALAN: Certainly. One of the things we wanted to do with *Watchmen* was to show the kind of congruity, the relationship of our world to the world of

Alexander, or the world of piracy we feature in the Black Freighter narrative. The world of piracy, at least the fictional world of piracy, is this black place where a lot of horrid, murderous deeds go on. It would be a mistake to imagine that such a world, even an imagined one, is removed from events in the contemporary world. So, we juxtaposed the pirate story with Nixon talking about fallout drifts and Ozymandias using Alexander as the first example of lateral thinking. I suppose the point here is that the more things change, the more they remain the same.

CHRIS: To go back for a moment to characters' personalities, it seems that Rorschach's alter ego and self-estimation is as large as Veidt's despite Rorschach's terrible origins. The fact is, this self-image allows him to do the most superhuman deeds, like climbing up a skyscraper or riding in the Antarctic with a trenchcoat on. Is the idea of ego a basic problem in the concept of the superhero?

ALAN: In a certain sense, perhaps. I've known various people who were capable of extraordinary physical acts simply because they were obsessed. I think we could have rethought the bit about Rorschach climbing up the skyscraper, which is within the bounds of possibility I suppose but a little too superheroish. Our point here was to show the man's obsession. Wearing a warm coat in the Antarctic would be a sign of softness to Rorschach, just as heating up a can of beans at Dreiberg's house would be a sign of softness. He sort of feels he would be betraying his principles to live in any manner other than one of total squalor and discomfort. This is probably a political thing as well. We've all known people who choose to live a very Spartan lifestyle and attempt to justify it on vaguely political grounds. It's a way of validating oneself. Veidt is a big opposite in his extravagant lifestyle, but there are similarities in regard to the way a person justifies a lifestyle and makes it correspond to a view of the world.

CHRIS: I'd like to talk to you about influences. William Burroughs is referred to several times in *Watchmen*, such as in the first page of issue #11 and through the magazine *Nova Express*. Could you describe your interest in Burroughs?

ALAN: Sure. If I had to single out one major influence on my work, it would probably be Burroughs. I would never attempt to duplicate his style of writing. I love his style, but it's unique to him. There have been various attempts to mimic his cut-up technique, most of which have been mannered imitations of Burroughs. I do admire his style, but I suppose the biggest influence is his thinking, his theoretical work, some of which has been wild and extreme, but the relationship he draws between the word and the image and the importance of both, I think, is significant. Burroughs tends to see the word and the image as the basis for our inner, and thus outer, realities. He suggests that the person who controls the word and the image controls reality. It seems to me a great pity that Burroughs hasn't done more comic-strip work himself given his interest in juxtaposition. There is one Burroughs comic strip in existence. It's a strip called "The Unspeakable Mr. Hart," done for a British underground comic called *Cyclops*. It was a poorly drawn but compelling little piece of work that was spotted by young David Chester Gibbons, who at the time was a surveyor and not involved in comics. He was interested in the idea of a comic shop. He went to the shop, eventually got involved in fandom, got involved in illustration, and finally gave up his job as a surveyor. Just an odd Burroughsian interconnection [laughter]. But, yeah, Burroughs is a strong influence, probably more in his thinking, the thinking that goes into writing, rather than the writing itself. I loved the last book. *The Place of Dead Roads*, sort of Wild Bill Burroughs [laughter].

CHRIS: I'm interested also in your knowledge of semiotic theory and the extent to which you've been influenced there. Your style shows some relation to the work of [Roland] Barthes and [Jacques] Derrida, and you actually mention semiotics in Chapter 11 of *Watchmen*.

ALAN: As an intellectual, I'm incredibly lazy, and also something of a dilettante. I tend to pick an idea out of a book, hypothesize the rest, and fake it. The only book on semiotics I've *ever* read is Roland Barthes's *Mythologies*, which I picked up about fifteen years ago. That was a revelation, this whole notion of the relationships of signals and signs. A book I'm looking forward to is Umberto Eco's *Travels in Hyperreality*, which I've got on order now. Yeah, I've got an interest in this, but it's a sort of uninformed layman's interest. My interest is mainly in terms of how I can manipulate, if you will, the underlanguage of comics, the language which occurs at the juncture of the word and the image. I'm interested in manipulating symbols and images in a way that will have a rather subliminal affect on the viewer. I think comics as a medium is ideally suited for this sort of thing, far more so than film, because with comics you can stare at the page for as long as you need in order to absorb all the little hints and suggestions going on in the background. With film, you're dragged along with the running speed of the projector, and unless you have a director like Alex Cox—who in *Repo Man* is able to cram the background with so many details you can't help but register them—you can lose some details of a film.

CHRIS: In the area of visuals, I'd like to go to the first six pages of the last chapter of *Watchmen*, those images of the New York holocaust. Those six pages are fairly unprecedented. I was thinking of images from Bruegel, Bosch, and Goya.

ALAN: We wanted to show the devastation of New York in as visual a way as possible. There have been quite a few holocausts in comics, but rarely is this kind of horror portrayed realistically. I mean, the first Superman comic begins with an entire planet being blown up. We're a little blasé about the death of millions. Comics have been even more blasé, I'm afraid, than other media in this regard. We wanted to transmit the impact of this devastation by giving the reader an actual physical shock. You noticed, no doubt, that this was the first time in the entire series that we used a full-page picture. There are no splash pages in *Watchmen*. We deliberately held off for eleven issues so that the impact of not one but six full-pages of images depicting in brutal detail this massive loss of life would be a bit devastating. I suppose that with all that intricate detail, all those little scenes of horror and such, it's rather difficult *not* to recall Bosch or Bruegel. I'm a big fan of those two gentlemen, and I'm sure Dave is too.

CHRIS: There's a sense at the end of the book that nothing has really changed.

ALAN: Well, no, at least not in our intent. I think there's an impression that things had changed quite a lot. For one thing the streets are rather empty. There are fewer people about. But beyond that, every sign, every little detail has changed. The spark hydrants have changed. The Gunga Diner is now Burgers and Borscht. *Tales of the Black Freighter* has been edged out by *Tales from the Morgue*. Even the wall graffiti has changed. "Who Watches the Watchmen?" has been replaced with "Watch the Skies." "One in Eight Go Mad" is replaced with "One in Three Go Mad." The change is relative not only to Veidt's action but to the whole world of the book, since we began, in a sense, with a pre-1960s America and ends with a post-1985 America. Whether or not this change is permanent is a different issue.

CHRIS: There's an issue of realism there. The holocaust takes place in early November, but New York is entirely back in shape by New Year's.

ALAN: I'm not sure. We do have a world there with slightly different technologies than our own, after all, and I think a mass devastation of New York would necessitate the immediate replacement of certain things. Say, for example, that you had planned to replace the spark hydrants anyway, and that the destruction of a large amount of them by cars smashing into them and so forth had expedited the process. Maybe we did collapse the time factor a bit there for dramatic effect. Maybe it could have been February or March when the epilogue takes place. It would have been a bit more credible, but I'm happy with the way it works.

CHRIS: It strikes me that you're not interested in a kind of Hitchcock ending, since you really telegraph the conclusion to us fairly early on, for people really paying attention.

ALAN: Our concern was that for people who read *Watchmen*, when they know who killed the Comedian, they could still find the book rewarding. On the simple MacGuffin level of the plot, there is a murder mystery, but that certainly isn't the end intention of the book. To us the most important thing is the semiotic substance, the things going on in the background, the meanings and intimations of meaning throughout the book. The plot was the skeleton over which we draped this flesh, the real substance of the book, and I think we got it about right in that most people I've spoken to who read it can go back two or three times and find new ideas or images they missed earlier on.

CHRIS: You really overturn expectations of the audience with that ending, in terms of the catastrophe that occurs. Most people were prepared, I think, for a real apocalypse.

ALAN: Well, yes, I think most readers fully expected the entire world to be wiped out and were disappointed when it was only five or six million people [laughter]. As I've said, we wanted to put the reader in the same moral dilemma as some of the characters. I think we were successful in that, from all I've read. On the Compuserve network, according to the review in the *Nation*, people are still debating whether or not Veidt was right in his scenario, whether he had the right to do it or not. Yeah. I think expectations were overturned concerning the nuclear war. All the signs pointed to it, Dr. Manhattan had strongly hinted as much, but then you end up with something that might be considered even more horrible. To think that someone could carry out such an act ruthlessly, cold-bloodedly, might be seen as more horrible than a catastrophe occurring due to our leaders' general mania and incompetence. We wanted to leave the reader with some moral questions about this act, questions which are problematical, I think, especially because the perpetrator is a liberal and a humanitarian! This issue raised here is not particularly new, of course. It's the same issue Rorschach brings up in his childhood essay, where he speaks highly of Truman for dropping the bomb on Hiroshima, this old argument concerning the sacrifice of lives as a price one pays for the betterment of the world.

CHRIS: Comparisons between *Dark Knight* [*Batman: The Dark Knight Returns*] and *Watchmen* are inevitable, especially in regard to the treatment of the superhero in both.

ALAN: Frank Miller and I are good friends, you know. We might have differences politically, although we've never found anything to argue about. We're both what might be termed "radical" to one degree or another, and as a result of that, yes, I suppose there are similarities in the two books. There are areas that, while thinking separately, we did come to some similar conclusions about. I think what's more interesting than the similarities are the differences in basic concerns of both books. Frank likes adventure fiction, and what he wanted with *Dark Knight* was to produce a very superior, very well executed, piece of adventure fiction. That wasn't our ambition in *Watchmen*. We produced a moral and political fable that used the icons of superhero adventure fiction to make its point. I don't know how to put this without sounding like I'm trivializing *Dark Knight*, which is the last thing I want to do, but *Dark Knight* includes moral and political ideas as part of its style, to make it more credible to the contemporary reader. It's basically adventure fiction with political ideas added to it. We came at it from the opposite direction. We were not concerned so much with adventure. There wasn't much action. There was no clear-cut hero. We were concerned with quieter things than *Dark Knight*. *Dark Knight* is a superhero adventure with moral and political ideas added in; *Watchmen* is a moral and political story with superheroes.

CHRIS: A predominant image of the book is the circle, since it appears in the central symbols of the clock, the smiley face, the radiation symbol, and there is also a circular kind of structure to the book.

ALAN: I think that the fact of those images being circles is more down to coincidence than any conscious attempt to refer to circularity. There is the clock, which simply helped underscore the tone of the book, a device that fit the title and concept in a kind of word-play relationship. The smiley button reflected the tone of the series on a number of levels. We found out while working on the book that the smiley face originated in a series of behavioral experiments with children. They were experiments to find the purest image of affection that a baby would respond to, and the smiley face is apparently it. The smiley face is evidently the purest symbol of innocence the human race has been able to come up with thus far. In that sense, putting a bloodstain across the eye of the face allows for a number of interpretations. There's the idea of smiling through the blood, the idea of a bloody joke, which, after all, is what Ozymandias perpetrates on humanity. Also, since the badge is a symbol of innocence, and since superheroes have also represented a certain naïveté and innocence, you have a sense of lost or bloodied innocence, the end of this idea of truth, justice, and the American way. The very naïve notion of superhero goodness gets bloodied and knocked about. There were a few other resonations there, but I think those were the principal ideas.

CHRIS: I wonder if you would discuss for a bit the relationship of *Watchmen* to *Miracleman* [née *Marvelman*] in terms of the image of the superhero.

ALAN: When I returned to *Miracleman* after working on *Watchmen*, it seemed that some of the ideas I began with on *Miracleman* had become old hat, since I'd developed them more fully in *Watchmen*, and in the intervening periods other creators had also come up with some very radical takes on the superhero. It was difficult to rethink this because I had already planned the plot outline of *Miracleman* and knew where it was going to go, but in Book Three I had to push the superhero even further than in *Watchmen*. *Miracleman* could not be as complex or intricate as *Watchmen*, of course, but it had to have a vision of the superhero that was even more radical. So I looked to the inspiration for superheroes in the motherlode, in the Greek myths, where you have an Olympus, you have a number of gods, each of whom govern an area of human endeavor. It's much more of a fantasy than *Watchmen*, but again a sort of very ambiguous utopia. *Miracleman* seems very benign, very decent, but some questions remain. I think I take it a step beyond *Watchmen*.

CHRIS: I'd like to wrap up by asking you some questions about your future plans. We know that you've parted company with DC, but there continue to be rumors that you're through with comics entirely.

ALAN: No, that's not true. I'll not be doing any more work for DC, but I'm not leaving comics. It's true I won't be doing much work in mainstream comics, and most people can't imagine comics outside the mainstream, so I suppose that's where the rumor comes from. It's true about DC, however. *V for Vendetta* will be coming out soon. The Batman/Joker graphic novel with Brian Bolland is finished [*Batman: The Killing Joke*], and I'll very likely do a Mr. Monster/Swamp Thing team-up, which I planned quite some time ago with Michael Gilbert. After that, in terms of future plans, I'm impressed with the development of the comics audience in the recent couple of years, the fact that we find comics in the book shops, and we've gained a fingerhold with the adult audience. If you would have asked me five years ago to describe my audience, I would have started by placing it between thirteen and eighteen years of age. Now, I'd place it between thirteen and thirty-five or forty. It has expanded a great deal. If we're going to keep that audience, we're going to have to be conscious of their interests, which aren't going to be the same as our captive audience. It's true that this new audience will occasionally enjoy a novel take on the superhero, but it won't want a steady diet of that. It would be like all the films being westerns, and unfortunately comics have had that kind of homogeneity. So, I'm finished with superheroes. After *V for Vendetta* and *Miracleman*, that will be it for the foreseeable future in terms of superheroes.

I'm certainly not through with comics. I might do the odd film script or novel or television play, but that's just because of my interest in experimenting with those media. Basically, I've no interest in films, no interest in television work. For me, comics is still the most exciting medium to work in, with the greatest possibilities.

CHRIS: What about the independent comic companies? Do you have any contract there?

ALAN: I haven't signed any new contracts with anyone. The independent companies have many of the same problems, in that the arrangements they make with the creators are usually shameful and antediluvian. If DC and Marvel comics now have pretensions regarding this adult market, they should adopt adult business practices. Instead, they continue to treat their creators as chattel. The idea of creators owning their own creations is something that DC Comics, even in its new enlightened mode refuses to entertain. They've set up a new concern called Piranha Press, which they optimistically hope will attract work of the quality of *Love and Rockets* and *Maus*, yet DC will continue to own rights to all characters, thank you very much. They simply must be taught a lesson. For my part, I might as well work with book companies and be treated as a proper author, so my ambition is really to write graphic novels for book companies, which will be going out to the book shops, with me owning the rights to my own creations, the company having the right to print the material once. This is a bit more reasonable and civilized. So, that's my strategy: comics for book companies, rather than comics for comic book companies. I also think it's a good idea to sort of stake out that area and consolidate it, to keep a steady stream of graphic novels which will continue to interest the widest possible adult audience and really give comics their proper place. Now, in terms of content, like I say, no superheroes. I'm much more interested in exploring our own world rather than creating new alien worlds and such. There are so many areas of our own landscape that seem like the first outpost of Mars, there is no need to create fantastic worlds. It strikes me as much more interesting to find the weird, bizarre, and fascinating aspects of mundane, everyday life.

CHRIS: That's very much the strategy of someone like Burroughs, and also J. G. Ballard.

ALAN: Absolutely. With Ballard it's easy to see how he's gotten away from fantasy in one respect, while finding things in the inner, psychic landscape that are every bit as fabulous and fascinating as his drowned worlds and crystal worlds. That's the kind of direction I'll be taking. I'm planning to do a graphic novel which I can't say too much about at the moment, but it might very well involve a shopping mall, an image which fascinates me and has been dealt with a bit in some books and films but not by any means exhausted. I'm also interested in using comics for other purposes, such as political journalism. I don't know if you've seen *Real War Comics*, but that's an example of the kind of work that I enjoy doing and has to my mind a lot of applications. I don't know what it's really like in your country, but if it's anything like over here, people would rather die than read a page of political analysis. Politics, for most people, has to be on the level of such meaningless gutter rubbish as Gary Hart–Donna Rice before people become interested. That's the kind of expectations and tastes people have cultivated. Politics has become some sort of quantum science which most people would like to leave to the big boys and the experts and not bother with otherwise, which I find a profoundly dangerous notion. Now, since comics are sort of inherently garish and sensational, it might be possible to get across complex political and moral ideas in a way that would be attractive to most people and cause people actually to sit down and read. Perhaps it's a small way of getting people to see how the study of politics actually applies to everyday life. I think this strategy has been validated somewhat by the Pentagon, which released a study saying that the most effective way of getting ideas across is in the form of a comic strip. We've believed it all the time, but now it's official [laughter]. So, our side has to have some role in this. I think much can be done here, and without vulgarizing or oversimplifying complex moral and political ideas so that they come out looking like some melodramatic made-for-TV movie or something. We'd want to avoid that, but I think comics could be a way of giving things back to the public, not just in the area of politics but in, for example, the area of literature. No one reads poetry, as a case in point. It's probably the easiest thing to get published and the last thing people want to read, perhaps because in school they've had hosts of golden daffodils crammed down their throats and came away thinking that's what poetry is all about. In *Swamp Thing*, you may not have good poetry, but there is poetry there which people can read and enjoy and perhaps see how poetry can be connected to a larger world of ideas. It might be possible actually to give back politics and poetry to people through this medium.

CHRIS: For some time, there's been a discussion about comics being the last outpost of literacy. With people like yourself, Frank Miller, Howard Chaykin, and others, that might finally be true. It's a shame that the major companies still have such poor policies.

ALAN: That's all got to change. I can see a domino effect happening. Basically, I see companies like DC and most of the others so far rooted in the past that they will continue to hang onto their rather dismal, grubby business practices for as long as possible, but in fact that won't be for much longer. When they see that people like me and Howard and Frank and the other top creators in the field can take work to book companies, they will see where their competition is. There will be no reason in the world why even *new* creators could not take their work to book companies, which I think will want to involve themselves in this new market more and more. I think the literacy idea is quite correct, and we'll be seeing a great deal of excellent work produced in the medium. There has to be a domino effect as comics companies realize what kind of competition they're faced with. In Britain, the situation is even worse in terms of company policy toward creators, worse than any of the American companies, but they will have to realize that with American companies coming over here regularly to hunt for talent, it's now an international market. The British comics companies will have to compete with the American comics companies who in turn will compete with the book companies. If it all works out—and of course there are many slips between cup and lip—but if it does work out, inevitably comics will be brought up to a perfectly respectable status with all other media, the kind of status other media have enjoyed for the past several decades. I'm quite optimistic about it and am looking forward to a very, very vital comics medium within the next ten years.

Alan Moore Interview

MATTHEW DE ABAITUA / 1998

The Idler 22 (February/March 1998). Reprinted by permission of Matthew De Abaitua.

The following is from the unedited transcript. The print edition was "highly truncated," as described online, where the unedited version has previously appeared, first at www.eddiecampbellcomics.com, and then at http://anamnesis.nl.eu.org/Alan-Moore-Interview-The-Idler-februari-1998.html. Mr. Abaitua notes that James Randi took exception to some of his portrayal in this interview. I elect to include the material anyway, with the understanding that it may be somewhat inaccurate and not completely indicative of Randi's thinking or behavior. Rather, the discussion of Randi sheds light on Alan Moore's thought and ideas, which is, ultimately, the purpose of this book. EB

We pull up in a pizza restaurant, where the waiters greet Moore with familiarity.

MDA: Is this a regular haunt then?

AM: Pretty much. I've been in most of the restaurants of Northampton. I tend to do them on a circuit. I'll eat at one of them for a couple of months and then get bored with it and go on to the next one. I'm less than electrifying today. I've been doing a lot of work this week and have not been getting to bed until four or five, and then getting up at nine, so I'm shell-shocked.

I've had some guys up. Alex Usborne, who has been producing the *Acid House Trilogy* for Irvine Welsh and "The Granton Star Cause," he is planning to do *Big Numbers* as a TV series, the full twelve-part colossus, like *Our Friends in the North*.

MDA: Has that all been published now?

AM: No, no it's never going to be published now. I've had two artists just run screaming into the night, and it becomes increasingly difficult to resurrect as a comic book with each one. I've written the scripts up to issue five. But what do you do? Do you get a new artist in? Do you start running it again from issue one and promise the readers that this time we are going to finish it. And what happens if the artist leaves halfway through again? I wonder, "Is it me?" Is it me doing this to these poor boys? I've been thinking, "What am I going to do about *Big Numbers*?" I don't want to leave it unfinished, and then when Alex Usborne approached me and asked me if I had anything suitable for television, I said "no," because most of it is either owned by other people or too peculiar. Then he started talking about *Big Numbers*, and I said, "Well that's even more of a problem, because I don't think I'm going to be able to finish that as a comic book."

While I was saying the words, I thought, "Maybe I could finish it as a television series." I've got the whole plot, the structure's practically done. So, we've been working with a scriptwriter to put the whole thing together. I've got this huge A1 sheet of paper with forty characters listed down one side and twelve numbers across the top, so there are twelve hundred squares filled with my little tiny mental-patient handwriting saying what was happening to each character in each issue. It is a wonderful piece of work in itself. It turns out to be a good schematic for the entire twelve-part series. If it goes anywhere.

MDA: Prospective TV and film projects are always so up in the air.
AM: It's barely even up in the air. It's in some vapourous nether dimension from which it may coalesce into something as sturdy as a soap bubble. The *From Hell* film is going to go into production in April, May, June. I understand Sean Connery has been signed for it, Hughes brothers to direct. It sounds like it might happen. But I've seen two of my books, *V for Vendetta* and *Watchmen*, go through various stages of Hollywood optimism. But I've not been that interested. I mean, it was nice to meet Terry Gilliam. The first thing he said to me over lunch was, "Well, how would you turn *Watchmen* into a film?" and I said, "Well to be honest Terry, I wouldn't." So we went on to talk about other things and just had a great lunch. But *Big Numbers* could work. It was always more like a TV series than a comic book anyway. All the visual elements, the backgrounds, were photo-referenced. It might have been a lot easier if we had just filmed it to begin with. But Hollywood, television, and film is not my prime area of interest, because I would never have any control, working in those areas. It's nice to get the money from a Hollywood project, but whatever they do with it, it would be their piece of work, and not mine. Someone said to Raymond Chandler, "How do you feel about Hollywood ruining all your books?" and he took them into his study, pointed to the shelves containing

Farewell, My Lovely and all the rest of them, and said, "There they are. They're alright. They're not ruined."

MDA: You said you'd been working quite hard this week. Is that the way you normally work, with long periods of research that snap into sudden flurries of activity?

AM: It doesn't really work like that. Because there are so many projects going on, when I'm researching one, I'm doing three others, so it tends to be pretty frenetic. Not many days go by without me actually writing a few pages, at the very least. I imagine it will be that way for the foreseeable future. I'd like to get the chance to slow down at some point, but on the other hand, it's surprising what you can do. I quite like working in this frenetic zone of ideas. As the ideas come up, you have to see which of the projects you are working on it is most applicable to, sort them properly. It's pleasurable. It doesn't feel stressful. It's kind of exhilarating to be able to do two or three things you are pleased with a week. It's also nice to be able to refresh the palette between courses. I mean, if you're writing something like *From Hell* without a break, I should imagine that would be horrible. But if I can take a few days off to write some baroque pornography like *Lost Girls*, or some harmless superhero fun, or do a bit of recording in the studio, stuff like that, there is a kind of synergy between the different forms of work. You'll learn things from one sort of work that will have tremendous application in another. They all tend to pull each other forward.

MDA: What I like about that form of work is that you are never trying to shoehorn various ideas and concepts into one project.

AM: When people first start out, and they've got all these wonderful ideas in their head with very few opportunities to vent them, you do find people who've got three very good ideas that they are trying to combine into one lousy idea. I did hear that Quentin Tarantino and Roger Avary had originally written a long, sprawling, and probably unusable screenplay containing the ideas for *True Romance*, *Pulp Fiction*, *Reservoir Dogs*, and *Natural Born Killers*. The *Natural Born Killers* was a fiction written by the characters in *True Romance*. So, you can imagine, in its original form, it was unreadable, but you come to learn how to discriminate between ideas. So, I have a more fractal way of working, if you like. It is more like the way most people's minds actually work. They don't work in any linear way. When your mind wanders, if you ever pay attention to some of the paths it takes, you generally find it's these paths of association that can link all over the place. Rudy Rucker, the mathematician, did an essay called "Life Is a Fractal in Hilbert Space," where he was talking about how, if you light up a cigarette, this may spark up any number of possible topics. You might start thinking about recent problems cigarette companies are having. You might start thinking about cancer . . .

[Quick break to order drinks]

The movements of the mind don't follow any linear pattern. They can't be explained with a mechanistic, clockwork view. You could find quantum models of how the mind works that might fit.

MDA: When we interviewed Bez [Mark Berry], he likened God to a particle in the corner of his mind.

AM: It's like The Copenhagen Interpretation that he [Niels Bohr] made [at] the Carlsberg Brewery, that all our scientific observations of the universe and quanta can only, in the end, be observations of ourselves. These are more interesting models of the mind than these deterministic models that a lot of biologists seem reluctant to let go of. They desperately want to explain all human thought processes as the squirt of a gland and some chemical reaction in the temporal lobe.

MDA: They are really stoked up in the press—the media always seizes upon genes for different forms of behaviour—the gay gene, the criminal gene, and these things always have more sinister sociological intents behind them.

AM: It's Nazi science, let's face it. People are more comfortable with that. I am currently writing this thing that is a study of some of my associates in this magic business. [We] are trying to formulate some quasi-rational thoughts on what we think of consciousness, language, magic, and art, and the relationships between them. And connect that with human development and show how these things are incredibly intertwined and inextricable from each other. We start out talking about how the "I" is its own blind spot. Mind has come up with this brilliant way of looking at the world, science, but it can't look at itself. Science has no place for the mind. The whole of our science is based upon empirical, repeatable experiments, whereas thought is not in that category. You can't take thought into a laboratory. The essential fact of our existence, perhaps the only fact of our existence—our own thought and perception—is ruled offside by the science it has invented. Science looks at the universe, doesn't see itself there, doesn't see mind there, so you have a world in which mind has no place. We are still no nearer to coming to terms with the actual dynamics of what consciousness is. In questing after artificial intelligence, we seem only to have learnt that normal intelligence is so far beyond our comprehension.

[picks up menu]

I've got to focus here, focus on food. I tend to forget to eat when I'm not sleeping, so I should shove something satisfying down my neck.

MDA: Have you come across the works of Rupert Sheldrake?

AM: Yeah, the morphogenetic field theory. You've got to admire a guy who has had *Nature* magazine recommend burning all his works. I've got a lot of sympathy for his ideas. My theories of Idea Space aren't necessarily complimentary to his notion of morphogenetic field theory, but they would probably have much the same effect.

MDA: When I reread *Swamp Thing*, your interpretation of his origins reminded me of Sheldrake's theories.

AM: Well, if I'm right, all these ideas are in the air, and if he's right, then there is morphic resonance around these in his morphogenetic field. Not unsurprisingly then, these ideas will turn up in fiction, comic books, cheap trash movies, scientific dissertations. I can't think of any other explanations for why these ideas should be so prevalent. It's what Charles Fort called Steam Engine Time. When James Watt invented the steam engine, there were about eight other guys who invented it around the same time but just not quite fast enough to make it down the patents office.

[We order food.]

MDA: I have a great attraction to theories like Sheldrake's morphic resonance. I read an interview with him, when he was talking about how there is no proof that memory is actually held in the brain. He posited a view that the brain is more like a radio tuner than a video recorder, receiving thoughts, memories—both those of the self and the collective—from localised morphic fields. These ideas are very attractive because they posit an alternative to straightforward mortality. You read it and feel that leap within, "Perhaps there might be more to life than just death." You have to be suspicious of your own motivations for seizing at these ideas—like a dying man reaching for miracle cures.

AM: Sheldrake's idea of the brain as a radio receiver—I feel something quite similar. But I'm still thinking it through, so this is a thought in progress. It strikes me that self, not just my self, but all self, the phenomenon of self, is perhaps one field, one consciousness. Perhaps there is only one "I." Perhaps our brains, our selves, our entire identity, is little more than a label on a waveband. We are only us when we are here. At this particular moment in space and time, this particular locus, the overall awareness of the entire continuum happens to believe it is Alan Moore. Over there (he points to another table in the pizza restaurant), it happens to believe it is something else.

I get the sense that if you can pull back from this particular locus, this website if you like, then you could be the whole net. All of us could be. That there is only one awareness here that is trying out different patterns. We are going to have to come to some resolution about a lot of things in the next twenty years' time: our notions of time, space, identity. The flowerings of seemingly outlandish concepts like Sheldrake's are what you would expect. At the scientific end of the spectrum—and I am a regular *New Scientist* reader— I like to balance the mad howling diabolism with a dose of scientific reality—I have noticed that the crossover is getting a bit extreme. The people at the cutting-edge of quantum physics and cosmology are trying to come up with a practical, workable model for the original expansion of the universe and what is happening now at a quantum level. They were saying that they are having to turn to these archaic belief structures, like Sufi beliefs, or the Qabbalah. They were talking about how this idea of expansion from a single point is the core of the Qabbalah—and the most accurate description of the Big Bang, knowing what we know now, would be Hokmah Binah. So, I was reading this in the *New Scientist*, and I was thinking, "Well surely this is the sort of idea I would expect from Robert Anton Wilson." All of us collectively are fumbling towards an apprehension of something that feels like a kind of group awareness. We are trying to feel the shape of it. It's not here yet, and a lot of us are probably saying a lot of silly things. That's understandable. There is something strange looming on the human horizon. If you draw a graph of all our consciousness, there is a point we seem to be heading towards. Our physics, our philosophy, our art, our literature—there is a kind of coherence there. It may look disorganised at first glance, but there is a fumbling towards a new way of apprehending of certain basic fundamentals. In postmodern literature, you can see similar things happening to what is happening, at the same time, in science, with the quantum theory advances. They are trying to come up with nonlinear ways of viewing things, trying to think our way outside of our own perceptions to find a new perception. Some people mistake this approaching new perception as the approach to Armageddon. In a certain sense, they might be right. There is a sense that we are reaching a critical point in the expansion of our inner worlds. For better or worse—I mean, I have no dreamy New Age notions of this—whatever awaits us up the road might not be all sunshine and smiles, pretty flowers everywhere. That all sounds a bit *Yellow Submarine* to me, but it will certainly be different. To me, when we talk about the world, we are talking about our ideas of the world. Our ideas of organisation, our different religions, our different economic systems, our ideas about it are the world. We are heading for a radical revision where you could say we are heading towards the end of the world, but more in the R.E.M. sense than the Revelation sense. That is what apocalypse means—revelation. I could square that with the end of the world, a revelation, a new way of looking at things, something that completely radicalises our notions of the where we were, when we were, what we were, something like that would constitute an end to the world in the kind of abstract, yet very real, sense—that I am talking about. A change in the language, a change in the thinking, a change in the music. It wouldn't take much—one big scientific idea, or artistic idea, one good book, one good painting—who knows? We are at a critical point where the ideas are coming thicker and faster and stranger and stranger than they ever were before. They are realised at a greater speed. Everything has become very fluid. I like to imagine setting a camera up in a field in the Bronze Age, taking a frame a week. I worked out the maths of this in a sad moment, if I can just remember it. Over the intervening two thousand years, you would have a two-hour film there. It would be very boring and slow for an hour and half: the buildings that were appearing very slowly, staying there for a long while, and then decaying very slowly. For the last half hour, buildings would be boiling, going up and down in seconds. Some of the more alarming possibilities for nanotechnology that people are talking about, you get that as a literal reality without needing a speeded-up film. You would be able to assemble and disassemble matter at the speed of thought. As far as I know, that is the definition of fluidity. We are approaching a more fluid state. I have talked about cultural boiling. The idea of the phase-transition period which, in fractal mathematics, is the chaotic flux between one state and another. Cold water is one state. You heat it up till boiling point. Then it reaches a phase-transition where there is this immense chaos—that mathematically, we still don't know what is going on when a kettle boils, in the boiling—and what comes out is steam. Which is nothing like hot water at all. An alien could not predict steam from water, anymore than he could predict water from ice. They are three different things, each with a phase-transition dividing them. Culturally, and as a species, we are approaching a phase-transition. I don't know quite what that means on a human level. A bronze-age hunter is analogous to cold water. We, with our very different lifestyle, are analogous to very hot water. But we are still both water. There is less difference between us and the bronze-age hunter than what is twenty years down the line.

MDA: The steam.

AM: The steam. Whatever that means. I can't conceive of vapour culture. I might not survive it. But that is where we are heading. I don't know quite what I mean by my own metaphor, but I have [a] feeling it may bring in an even greater, faster space of fluid transmission, where no structures, as we used to understand structure, will sustain itself. We will have to come up with new notions of structure where things can change by the moment. I'm talking about physical structures, political structures. I can't see coherent political structures in the traditional sense lasting beyond the next twenty years. I don't think that would be possible.

MDA: But there are lot[s] of recessive genes. The Fundamentalist Christians exist to hold the novelty in American society in check. In this country, the traditions of monarchy and parliament function in a similar way. There is a lot of inertia within traditional political and economic structures designed to hold culture and society in place, where they are now. I can't see how any force of change could overcome these historical power bases.

AM: In terms of almost everything, things are getting more vaporous, more fluid. National boundaries are being eroded by technology and economics. Most of us work for companies that, if you trace it back, exist within another country. You are paid in an abstract swarm of bytes. Consequently, the line on a map means less and less. The territorial imperatives that until very recently have been the main reason for war start to make way. As the physical and material world gives way to this infosphere, these things become less and less important. The nationalists then go into a kind of death spasm, where they realise where the map is evaporating, and their only response to that is to dig their hooves in, to stick with nationalism at its most primitive, brutal form. The same thing happens with religion, and that is the reason behind the Fundamentalist Christians. If you look at the power of the Church, starting from the end of the Dark Ages up until the end of the nineteenth century, you can see a solid power base there, with a guaranteed influence over the development of society. If you look at this century, it is a third division team facing relegation. Fundamentalism in religion is the same as the political fundamentalism represented by various nationalist groups, or in science. Take the Committee for Scientific Investigation for Claims of the Paranormal: the ones who hounded Uri Geller. James Randi, The Amazing Randi, persecuted Uri Geller, and when he found he couldn't disprove Geller's claims, resorted to suggesting Geller was a pedophile and getting his ass sued, quite justifiably.

MDA: Was he the man who put up the reward for anyone who could perform a paranormal act that he couldn't replicate with conjuring?
AM: Yes. As if that proved anything.

MDA: It was an amazingly effective stunt though. It lodges in their mind, and when you talk about paranormal acts, they respond with, "Well, why hasn't that person taken Randi's money?"
AM: Randi says he can do it by tricks, so the person making the claim must have done it by tricks, which is fallacious.

MDA: I've been researching the CIA programme into Remote Viewing and came across the people involved in this programme.
AM: Ingo Swann and the other guys. Yeah, interesting shit that. I only found out about that a few years ago. I wasn't surprised that the CIA would be doing something like that. Once anyone has had any sort of intimations that that type of stuff might be possible, an intelligent person presumes that other people have probably figured this out before me, and if it's got any military application, they are probably doing it.

MDA: Did you follow how the remote viewing group was closed down by the CIA?
AM: There was a guy, I believe he was an admiral, who took over the remote viewing project in the seventies, and he might have committed suicide. Maybe he just died, and I saw them on TV talking to one of the heads of the CIA. It might have been Stansfield Turner, and they were talking about the remote viewing, and how the admiral had set up a splinter group, apart from the original remote viewing group. Then he died, and his group was closed down. The interviewer asked what this splinter remote viewing group was up to, and Turner was saying, "No, no. Their work was not connected to remote viewing, per se." The interviewer then asked, "What was it concerned with?" and he said, "Well, I suppose you could say it was concerned with contacting entities." Then the camera moved away, and I thought: "Entities? What are they doing there?" It makes you understand why the Pentagon is that shape!

MDA: I found out that to test the range of the remote viewing, they got the team of psychics to focus on the NASA probe that—at that time—was orbiting Jupiter. The team said they saw rings around Jupiter and mountainous formations, and these observations were contrary to both accepted scientific orthodoxy and the information coming from the probe. So, the experiment was deemed a failure. It [is] only in the last ten years that rings have, in fact, been discovered around Jupiter, and there are even workable theories about how a mountainous structure could have come about. By the time these cosmological discoveries were made, the team had been disbanded—so those that are still alive are sorting through their old observations to see if they were, in fact, true.

AM: The problem is, you also get remote viewers, like that guy who was remote viewing the Hale-Bopp Comet, who was convinced there was a spaceship full of evil reptiloids following on behind it. That sort of stuff tends to come from a misunderstanding of the nature of mental space. Mental space, and its existence, is what makes things like remote viewing possible. There shouldn't be any limit to it. As I understand mental space, one of the differences between it and physical space is that there is no space in it. All the distances are associative. In the real world, Land's End and John O'Groats are famously far apart. Yet you can't say one without thinking of the other. In conceptual space, they are right next to one another. Distances can only be associative, even vast interstellar distances shouldn't be a problem. Time would also function like this.

MDA: If it is associatively linked, then presumably it would be predicated upon language. If you say to someone, "Focus on Jupiter," then they would have to find an alien planet in the vastness of interstellar space, with just that English word.

AM: As I understand, or as I hallucinate, conceptual space, nearly all form in conceptual space, is language. I might even say all the form in nonconceptual space is language. I'm not even sure of what the difference between physical space and conceptual space is anymore in the interface. All form is language. The forms that we see, or imagine, or perceive, or whatever it is remote viewers are doing, in conceptual space, are mindforms made from language, and by language I also mean images, sounds. We dress these basic ideas in language we can understand. Sometimes there are sizable errors of translation.

[BREAK]

AM: A lot of conspiracy theorists, they find it comforting, secretly: the idea of the Illuminati, and the CIA, and whoever, controlling our lives and destinies. You know, because that means that at least someone is in control, at least someone is at the steering wheel, and it's not a runaway train. Paranoia is a security blanket, a massive security blanket. Whereas I think that, yes, these people do try to have an influence, and they often do have a very big influence. The CIA's unique method of funding its wars over the last thirty years has contributed to the crippling drug problems of most of the Western world. So, yes they have an effect. Do they control our destinies? No, they don't. They are nowhere near that powerful or organised. Does anything human control our destinies? No. Does this mean that God does? No. For all I know, God might just be a simple, two-line, iterative equation, with no more awareness of itself than that.

MDA: It is difficult to locate the exact beginnings of money. I think of money as being that nonhuman force that controls our destinies, a self-replicating viral idea that—at the moment—runs us as a species.

AM: The origin of money is something to do with representational thinking. Representational thinking is the real leap, where somebody says, "Hey, I can draw this shape on the cave wall, and it is, in some way, the bison we saw at the meadow. These lines are the bison." That, of course, led to language, "This squiggle is, of course, a tree, or something. Is the tree." Money is code for the whole of life. You can bind in everything that is contained within life for money. Money is a certain amount of sex, a certain amount of shelter, a certain amount of sustenance. I had those wacky K2 boys up at my house. I was part of the itinerary of their star-studded tour of Britain. In the book, *Watch the K Foundation Burn a Million Quid*, they have a list of venues that they showed the film at, and they've got Alan Moore's Living Room, Northampton, and I thought that was an interesting film because it was the apocalypse in miniature. Money is the code for the entire world. Money is the world, the world in the sense I was talking about earlier: our abstract ideas about the world. Money is a perfect symbol for all that, and if you don't believe in it, and you set a match to it, it's just firewood. It doesn't mean anything anymore. I thought that was a great film. I like a film where you can see every penny of the budget up there on the screen.

MDA: Bill Drummond now writes for us, which [is] the fulfillment of a long-term ambition of mine.

AM: I like Bill, but he's as mad as a fucking snake. But I like him. He's great. We were having dinner here last month, and he was planning to bulldoze Stonehenge at that time, I think, on January 1st, year 2000, but that just [may] have been the Peroni talking.

MDA: He's discussing building a giant pyramid at the moment.

AM: I thought that was a nicer idea, the People's Pyramid. He can go and build it on that island out at Althorp. This only gets in the Northampton papers but doesn't get in all the rest of them. I was hearing rumours in my psychic web that extends over the entire county. I was hearing rumours from Brinton, couple of days after Diana's funeral, a big van, police escort round the back of Brinton churchyard for a couple of hours, then out again. I was also hearing people saying, "Well how did they get the coffin out to the island." The official explanation was that we had this crack team of marines who built this special, portable bridge, floated her out to the island, then dismantled the bridge again afterwards. One of the waiters here, he was having a party in this pub, which is on this lonely little road and is the only access to the rear of Althorp House, and he said, "Well there were no army vehicles going either way for twenty-four hours." Then all these other rumours started coming out. "She's not out on the lake at Althorp. She's in the churchyard at Brinton, where she wanted to be." So I thought these were just rumours until, in the local paper, they had a headline saying, "Stop these sick rumours." Then, I thought, "gotta be true." There was a signed statement from the Bishop saying, "Yes, I definitely buried her on the island." Again, this made me think the rumours were true. It's like the Queen Mother. Her husband died, and they went through the funeral, but she's a little eccentric and wouldn't let him be buried for months. She kept her husband on a slab. The Bishops had to say he'd been buried, because the Queen's head of Church of England. So anyway, that's where he should build the People's Pyramid, out on Althorp, because there's fuck all else there.

The K Foundation are interesting and lively, a good laugh, and they mean it. They are very dedicated to their irrational ideas, which I am wholeheartedly in favour of. Gimpo [Alan Goodrick], the man who filmed it, is a pretty extraordinary character as well. Me and my people were doing one of our one-off performances in Highbury Garage in November. It was quite intense—a forty-minute piece with music and words and a dancer—and Gimpo happened to be there, and he filmed it for us. There is an underground again. Probably kill it stone dead to call it that. But I get the sense that there is an underground again. It's not as self-conscious as it was in the sixties. There are some subterranean people about—people who only pop their head above the ground infrequently—Iain Sinclair and Stewart Home's art mafia crowd. It's a lot healthier than the Groucho Club.

MDA: When I was coming here, I sat outside St. Pancras church. I had a headful of the psychogeographical theories, and your own writing on the significance of London's churches, and I had one of those moments when all the theories and information I had absorbed about this church focused about the faces of the caryatids. There was a haze about their faces. The statues seemed to be not quite stone. These are the great moments in life.

AM: The moments where you are actually there for a moment or two. I tell you what, man, one of the greatest, most mentally enriching, physically debilitating experiences of my life was going on a walk with Iain Sinclair, when he was doing this art exhibition at a gallery on Shoreditch High Street. He was getting together four male artists and four female artists, and the idea was, he was picking sites from his AA road atlas of London, and he got them all to pick a site, and he would either meet them there, or he would do a walk there. One of them was Michael Moorcock, who had come up from California. I was the only one who was actually doing the walk with Iain. The site I had chosen was Moorgate Churchyard, John Dee's place. I went to Iain's place at half eight in the morning, and we walked the twenty miles through London, up the river to Moorgate. He had his special psychogeography socks. He was skipping. I was crawling along, sobbing. It was incredible. It's not just the walk; it was doing the walk with Iain.

He would say, "Oh, see that grating over there. That's the grating that T. S. Eliot used to peer up women's skirts from under." "Oh, this is where they used to push Ezra Pound along the pavement while he was cursing about the Jews." You suddenly get this sort of . . . everything becomes light. New age, woolly-hat, Glastonbury mystics weary me, sometimes, but they talk about energy—the energy of a place, of a person. We all know what they mean, but, at the same time, it has to be said that this is not energy that is going to show up on an autometer. We're not talking about energy in the conventional sense that physics talks about energy. To me, energy is information. I think you can make that bold a statement. The only lines of energy that link up disparate sites in London are lines of information that have been drawn by an informed mind. The energy that we put forth is information we have taken in. We will see a work of art, and it will give us inspiration; it will give us energy. It's given us information that we can turn to our own use and put out as something else. That's the kind of energy that we—and psychogeography—are talking about. So, Iain Sinclair's London is a much richer, more extraordinary, place than almost anyone else's.

I have been reading about the ancient Egyptians and trying to get into their mindset. They used to have this really complex symbol matrix that they lived within. They get up in the morning. They want to put a bit of slap on, put coal around their eyes, and look into a mirror. A mirror to them symbolises a pool of water. Now, to them, a pool of water represents the eye of the Goddess. So you've this other cosmological idea coming in. Just having a shave and putting on your make-up means you have a lot of concepts to play with. You are looking at your reflection in the eye of the Goddess. What does this mean? Does this mean that how I see myself is how the Goddess sees me? Does this entail saying that I am the Goddess in some sense? Now, I'm not saying any of these ideas are earth shattering, but they are interesting to play with while you're having a shave. It makes shaving a richer experience. That's just the mirror. Everything else that they touch or see, during that day, during their entire lives, was part of this learned alphabet of symbols that came from a rich symbolic language with which to approach the symbological world if you like, the conceptual world. A stone picked up on a beach is a unit of information. If a child picks it up, the information the child is drawing from the stone is probably how heavy it is, how far it would go if you threw it, whether it is the right shape to skim a couple of times across the waves. That is information. Obviously, a geologist picking up that stone is going to be able to abstract more information from it. It is possible that an archaeologist noticing an imprint in the stone—that would tell him a lot more. A quantum physicist considering the stone would be able to get different levels of information from it. A William Blake picking up the stone is going to have a whole new channel of information from which he can draw from it. To some degree, the stone is only the compound sum of its information. As are any of us. We are all the aggregate of the ideas about us, including our own ideas about us. That is all that any of us can be considered as—units of information in a sea of information. When you get to a certain point, there is not much more to it than information. Which for our terms is practically synonymous with language, because that is the only way we understand information, in one sort of language or another. Yeah, well that's not bad. We've managed to dissolve the entire universe in a sea of language before I've finished my coffee.

MDA: Do you mind if I take a single picture?
AM: Whatever you want.

MDA: I was interested in what you were saying about how the return of a[n economic boom] was going to squash people out the way again. Hopefully that won't be the case.

AM: The economic boom is only there for such a small percentage of the population that I don't think that will be the case. Excuse me, I'm just trying not to look self-conscious.

MDA: That was what was troubling me when I went back to Liverpool over Christmas. I realised that for the first time, the power base in this country just doesn't need it. The North and South of this country, while being locked in an admittedly antagonistic relationship, nevertheless had to maintain a relationship. They needed each other. But without an industrial base, without the docks, the North is redundant to the economic needs of the South.

AM: Liverpool, in that sense, is a symbol for the working class in general. While we were needed to actually man the conveyor belts . . . that was where the ruling class made its big mistake, you know: "Hey let's educate the brutes. We know we are superior to them anyway. Just through genetics, we are genetically superior to the working class. They are a shaved monkey. If we educate them, they will be able to read instructions, turn up on time, and man the conveyor belts. Sorted." So, they started to educate the working class and giving them a proper diet, things like school milk. All of a sudden it turned out that this genetic thing didn't hold up. Often, the working class seemed to be stronger, physically and mentally, than these products of long-term inbreeding experiments. Now, of course, they are not needed to turn up at the conveyor belts any more. But they are educated. They have high expectations. This is a problem. "How do we tell them they are not needed?"

I can remember my Dad, God bless him, and he was telling me—when I was growing up—that machines would do everything. It would be great. There wouldn't be any need to go to work because the machines would do everything. He thought that the working class would then be given a holiday, to Yarmouth or somewhere, forever. He was right except about the holiday to Yarmouth. He hadn't really thought it through. He still trusted the society he was in. That he would be looked after. It turns out to have been a much more pragmatic relationship all along. I think we should have taken the clue when Thatcher said there is no such thing as society. What she meant was— just like the London-Liverpool thing—"We don't need there to be a society anymore." "We are getting what we want anyway, therefore we do not need your support. Therefore we do not need to maintain the illusion of society anymore."

MDA: My first thought on leaving London to come to Northampton was, "Oh I'm back in England again."

AM: It's the city. It doesn't matter what country you are in. There is only one city. They all have their own type of populace. It's the same city, the same derelicts on the street, whether you are in New York, Paris, or London. New York is three Londons stacked on top of each other. Different accents, slightly better food—but it's the same city. Doesn't matter. Tokyo—doesn't matter. I find London fascinating and horrifying. I would never want to live there. There is a deeper emotional reality here, in Northampton. The city is designed to be concentration living. There is something funny happening there.

There is no need for cities anymore. There was when we had to get everyone near the factories. It made sense. I see cities over the next fifty years becoming like theme parks. They will have less actual function. I mean, who needs to rent office space in the city these days?

MDA: But social hierarchies require a certain amount of physical proximity to operate.

AM: Yeah, you'd have your square mile. Traditionally, everywhere has needed a certain amount of physical proximity to operate, but whether that will be true in the future . . . The virtual office is cheaper to run than the London office. I can see practical reasons for that making cities obsolete. It will lead to crater culture. I mean, look at Liverpool. Despite attempts to reinvigorate it, it has never really attracted the big business option that it hoped to. Consequently, you have a crater, and everybody is moving to the rim. In the middle, you've just got the urban despoilment. [Alvin] Toffler talks about a return to rural areas, the electronic cottage.

MDA: But what people get out of work, the power and the status, I think that requires an office environment, the strange greenhouse some thrive on.

AM: It's difficult to say. We only know the world as we have lived in it. A lot of things we thought were givens have turned out to be local and temporary phenomena. Capitalism and communism felt like they were always going to be around, but it turns out they were just two ways of ordering an industrial society. If you were looking for more fundamental human political poles, you'd take anarchy and fascism, for my money. Which are not dependent upon economic trends because they are both a bit mad. One of them is complete abdication of individual responsibility into the collective, and one of them absolute responsibility for the individual. I think these will both still be with us, but fascism becomes less and less possible. We have to accept that we are moving towards some sort of anarchy.

MDA: But earlier you were talking about a coming together in society, a more holistic realisation of one another, but against that, there is the prevalent cultural trend of difference, that over the eighties we became aware of our ethnic, sexual, religious difference. To me, these seem opposing trends.

AM: Take disintegration far enough and you get a new form of integration. I tend to see all this in neural terms. It doesn't matter how big your brain is, or how many cells or neurons in it, what matters is the synaptic fusions, the connections that determine how intelligent you are. "As with the individual, so with the macrocosm." That's how the kind of society I live in works. Me and my friends and my contacts, we don't work in any hierarchical sense. No one wants a boss, to be a boss, to work under a boss. The people you like working with are the people you respect as individuals.

Sometimes in connecting up—and I've worked a lot in collaborative media—you get something that is better than either of you could do. I couldn't have done the *Watchmen* without Dave Gibbons, and he couldn't have done it without me. That was the result of an almost sexual union. Dave will be very surprised to hear about it in those terms, but in the creative sense, the pro-creative sense. His and mine mental genetics producing a healthy bouncing baby boy. The sexuality of creativity—on that level, human interaction becomes less of an oppressive pyramid and more of a dance, an orgy, something that you can imagine being a bit of fun. It seems to work naturally, except when order is imposed upon it, from above, and then everything starts getting a bit screwed up. The information, the energy, starts to get messed up.

The only organisation I have ever enjoyed being a part of was the Northampton Arts Lab, when I was seventeen. Arts Labs are a phenomenon that no longer exist. They only existed for the late sixties, early seventies. I can't even begin to describe the effect that had upon me, and I suspect that it would be difficult to measure the effect they had on British culture. It was basically the idea that in any town, anywhere, there was nothing to stop like-minded people who were interested in any form of art, getting together and forming completely anarchic experimental arts workshops—magazines, live events, whatever they could imagine doing. And it was completely nonhierarchical, and it worked fine. There would be other artists you respect, and you would talk about possible collaborations. I've not seen another organisation like that, and therefore I've never joined another organisation until this magic cabal, which we've just made up as we went along. It's pretty much the same to me—art and magic are synonymous. It's just that this is a magic lab, rather than an arts lab. That sort of organisation, where it is arranged in a natural, neurological pattern—I mean it was the Arts Labs that gave us David Bowie, from Beckenham Arts Lab—, and I can see that kind of consciousness that he was bringing to it, the mixed media. To me, that is the only organisation that works. To me, any other organisation has got a whiff of fascism. I'm not using the word in the sense of, "All politicians are fascist." I think all girl guides are fascists. It's "facia," the roman word for a bunch of bound twigs, and that was the original symbol for fascism, and the symbolism of it is that one twig can be broken but in unity, there is strength. Inevitably, this translates as, "In uniformity there is strength." The twigs will be tied together in a neater and stronger bundle if they are all the same size and length. That's fascism. It suggests that you have two contrary organisational principles involved in anarchy. One is a kind of linear, meccano-like organization—tie up all the sticks, make sure they are the same length, and you have a brick wall or something. The other one—anarchy—is a more fractal, more natural, more human organisational system in that it organises society in much the same way that we organise our personalities, where it is purely the interplay of neurons. We haven't got a king neuron that tells all the other neurons what to do. It seems to me to be a more emotionally natural way of working with other people.

MDA: That might be why some of the collective social experiments of the twenties didn't work, because they wrote down the rules beforehand. They were focused around figureheads like Bernard Shaw.

AM: Anarchy—anarchon—no leaders. Which means, everybody is a leader. You can't have an official set of rules for anarchy. I tend to think such connections casually break and form, and break and form, throughout our lives. If you look back ten years, you will remember a group of friends who you were productively involved with at that time. Now some of them have drifted away. New people have come in. These are more naturalistic linkages, which exist while there is a need for them to exist. It's more like the way ants work. Douglas Hofstadter did an illuminating piece called *Ant Fugue*, which is actually a picture by M. C. Escher. What Hofstadter does is frame it as one of his dialogues between Achilles, a tortoise, an anteater, and one other creature. It is a four-handed conversation about the idea of fugues, and it is talking about how, with a fugue, if you listen to one voice within it, you can follow it perfectly, but you can't hear the overall music. If you listen to the whole fugue, it makes perfect sense and is beautiful, but you can't hear the individual voice. Then they start talking about how this applies to consciousness, and they start talking about anthills. On the scent level, where a scent will be released—the signal level—ants will stop what they are doing and follow the scent until they reach a place in the nest where they are needed. At which point, the scent will break down. So you've got this perfect organisation going on. None of the ants are conscious, but the next level up is the signal level. And if you go right to the top, he says there is the symbol level of the anthill, which is what you could call the mass consciousness of the anthill, which no individual ant has. But it is what is really going on there. That seems natural—that we all follow our little scents and do what we need to do, and when there isn't a need for us anymore, we move onto something else. Things tend to organise themselves. If there is any message from contemporary science, it is surely that. I am very fond of the anarchist proverb regarding laws, "Good people have no need for them. Bad people pay no attention to them. What are they there for, other than as a symbol of power?" We can say, "This is law." I could say, "I rule the universe." It depends on whether anyone believes me or not. To some degree, I don't think the authorities care whether the law is observed or not, as long as it is there, and everyone accepts the idea of Law. As long as they buy into the idea of Law.

These days it's difficult to actually define anything as underground culture, but I can see things like this [holds up *The Idler*]—if the same impulse had been expressed thirty years ago, it would probably have been an underground magazine. They don't really exist anymore, apart from on a fanzine level. So it has to be something like this. I can see that, you know. There is an eclecticism returning to a culture that I like. On one level, you get Qabbala turning up in *New Scientist*. Certain fundamental barriers don't seem to exist anymore. There has been an integration of gay culture into mainstream culture. There is not the same level of heterosexual assumption. Even in the personal ads in local newspapers, you'll have a "men seeking men" category. Which is a small thing, but it's a step. We don't need, to the same degree, special interest magazines. You can get to this level of simple human integration that we were talking about earlier. Break us all up until we are a different organisation, a different category in our own right, then fine, we can start working together.

MDA: Is your cabal focused around Northampton?

AM: It's not really around Northampton. It started about five years ago when I decided to become a magician. It was largely, to begin with, me and Steve Moore, no relation. He's a longstanding editor on *Fortean Times*. He handles *Fortean Studies*, which is the academic part of it. He used to be a comic book writer, friend of mine since I was fourteen, fellow of the Royal Asiatic Society. He's a heavyweight intellectual, Steve, with an interest in gods, magic, and we initially formed a secret society of two. Within which context, we could discuss our emerging ideas of magic, language, consciousness, and art. As these developed, we found ourselves discussing them with other people. It started to expand into this loose-knit cabal, which now includes various artists and musicians that I've worked with, various occultists that each of us have been in contact with. It's the idea of all of us having our different areas of specialty, our different talents, but all of us being able to call upon the information, knowledge, or talents of the others, should we need to extend ourselves into that area. This has led to some interesting performances with me and Dave J from Love and Rockets, Bauhaus. Dave is somebody who is very definitely part of the cabal that we generally refer to as "The Moon and Serpent Grand Egyptian Theatre of Marvels." Just 'cos we thought it sounded like a good name. We just wanted something grandiloquent, a bit mad, with an air of fraud about it, an air of charlatanry, mountebanquery, because there is a certain amount of sham in shamanism. There is a certain amount of theatre. It's as loosely knit as that. We're sort of coming out of the closet a bit more over the next couple of years. We're going to be bringing out—manifesto's too pushy a word. If it's a theatre of marvels, we're bringing out a theatre programme in the next couple of years. We're working on it at the moment—our unified field theory of spookiness, where we try to explain everything from language, consciousness, grey aliens, to Rosicrucianism or whatever. It is a grand, mad theory, which I'm working my best on at the moment to make it rational. It is an antirationalistic theory, but I'm trying to couch it in rational terms so that it is not as insular as a lot of magic stuff. I understand that the word "occult" means hidden, but surely that is not meant to be the final state of all this information, hidden forever. I don't see why there is any need to further obscure things that are actually lucid and bright. Language and strange terminology—to keep them as some private mystery. I think there is too much darkness in magic. I can understand that it is part of the theatre. I can understand Aleister Crowley, who I think was a great intellect that was sometimes let down by his own flair for showmanship, but he did a lot to generate the scary aura of the magician that you find these sad, Crowleyite fucks making a fetish of. The ones who say, "Oh we're into Aleister Crowley, because he was the wickedest man in the world, and we're also into Charles Manson because we're bad. And we are middle-class as well, but we're bad." There are some people who seek evil. I don't think there is such a thing as evil, but there are people who seek it as a kind of Goth thing. That just adds to the murk to what to me is a very lucid and fluorescent subject. What occultism needs is someone to open the window. It's too stuffy and it smells. Let's get some fresh air, throw open the curtains. I can't go for that posturing, spooky guy stuff. When they wanted me to do Fortean TV it became apparent that they wanted me to be Spooky Bloke. But I'm not actually trying to look spooky. I dress in black because it makes me look less fat. It's as simple as that. It's not a gothic flourish. I don't want to be thought of as a figure of mystery, or a master of the occult. Surely this is about illumination, casting light on things. I'm an illuminist. That'd do for me.

MDA: The cabal seems to be like an artistic movement, like the Surrealists, in which you have a philosophy and a worldview that unites around an artistic practise, as a particular way of seeing and portraying things.

AM: The Surrealists are a good example. The more I look at most of the art movements, it's all occultism, when you get down to it. The Surrealists were openly talking about being magicians. Duchamp's "Bride Stripped Bare by Her Bachelors" makes no sense except in alchemical terms. Ernst, Magritte, Dali—these were people who were taking their inspiration from magic. That's just the Surrealists. Turns out Annie Besant's book, where she put forward the idea that theosophical mystical energies could be portrayed as colours or abstract shapes, was practically the invention of abstract art. A lot of artists rushed out and read it and suddenly thought, "Oh God, you could, you could portray love as a colour, or depression as a colour." All of a sudden, abstract art happens, a flowering out of occultism. What we tend to do is cover the waterfront. I like a form of occultism that has some result that you can show people. Now if I tell people that I've been doing lots and lots of initiatory work inside my head, inside my bedroom, and that I've risen to the level of Magestic Templi and blah blah blah, then they'll think, "Yeah, I guess you're right Al. You have done that," but what's it mean to them? "Show me. You say you're a magician. You say you can do this or that. Show me some magic." What I would prefer to have is to have a kind of magic where we say, "OK, we're going to do a magical performance on this night, at this time. You come along. If you don't think it's magical, that's fine. We'll show you. We'll show you what we mean, and you judge for yourself." That's only fair. So a lot of the magic we do tends to gravitate toward the practical end, toward something that is tangible, where you've got a record at the end of it, a performance at the end of it, a painting at the end of it. You've conjured some energy, some idea, some information from somewhere and put it in a tangible form. You conjure something into existence in a literal sense. A rabbit out of a hat. Something out of nothing. That's one level to it, but there's a lot of background to that. That's the stuff that people see. That's the end result of the process. But we also do a lot of ritual work purely on our own. Last time I was up with Steve, we started messing around with John Dee's Enochian language system. It was John Dee and Edward Kelly [née Talbot], the Elizabethan magus and his assistant, who turned up with the language spoken by angels, or what they referred to as angels. Me and Steve had never tried it before, so we got into Enochian for a couple of days. It turns out to be very easy to use, very simple, very powerful, very direct. You get results straight away. You don't even have to be on drugs. I'll put that on the backburner for a while, because it looks like a big system that will need a lot of investigation. At the moment, I'm still too immersed in the Qabbalah, the Jewish mystical system, and it's a separate one. They are two different ways of looking at the universe, but with the Qabbalah, we are working through numerous different exercises, and the information we are getting from these we are channeling into this project we are doing at the moment, the Disco Qabbalah, where we are trying to translate these different states as described in the Qabbalah into dance tracks. Because there has always been a dance element in my mysticism. We just think, "Why not?" Music is imposing a state of consciousness by its very nature. If what this Tree of Life is, is a hierarchy of different states of consciousness, would it be possible to simulate and stimulate those states of consciousness in the listener by producing the right sorts of music? Is it possible? We don't know, but we're working on it.

MDA: Writers are deliberately using language to induce a different state of mind, whether it be disorientation, a certain disjointed set of emotions. It's not like Joyce, where the moment you look at it, you know it is trying to play with your mind. It is demonstrably difficult, so it doesn't quite insinuate itself into your mind if you're doing it rhythmically.

AM: I come from the Arts Lab. Most of the writing I used to do was used for performance, so consequently I learnt that when you are reading a poem it has to read properly, which is to do with syllables and stresses. What takes me the longest with my fine writing, like say *Voice of the Fire*, is reading it through and finding the bits where it clunks, where it's one syllable too long, and once you find that rhythm—the reader probably won't be aware of it, consciously, but there is a tidal wave embedded in the prose that the reader is responding to. In the last chapter of *Voice of the Fire*, where it is actually me talking in my own voice, I don't use the word "I" or "me" or "mine." I don't know why—perhaps I had been reading that *Private Eye* column where it is all "I, I, I," and started to feel a bit self-conscious about it—, but I thought, if I can still be the central voice but without having an "I" there, and by not having it there, it makes it easier for the reader to slip into the consciousness of the narrator. If you remove the letter "I," it becomes a universal "I." Everybody is the author walking down those streets while they are in the prose. The reason I got into magic was that it seemed to be what was lying at the end of the path of writing. If I wanted to continue on that path, I was going to have to get into that territory, because I had followed writing as far as I thought I could without taking a step over the edges of rationality. The path led out of rational confines. When you start thinking about art and creativity, rationality is not big enough to contain it all. Otherwise, you end up at a B. F. Skinner hypothesis, where it is all purely to do with stimulus and response. B. F. Skinner actually put forward—and this is a measure of scientific desperation over consciousness—the idea that consciousness was a weird vibrational byproduct of the vocal cords. That we did not actually think. We thought we thought because of this weird vibration caused by the vocal cords. This shows the lengths that hard science will go to banish the ghost from the machine.

MDA: Like Biblical exegesis—you end up with absurdities of angels on a pinhead.

AM: To me, consciousness, the mind, language is the prime channel—part of this thing I am doing with the Moon and Serpent, this theory with Steve Moore, is any nascent consciousness, whether you are talking about an emerging culture or a single human infant, what they first have to do is undergo a process of discrimination when they are trying to come up with a worldview. What you have to do first is separate yourself from the world. Most newborn babies don't see any difference between them, their playpen, and their Dad. It's all them. Only after a little while do they start to realise that it's not all me, just this bit is me. So by the invention of something similar to the word or concept "I," we separate ourselves from the universe. Then we start to separate up the universe. We will divide sky from ground, the organic from inorganic. Looked at like this, doesn't it provide a literal interpretation of the Biblical Creation story? If you take the idea of God in the Bible as a metaphor for any nascent, formative, just-created intelligence, is that not how we all create the universe? We divide the firmament up from the waters of the abyss, and the key to how to do this is in the first line, "In the beginning, there was the word." By giving "sky" one word, the ground into another, we break the universe down into manageable things that we can interact with through language.

MDA: That's very clear in what Adam does. He is standing there pointing, going "sheep," "cow."

AM: He is almost creating them by pointing. It's a process of finer and finer discrimination. In the beginning, there is just universe. There is no us. There is just God in His or Her universe. Then we separate God from the universe, until we are trapped in it, in the universe we have created.

MDA: So how does this relate to your practice as a magician? My understanding of magic is that, through words you can create events. If events are a consequence of perception, and perception is composed of language, then language can change perception, and therefore change events.

AM: Here I think we are getting down to the difference between traditional perceptions of language and one that I would be comfortable with. The traditional definition of magic—and I think this comes from Crowley who laid down a lot of the ground rules—he defined magic as bringing about change in accordance with the will. I'm not sure about that. It's certainly part of it, but to bring about change in the universe in accordance with your will seems to me to be misunderstanding the relationship between the individual and the universe. In my relationship with the universe, I do tend to see myself as very much the Junior Partner. I don't want to impose my will on the universe. I'd rather the universe imposed its will on me. I would rather that what I wanted was more in tune with what the universe wanted. So my definition of magic is a bit less invasive and intrusive.

MDA: It's less of a power fantasy than Crowley's?

AM: It's more exploratory with me. I see magic as a vantage point from which one can look down on the rest of consciousness. It's a point outside normal consciousness from which you can look at normal consciousness. It's a point outside beliefs from which you can look at beliefs. All beliefs are reality tunnels, to use Anton Wilson's phrase. There is the Communist reality tunnel, the Feminist reality tunnel, all of which seem to be the whole of reality when you are in the middle of them. The whole universe is based on Marxist theory if you're an intent Marxist. Magic is having a plan of all the tunnels and seeing the overall condition in which they all work. Being aware of different possibilities. If the universe is as a magician sees it, then there are wider possibilities. For example, do I believe I can raise the dead and talk to them? Yes, I do. Not in any physical sense, because that would smell. I don't see any point in that. You don't want a maggot bag walking around your living room. But could I reanimate the idea of a person in the useful sense and be able to communicate with that person—or, at least, to believe that I was communicating with that person to such an extent that the information I received was as good as if that person was talking to me? Yes, I do. Most of the effects described in classical magical tradition, I believe I can duplicate with art, possibly drugs—or some other means of integrating myself more deeply with that sort of reality, that sort of consciousness. I believe I could do most of the things that are described in traditional magic. This opens up wider possibilities. It also enables me to understand myself on a deeper level. By accepting the idea of endless pantheons of gods, I somehow accept these creatures as being distinct and separate from me and not as being, to some degree, higher functions of me. Iain Sinclair was asking me about this. He asked me, "Do you think they are inside you, or outside you?" The only answer I could come up with was, "The more I think about it, the inside is the outside," that the objective world and the nonobjective world are the same thing, to some degree. Idea Space and this space are the same space, just different ends of the scale. That's not a very good explanation, but the best I can come up with so far. All of these things are exploratory. They are exploring me, exploring the world of ideas, attempting to contact what I believe may be potent forms of energy. Like for example, I might do a work to put me in contact with the god Mercury. If the information I get from that is valuable to me, and new enough, it doesn't really matter whether the god Mercury is there at all, does it? There is a channel that I have called the god Mercury, some sort of information source I have named.

MDA: I can understand that on an abstract level. If the information provided is useful, why question the actual existence of whatever is providing that information. But on a personal level, if you were receiving information that you couldn't immediately attribute to as coming from yourself, wouldn't you feel absolute terror?

AM: In my own experience—and this is where we get into the complete madness here—I have only met about four gods, a couple of other classes of entity as well. I'm quite prepared to admit this might have been a hallucination. On most of the instances, I was on hallucinogenic drugs. That's the logical explanation—that it was purely an hallucinatory experience. I can only talk about my subjective experience, however, and the fact that having had some experience of hallucinations over the last twenty-five years or so, I'd have to say that it seemed to me to be a different class of hallucination. It seemed to me to be outside of me. It seemed to be real. It is a terrifying experience, and a wonderful one, all at once. It is everything you'd imagine it to be. As a result of this, there is one particular entity that I feel a particular affinity with. There is [a] late Roman snake god, called Glycon. He was an invention of the False Prophet Alexander. Which is a lousy name to go into business under. He had an image problem. He could have done with a spin doctor there.

Anyway, the False Prophet Alexander is a Moon and Serpent hero, a saint if you like. He was running what seemed to be a travelling Seleni medicine show. He would do a performance of the mysteries of the goddess Soi. The only reference to him is in the works of Lucian, who calls him a complete charlatan and fraud. At some point, Alexander the False Prophet said he was going to preside over the second coming of the god Aeschepylus [or Ascle-pius], the serpent god of medicine. He said this is going to happen at noon tomorrow, in the marketplace. So everyone said, "Sounds good," and they all went down there. After a little while, they said, "Come on, False Prophet Alexander, where is the second coming of Aeschepylus?" At which point, the False Prophet Alexander bent down, reached into a puddle at his feet, pulled up an egg, split it with his thumbnail, and there was a tiny snake inside, and said, "Behold, the new Aeschepylus," took it home with him, where over a week it apparently grew to a prodigious size until it was taller than a man and had the head and features of a man. It had long blonde hair, ears, eyelids, a nose. At this point, he started to exhibit it in his temple, providing religious meeting with this incarnate god. At which point, Lucian said, it was obvious, "I could have done that." Lucian is another James Randi, you know, "I could have done that." He got the snake's head under his arm, speaking tube over his shoulder, child's play. And he's probably right, that's probably how he did it. If I'm going to adopt a god, I'd rather know starting out that it was a glove puppet. To me, it's a real god. There's nothing that precludes a glove puppet from being a real god. How else would you explain the cult of Sooty? But a god is the idea of a god. The idea of a god is a god. The idea of Glycon is Glycon. If I can enhance that idea with an anaconda and a speaking tube, fair enough. I am unlikely to start believing that this glove puppet created the universe. It's a fiction. All gods are fiction. It's just that I happen to think that fiction's real. Or that it has its own reality that is just as valid as ours. I happen to believe that most of the important things in the material world start out as fiction. That everything around us was once fiction—before there was the table, there was the idea of a table, and the idea of a table before tables was fiction. This is the most important world, the world of fictional things. That's the world where all this starts. So I had an experience which seems to be an experience of this made-up, Basil-Brush type entity. It was devastating.

MDA: This was the pivotal experience. You were forty when you had this oc-cult Road to Damascus.

AM: Yes. On the day I was forty, I decided I was going to become a magician. That was on November 18. On January 7 the following year, that was when

From *From Hell*, chapter 4,
page 18 (partial), by Alan
Moore and Eddie Campbell.
Copyright © 1989, 1999,
2000, 2001, 2004, 2006 Alan
Moore and Eddie Campbell,
used by permission.

all of a sudden the lightning bolt hit. It all got a bit strange. For a couple of months after that, I was, looking back, probably in some borderline schizophrenic state. I was very spaced out—godstruck. You babble for a while. It's a natural response. Babble like an idiot. I'm surprised that—when I look back at what I was saying—that so much of it at least makes a fragment of sense, because I was in some divine haze. "I see it all now," you know. I must have been unbearable for two or three months. I've integrated that now into the rest of my life. Now I can deal with functionality on a practical level. And I still have this relationship with this imaginary snake. My imaginary pal. If I'm going to be dealing in totally imaginary territory, it struck me that it would be useful to have a native as a guide. So, I can have my imaginary conversations with my imaginary snake, and maybe it gives me information I already knew in part of myself, and maybe I just needed to make up an imaginary snake to tell me it.

MDA: Do you have a ritual during which these various conversations take place?

AM: Increasingly, with that particular god, it becomes more casual. I will be talking to the giant imaginary snake god much in the same way you talked to God when you were six, in the quiet silence of bed. If I wanted a full-scale manifestation, one that was apparent to other people, then I would do a ritual. I have displayed the snake god to other people. Or I have consciously hypnotised them into accepting my psychotic belief system, given them drugs, and made them think they are having the experience I have. Whatever you want. I'm not fussed.

MDA: How did they react? I mean, they're your friends. They are going to be curious. They are going to want to see what is going on.
AM: They want to know if I'm mad or not.

MDA: So, you organised a ritual with them in which you said, "Well, let's find out."
AM: I went through it with numerous friends. Most of which seemed to experience something, something they had never experienced before. It got very weird. It's surprising, you don't have to believe in this stuff very much to get extraordinary stuff out of it. I was surprised by how easy it was to reproduce these effects for other people to experience. I remember one guy—I hadn't even told him the details of what I believed. He didn't particularly like the mushrooms, so he only took a couple. I did the invocation, and he got a bit giggly. He said, "I'm trying to listen to what you are saying, but I've got this Hanna Barbera cartoon in my head, a sort of Jungle Book type animals, and there's this one thing . . ." And I said, "Can you describe these Jungle Book animals?" And he said, "Well, it's just cheap animation that I can see. It's just cartoons. There is nothing mystical about it. There is this one particular animal. It's a snake, but it's got a tea towel over its head." And I drew a snake, drew the tea towel, and I said, "Does it look like this?" And he said, "Yeah, like that." Then I pulled out this picture I had done—one I had drawn earlier—a fully rendered crowned drawing of the snake as I saw it, with the long hair. He went, "Oh Jesus Christ." I said, "Don't worry about it. This is the snake god. This is Glycon. He's in your head now talking to you. Don't worry about it." Yeah, so it was that sort of thing. It's proven very easy to work with, frighteningly easy. All you have to do is take that step from "This can't possibly happen" to "Oh, maybe it could happen."

Also, I can understand why magicians have such a high insanity rate. We don't end well, most of us, it has to be said. Paul Daniels might escape the worst effects, but the rest of us are pretty obviously doomed. Once you step over that line, you are in danger from a lot of stuff, delusion, obviously, being the main thing. When I started to get into magic, I said to a lot of friends, "Well, I'm not going to know if I go mad, am I?" So, let's think about this. I want you all to keep an eye on me. If I am happy, that in itself is no indication of not being mad. You can be drawing pictures on the wall in your own shit and be completely happy. The only thing I can use as a yardstick is if I am happy and functional and productive. If I am producing more work than I did in the past, then that's a good sign. And if it's better work. Madness and insanity are two terms that are so vague and relative that you can't really apportion proper values to them. The only thing I can think of that has any use is "functional" and "dysfunctional." Are you working as well? In which case, it doesn't matter if you are mad. So it was quite an experience. I was also surprised to find out how frightening it was for everyone else, how much [more] powerful the magic has got when we were all, officially, not supposed to believe in it anymore. But if you start saying, "Actually, I've become a magician," there is a look of terror on people's faces, which I understand. You can divide them into two categories. There were some people who had fear and worry on their faces because they were afraid I had gone mad, which is understandable. Then there were the other people who were afraid that I hadn't. Who were faced with a dilemma, because they were faced with somebody who seemed relatively articulate, relatively sane, and who they respected, intellectually, who was suddenly saying they were a magician and talking to a snake, an imaginary snake. I can see why that would worry them, because they are faced with a choice. Either they have to decide I am deluded, or if I'm not deluded, then that opens up a whole can of worms—or snakes—because they have to readjust their view of the universe to include that possibility. If I realised the power of magic to worry and terrify people before, then I certainly would have used it before. Everyone freezes before it for different reasons—perhaps because it means madness to them, or because it means opening the door to a whole lot of stuff that the Age of Reason should have firmly bolted the door upon. A lot of concepts that we got rid of a long time ago, that would be a bit creepy to have them back.

MDA: The reason why I'm interviewing you on this subject, in very straight-forward terms, is that a lot of the questions it raises are cropping up else-where, in other more "respectable" fields. It is serendipitous, or fortunate, that your declaration has come at a time when a lot of people are considering the idea that things are other than what they seem, or other than what we have previously believed them to be.
AM: If there is an Idea Space, then there is no serendipity. I know exactly what you mean. Aren't we all creatures of our times? If there is an overlying mental space in which we all exist, then presumably it would have its own weather: weathers of ideas that just blow in. Certain storms of ideas—the Renaissance, things like that. It would be only natural that any mind that is actively involved in trying to find that frontier should not be surprised if it

suddenly has luminous snakes thrumming into its head. I think that we are approaching a kind of event field—fifteen years, twenty years up the road. There is a big event in the future and because time is not what we think it is, that event radiates in all directions. We are entering its field and have been for hundreds of years. We are starting to approach the core of it.

MDA: We were discussing madness, and why I don't think you are mad. A friend of mine once described the insane as giving off a high-octane whiff like cat urine, which I don't pick up from you.

AM: I've known a lot of people go mad over the years, and it is more distressing than people dying. People dying is quite natural. People going mad is the complete antithesis of that. Just after I became a magician, the son of a close friend of mine—who was a kind of rave culture casualty—had quite a powerful and florid breakdown. Very grim. I was going to visit him every day in the local loony bin—I wouldn't dignify it with the term "mental home"—, and his florid beliefs, his messianic fantasies, and I was listening to him and thinking, "Well, he's putting it in different terms, but this is pretty much what I believe. Where are we going with this? I cannot stand here with my hand on my heart and say that my perceptions of reality are any madder than his, or less mad. What's this about?" The best description I could come up with was that somebody had said, "All of us, as human beings, through our accumulated perceptions, that could be considered to be our window on reality—what we perceive. We know that it is limited, what we perceive, but it is still our window upon reality. Just as if you are looking out of a window from your house, you can see a little bit of the houses across the street, a little bit of sky. You know there is a whole universe out there, but the limits of your window just show you that view. What the magician is attempting to do is alter the dimension or the angle of that window, broaden it perhaps, tilt it so it can see different things. The schizophrenic has had their window kicked in. The magician has got a body of law—probably most of it bollocks, it doesn't matter. The magician's got a system into which the alien information that will be pouring into him or her will be fitted. They've got a filing cabinet, like the Qabbalah, which is a filing cabinet for ideas. It divides the whole universe up into ten drawers. Any experience can be passed into one of the drawers. The schizophrenic is probably having exactly the same experience as the magician but has no context in which to understand it. If I see some particularly florid vision, I can think "Right, Qabbalistically, because I saw this number of flying talking fishes, then this number relates to here on the Qabbalah. The fact that they were fishes would mean they tend to relate to this," and I can start to make sense of this apparently incoherent vision. The schizophrenic can't. They get the same feeling. The schizophrenics I have known, the most evident thing about it is the interconnectedness of everything. That's standard lunacy. It's also standard magic. But with one of them, it is uncontrollable. You are lost in a world in which everything is obviously connected by symbolic threads. That is what the magician is seeking, to see these threads that connect things up. If you've got a system—even if it's a completely made-up bogus system—then you've at least got a filing cabinet to sort this stuff into. You don't have to get crushed under it. It's like what we were saying earlier about signal and noise. In linguistic terms, there is this weird paradox that I think Alfred Kazinsky pointed out. Ironically, something that is pure signal will have almost no information content. Pure signal is a *Janet and John* book. Something that has got noise, up to a certain level, like a page of *Ulysses* or a page of Iain Sinclair, when you look at it, it makes no sense whatsoever, but has actually got an incredible amount of information in it. Information is a product of noise, to some degree, as much as it is of signal. It just depends on whether you've got a decoding mechanism. This is why a lot of people don't get on with Iain Sinclair's books. The stuff he is talking about is so far outside their grasp of reality that it is noise, noisy babbling about these churches, these sixties film makers, these historical figures. It doesn't make any sense. But if someone takes it as signal, sees the point of how one thing connects to another, then they are going to get a wealth of information out of it. The same thing goes for magic. If you've got a decoding system, the manual, the information can flood over you in a tidal burst and you won't drown.

MDA: This reminds me of Lester Grinspoon's experiments, when he compared transcripts between people under the influence of LSD and people under the influence of schizophrenia, and he concluded that the difference was that the people tripping had chosen to be dosed. That choice was what kept them sane. They knew what was happening to them. This is why they could come out of it afterwards. Right the way through the experience, you could always attribute it back to that choice to go into that area.

AM: The magician, to some degree, is trying to drive him or herself mad in a controlled setting, within controlled laws. You ask the protective spirits to look after you, or whatever. This provides a framework over an essentially amorphous experience. You are setting up your terms, your ritual, your channels—but you deliberately step over the edge into the madness. You are not falling over the edge, or tripping over the edge. When I was a kid, I used to go to the seaside and play in the waves. The thing you learn about waves is that when you see a big one coming, you run towards it. You try and get out of its way, and you'll end up twenty yards up the beach covered in scratches. Dive into it, and then you can get behind it. You get on top it, you won't be hurt. It is counterintuitive. The impulse is to run away, but the right thing to do is to plunge into it deliberately, and be in control when you do it. Magic is a response to the madness of the twentieth century.

MDA: Is it a safety mechanism for you? Is it a safety response kicking in against what might have been happening in your mind beforehand?

AM: Well, I don't distinguish between magic and art. When I got into magic, I realised I had been doing it all along, ever since I wrote my first pathetic story or poem when I was twelve or whatever. This has all been my magic, my way of dealing with it. Actually stepping into it as magic with a capital "M" was just a clarification of something I think a lot of us do, if we are creative. It's the standard moron's question that drove me away from comic conventions, "Where do you get your ideas from?" And yet, it is the only question worth asking. Where do we get these ideas from? Something is not there, then it is an idea form, then it is a book you pick up and read. Where is this nothing, this pregnant vacuum, that these things come from? Once you've noticed that, then sooner or later you are going to have to come to terms with it. You've got something that is pouring ideas down into you. When I was twenty-five, my big problem was that I had so many ideas, I couldn't finish any of them. Everyone has been through that phase. The big sprawling projects laying around in your head that vaguely depress you because you know you are never going to finish it. You need to get this raw energy into some form of acceptable, digestible form for the rest of the population. We tend to think of creativity and art, pop music, as a twentieth-century thing. We don't give them the same power that they've always had. This is all entertainment. This is all commerce. This is all culture. We forget what power these things originally had. The bardic tradition of magic, whereby if someone puts a curse on you, it may sour your milk for a month, or burn your house down, "yeah, yeah, yeah." Someone puts a satire on you that will destroy you in the eyes of your friends, in the eyes of your family, in your own eyes. If it's a particular good satire that's well worded and funny and clever, then five hundred years after you are dead, people will still be laughing at what a shit you were. That is destroyed. That's not just making your cow sick. People understood that as a real power, which, of course, it is. There are books that have devastated continents, destroyed thousands. What war hasn't been a war of fiction? All the religious wars, certainly, or the fiction of communism versus the fiction of capitalism—ideas, fictions, shit that people make. They have made a vast impression on the real world. It is the real world. Are thoughts not real? I believe it was Wittgenstein who said a thought is a real event in space and time. I don't quite agree about the space and time bit, Ludwig, but certainly a real event. It's only science that cannot consider thought as a real event, and science is not reality. It's a map of reality and not a very good one. It's good. It's useful, but it has its limits. We have to realise that the map has its edges. One thing that is past the edge is any personal experience. That is why magic is a broader map to me. It includes science. It's the kind of map we need if we are to survive psychologically in the age that is to come, whatever that is. We need a bigger map because the old one is based on an old universe where not many of us live anymore. We have to understand what we are dealing with here, because it is dangerous. It kills people. Art kills.

In the bardic tradition, art was understood as magic. The guy who could paint on the cave wall, he was a magician. The idea of representation was a magical idea. Then something happened, and then we all started to believe we were entertainers, and it was just a job. An aesthetic Thatcherism was imposed, and we all thought, "Oh shit, there isn't an art union, and we're lucky to have a job. We better accept that we're just the court jesters, and all we are here to do is keep the masses happy, write some more potboilers. We are magicians. We are not gods." Which in fact we are. We just forget that. We forgot our searing power and lost it, as a result. This is not a searing power coming from an elite of artists that I'm talking about. This is an inherent human power that all of us have the possibility of contacting. If you look at early shamanic texts and cultures, the magical powers that the shaman hopes the gods might give him, flying, turning into animals, invisibility, poetry— as if poetry was a magic power, as if it was the equivalent of turning into a dog or flying. As if. What does this tell us? Maybe there was a time when we could legitimately ask the gods for it as a gift. But we know there aren't any gods, and that they can't give those gifts, so the best thing we can do is go to church, listen to the lesson, and hope we don't burn. Have no direct contact with whatever form of god we choose to worship. It's like the magical or spiritual equivalent of the big flaw in Marxism. Karl Marx, lovely geezer, very humane, a bit middle class, but we'll gloss over that, but his big flaw was that when he said, "The reins of society will inevitably rest in the hands of those who control the means of production," [he] didn't take into account middle management, all the people who get between those with the means of production and the society. That translates onto a spiritual level as the shift from our earliest beliefs, which are all shamanic. The shaman is not a priest.

The shaman has no secret knowledge. He is equivalent to the hunter. He has a specific skill that is subjugated to the needs of the group. He is prepared to take drugs, go loopy, visit the underworld, bring back knowledge, and tell everybody. He's not keeping a secret knowledge. Originally, priests were instructors. They passed out the mysteries and revelations to the masses. Increasingly, they say, "You don't need to have a religious experience, we are having that for you. That's what we are here for." Eventually, they start saying, "You don't need to have a religious experience, and neither do we. We've got this book about some people who—a thousand years ago—had a religious experience. And if you come in on Sunday, we'll read you a bit of that, and you'll be sorted. Don't you worry." Effectively, a portcullis has slammed down between the individual and their godhead. "You can't approach your godhead except through us now. We are the only path. Our church is the only path." But that is every human being's birthright, to have ingress to their godhead. Organised religion has corrupted one of the purest, most powerful, and sustaining things in the human condition. It has imposed a middle management, not only in our politics and in our finances, but in our spirituality as well. The difference between religion and magic is the same as what we were talking about earlier. I think you could map that over those two poles of fascism and anarchism. Magic is closer to anarchism.

Moore in *The Onion* Edits

TASHA ROBINSON / 2001

The Onion AV Club. October 25, 2001. Reprinted by permission of Tasha Robinson at *The Onion*.

Tasha Robinson's 2001 interview was published in excerpted form as "Interview: Alan Moore" in *The Onion AV Club* print edition on October 24, 2001. The remainder of the interview was published exclusively at the *AV Club* website on October 25, 2001, as "Moore in *The Onion* Edits." Robinson's introduction below comes from the print interview, but the Q & A is from the edits. The original print content is currently available online, at http://www.avclub.com/articles/alan-moore,13740/, but the edits have, until now, disappeared into the Internet ether. EB

British writer Alan Moore was a comics fan from a very young age—"If you were working-class, you had comics. It was like rickets," he says—and by the time he was in his twenties, he was making a living writing comics and comic strips. After winning awards for his *V for Vendetta* series, a grim story about a poetry-spouting terrorist spreading anarchy in a fascistic future England, he attracted the attention of DC Comics, which recruited him to take over *Swamp Thing*. The company also gave him a launching pad for *Watchmen*, an intricately executed, seminal series that changed how literate comic-book readers thought about the superhero genre. Currently, Moore is writing half a dozen miniseries and ongoing monthly titles for DC Comics, including the psychedelic superhero comic *Promethea*, the retro-flavored *Tom Strong* titles, and the anthology *Tomorrow Stories*. But, apart from *Watchmen*, his greatest work to date remains *From Hell*, a massive exploration of the Jack the Ripper murders that incorporates British history, Masonic ritual, and London geography in a fascinating and horrifying conspiracy theory. The Hughes brothers' film adaptation of *From Hell* opened in America on October 19. From his home in Northampton, England, Moore spoke to *The Onion A.V. Club* about the *From Hell* movie, how the bad mood he was in fifteen years ago has warped the comics industry, and his worship of a second-century sock puppet.

Due to space constraints in *The Onion A.V. Club*'s print edition, the Alan Moore interview was cut considerably. Here's more of the transcript.

The Onion: When you first started reading comics as a child, and thinking about becoming a comics writer, did you ever consider the kind of deconstruction you've made into a career. Or were you just interested in imitating existing works back then?

Alan Moore: I was eight. The deconstruction of comics was when the staples came out, for that age. But probably, I started out like any other child of that age, just purely obsessed with the characters. I wanted to know what Batman was doing this month, whether he was hanging out with Superman, or whether he was with the Justice League. Given a couple of years, I discovered things like Harvey Kurtzman's original *Mad* comic, which was reprinted in paperbacks that were available over here. I discovered Will Eisner's *Spirit*. These were an incredible jolt, because for the first time, I was suddenly aware of the fantastic intelligence that could be invested in comics, given a talented enough creator. People like Kurtzman or Eisner were telling stories that could only be told in the comics form, but they were telling them with such style and power that I began to grasp what comics might be capable of. I started to realize how comics didn't need to be the way that the more normal comics that made up my reading diet always seemed to be, that you could do fantastic things. Who knew exactly what you could do with them? I certainly thought they could probably be made more realistic. I thought they could probably be given greater atmosphere, and that the writing of them could perhaps be improved. I think I was aware, even at that time, that the writing in comics, on some level, wasn't as good as the writing in some of the books I'd begun to stumble across. And I didn't see why literary values shouldn't be transplanted to comics. But during those days, this was only on a very amateur level. I'd do sort of incoherent experimental comic strips for local arts magazines, or local quasi-underground papers. Which were, I suppose, an attempt at learning my craft, but they weren't deconstructed. They were just messy. But, yeah, probably from an early age, there was a desire to do a different kind of comic book. But whether I'd have really dignified it with . . . I can't really claim to have any intelligent master plan. I probably didn't even realize that I was deconstructing superheroes until I was about halfway through *Watchmen*. Afterwards, it seemed a lot more obvious, but at the time we were just trying, initially, to do a cleverer-than-usual, more-stylish-than-usual, superhero comic. But two or three issues in, it had become a sort of semiotic nightmare that I still get hounded by literature professors over to this day. It obviously, halfway through the telling, became a very different sort of animal.

O: Did that realization actually alter *Watchmen* in the writing? Did you end up changing the story midway through as you realized what you were doing?

AM: We didn't. It was funny. The basic plot was there from before we started work on it. And we knew that we were going to be treating these superheroes in a way that was probably a little more dark, and perhaps a little more naturalistic, than the way they'd been treated usually. I was writing the opening pages, and as is my custom, I was making tiny little thumbnail sketches to actually be able to envisage what the page would finally look like when it was drawn. I had two or three strains of narrative going on in the same page. I had a truculent newsvendor giving his fairly uninformed commentary on the political state of the world, the likelihood of a coming war. Across the street, in the background, we have two people fixing a radiation sign to a wall. Sitting with his back to a hydrant near the newsvendor, there's a small boy reading a comic, which is a pirate comic. And I think while I was doodling, I noticed that an extreme close-up of the radiation symbol, if you put the right sort of caption with it, could look almost like the black sail of a ship against a yellow sky. So I dropped in a caption in the comic that the child was reading about a hellbound ship's black sails against a yellow Indies sky. And I have a word balloon coming from off-panel, which is actually the balloon of the newsvendor, which is talking about war. The narrative of the pirate comic is talking about a different sort of war. As we pull back, we realize that we're looking at a radiation symbol that's being tacked to the wall of a newly created fallout shelter. And finally, when we pull back into the beginning, into the foreground, we realize that these pirate captions that we've been reading are those in the comic that is being read by the small boy. This was exciting. There was something going on here. There was an interplay between the imagery, between the strands of narrative, the pirate narrative, the dialogue going on in the street. They were striking sparks off of each other, and they were doing something which I hadn't actually seen a comic do before. I think it was around those first three pages of *Watchmen* #3 that I started to realize that we'd got something different on our hands here. There were storytelling techniques that were starting to suggest themselves that simply hadn't been done before. There were complexities of narrative that suddenly seemed possible. We took that and ran with it. By the next issue, we had this incredibly complex kind of multifaceted view of time, where everything is kind of happening at once—at least in the mind of the central character. Which, again, opened up possibilities for new narrative tricks, which we pretty much kept up until the end of the series. But, like I said, it was purely while I was scribbling, doodling, writing bits of dialogue and crossing them out that I suddenly noticed these possibilities for things that could be done in a comic and nowhere else.

O: What was your work process like when you were creating the parallel scenes in *Watchmen* and *From Hell*? Did you write the subplots separately, or was it all a panel-by-panel realization of where your connections were?

AM: We knew broadly what was happening in plot terms in each issue, but in terms of fine details, all of the symbols and signs, word juxtapositions, that was pretty much panel-by-panel. By the time I'd got *From Hell* . . . I remember jotting down the titles of sixteen chapters, because I thought I could tell the whole story in sixteen chapters, including a prologue and an epilogue. So, I knew roughly what I'd be covering in each one, but I left it open in terms of the length of each episode. When I started out, when I was writing *Swamp Thing*, I would be very meticulous, in that for each issue, before I started it, I would map out twenty-four pages. I would know pretty much exactly what was going to happen on each page, what the ending of that particular episode would be. By the time I was doing *Watchmen*, I'd been writing for long enough to trust my own processes, so I was able to relax that a little bit. I'd have a vague idea, but I'd kind of . . . Because there really wasn't any limit on how many pages I could take, I would let the story evolve itself. That's gone even further with my current work, with a lot of the ABC titles, where they're more or less all improvised. Yes, I have got a vague idea, the very vaguest of ideas, about how certain plot threads might resolve themselves, but I find something quite exciting about the spontaneity of just not having any idea where you're going to end up. I find that forces stranger, better story resolutions out of me. I prefer working without the safety net of a preexisting structure at the moment. With *Watchmen*, it was pretty tightly planned; with *From Hell*, half and half. It had a structure that existed from the beginning, but there was still a lot of room to move within that structure. The things that I'm writing now, the structure is fairly vaporous.

O: You say "we" knew what the plot was going to be. Was Dave Gibbons involved in creating the narrative? Did his art affect your . . .

AM: Oh, absolutely. The thing is, when I started working in comics, I was not very often privileged to know which artist would be drawing the script. I more

Watchmen #3, page 1 by Alan Moore and Dave Gibbons. Copyright © 1986 DC Comics. All Rights Reserved, used by permission.

or less had to write an artist-proof script, so even if it went to the worst artist in the world, he would at least be able to get some sense out of it. This didn't give me a lot of control over what the finished product looked like. Whereas, if I know that I'm going to be working with an artist like David Lloyd on *V For Vendetta*, or Dave Gibbons on *Watchmen*, then I can write the entire script suited specifically to that artist. Now, I'd worked with Dave before. I knew that he did have this surveyor's precision when it came to placing objects into a panel, fitting them in somehow, with lots of filigree and detail. So, with *Watchmen*, I was able to exploit that. I mean, this is certainly true on *From Hell*. I don't imagine that I could have done *From Hell* with any artist other than Eddie Campbell. I mean, Eddie's style is, even in comics, unique. It was a style that was exactly necessary to get away with some of the stuff we got away with. I mean, we did get away with murder. The standard horror comic has got a lot in common with the modern horror film. There is this gross-out element, where if you see a severed head, you won't just see the severed head. You'll see all of the little veins dangling underneath it, the dripping blood, and it'll all be done in loving detail. This is the same thing we get in cinema, where the gore is spectacular, and where the reaction of the audience, generally, is the same as it was with those EC comics: It's to laugh. In a kind of a dark and morbid fashion, perhaps, but to laugh nonetheless. I think that's because there's something about the signals and symbols that we surround our various genres with. And with a horror comic or a horror film, right from the title lettering, you're going to know that this is what you're looking at. If the title lettering is red and kind of drippy, then this is a horror book, this is a horror film, this is a horror comic. And I think at that point, we all kind of switch over into horror mode, where we understand that what we're being shown on the screen is a kind of entertainment. It's all ketchup. There's no blood. It's a kind of vicarious thrill. It's a kind of roller-coaster ride. We're not in any danger of being harmed, and yet we can have that vicarious thrill of fear, followed by the release of laughter. Sort of, "No, that's not actually very horrifying." That's taking the coward's way out, as far as I'm concerned. With *From Hell*, given the nature of the material, given that this is essentially about one man killing five fairly anonymous women in the back streets of London's poorest quarter during the late 1880s, it didn't seem appropriate to me to dress it up in that kind of jokey clothing that the horror genre generally comes equipped with. I'd seen a number of Ripper films that almost became a kind of pornography, where the images were always the same. They would show you the unrealistically attractive 1880s prostitute walking down a street after dark, perhaps tunelessly and drunkenly singing some English song of the period.

Then perhaps you'll see a shadow of a man in a top hat with a Gladstone bag, cast upon a glistening cold wall. She notices someone behind her. Her steps increase, echoing upon the cobbles. His steps increase. She ducks down alleyways. She's breathing faster now. He's following her. We perhaps get a shot of the knife upraised, her face. She screams, then blood splashes over, perhaps, a musical poster. The next shot is the policeman turning up, saying, "Oh my god," then blowing his whistle. This is making it exciting. I mean, this is a very sordid, miserable, unfair little death in a back alleyway in London. I don't think that it is appropriate to make it part of this teasing dance. What I wanted to do was to actually make this a genuine horror book, if you like, in that I wouldn't allow the readers that escape. If they wanted to see what it was like to cut up women, then I wanted to show them the plain and awful truth of it, unadorned, particularly in the Mary Kelly chapter, where we spend almost the entire forty-page episode in a room with him cutting up the final victim. By the end of it, I'm sure that the readers, just like me and Eddie, were begging to get out of that room. It's something where I think I felt a responsibility to myself, to the book, and weirdly, I think, to the women, to actually show this in as cold and unemotional a light as possible. To not adorn it or trick it out. Eddie's style is so matter-of-fact that it is the opposite of the standard horror-comic style. What Eddie's material brings to *From Hell*—you see characters chatting in the street. You see characters going into the shop to buy a candle, or talking in the pub. You see characters discussing points of philosophy. You see characters being ritually disemboweled by some strange Masonic maniac. And all of this is happening in the same world. Characters are eating, sleeping, having sex, being murdered, murdering, and it's all in the same universe. With horror films, I think it's very easy for us to be able to switch over our perceptions and think, "Right, this is happening in the horror-film universe. This sort of stuff doesn't happen in my universe." It's a way of making the film safe. It's a kind of prophylactic measure. The fact that all of the blood and the gothic staging immediately puts it in a completely different world from ours. I think that *From Hell* and Eddie's style is more insidious, in that there is no actual point where you can say, "No, this definitely couldn't have happened in our world." That's a very good example of the artist, to a large degree, governing how I wrote the work.

O: Given that you work without revising or editing, how do you feel about your final product when you go back and look at it?

AM: There's never anything that I'd change. They're all accurate representations of where I was at that particular time. It's funny, you tend to find that your reaction to your past work is almost tidal. Sometimes I'll pick up *Watch-men* and flip through it and think, "Oh, God, I can't be bothered to read all this. It's so wordy, and there are so many pictures. Nah." And then, maybe a year later, I'll pick it up again and will be sucked straight into the story and will think, "Actually, this is pretty good." Maybe two years after that, I'll be back to thinking that it's dull, or less than satisfying. Generally, I'm pretty pleased with most of my past work. That's not to say that it's all good, because I've done some terrible stories. Most of the more significant ones, I'm very pleased with, and I wouldn't want to change them. They sometimes show naiveté, political naiveté or emotional naiveté, but at least it was an honest naiveté. I wouldn't want to go back and do any cosmetic work to edit out my clumsy beginnings, because I find them kind of charming myself. When I read my past work, I generally read it with a certain amount of pleasure.

O: Your current series, *Tomorrow Stories*, is unusual for you, in that it's a lot sillier and more random than most of your work. Does it have a purpose for you beyond satire?

AM: Well, it's basically a place where I can do very short little experimental stories. Sometimes I can just have silly fun, and I have a great deal of silly fun with *Tomorrow Stories*. Sometimes I can do something a bit more serious. In one of the Greyshirt stories in *Tomorrow Stories*, we did something very peculiar with the panel layouts. We had an apartment building, the same building, upon every page. There are four horizontal panels on each page. Each of those panels corresponds to one floor of the building upon each page. Then, to add another element, we made it so that the top panels are all taking place in 1999, the second panel down on each page is taking place in 1979, the panel beneath that takes place in 1959, and on the bottom panel of each page, you're seeing the bottom of the building as it was in 1939, when it was a fairly new building. We're able to tell, by some quite complicated story gymnastics, quite an interesting little story that is told over nearly sixty years of this building's life, with characters getting older depending upon which panel and which time period they're in. There's something that you couldn't do in any medium other than comics. I enjoy the satire in *Tomorrow Stories*, but it also gives me the opportunity to pull short little one-off stories out of a hat that are just a moment's inspiration that wouldn't lend themselves to the longer stories of some of the other books, but which might fill six pages in an interesting fashion. I enjoy short work, especially after spending ten years doing *From Hell* and twelve or thirteen years before *Lost Girls* is finished. The idea of something that I can more or less write in a couple of days is very refreshing.

Tomorrow Stories #2, page 1, by Alan Moore and Rick Veitch. Copyright © 1999 America's Best Comics, LLC, used by permission of DC Comics. All Rights Reserved.

O: When you're talking about getting into that kind of structural experiment, you're talking about something people probably won't appreciate on first glance, that they actually have to go through and mine out the details in order to understand what you're doing. Do you think people appreciate that sort of thing on a different mental level than simply reading a book or seeing a movie?

AM: I think they do. I've got my own kind of highfalutin' theories on it. One thing that strikes me is that the brain, as I understand it, is divided into roughly two lobes. Roughly speaking, the left side of our brain deals with rational cognitive thinking, language, forming sentences, speaking, things like that. The right side of our brain deals more with unconscious imagery. Dreams, the unconscious, the irrational, that side of us. I tend to think that maybe you could expand from that to think that perhaps, in the left side of our brain, words are the primary unit of currency. Perhaps in the right side of our brain, the image, the picture, is the primary unit of currency, because the right side of the brain is pre-verbal. There's something unique in the way that comics will connect a single image with a single group of words. I know that they did tests at the Pentagon where they were trying to find what form of instructional leaflet would spread information in the most direct way, and the way that it was most likely to be retained. They chose several different forms. They chose straight text, text with occasional illustrations, illustrated photographs, or photographs with captions, and they tried comics. They found that comics was far and away the best way for people to take in information and retain it. I think people would remember the picture, and that would cue the words they had read going along with that picture. I think that this might be because comics engage both halves of the brain simultaneously. One half is concerned with words. One half is concerned with images. With comics, you do have single static images, single clumps of words. Maybe the two halves are engaged in a different way than they are with other art forms, and this accounts for the kind of imprinting that comics are capable of. This is only speculation. I try to keep up with science and neurology, and how the brain works, but at the end of the day, I am largely a comic writer, so you probably shouldn't trust me to perform extensive brain surgery or anything like that.

O: When you experiment with this sort of thing, is it a scientific experiment? Are you interested in the effect, or are you doing it for your own satisfaction, to see if it can be done?

AM: A bit of both. I like to show off, even if it's only going to be to, in some cases, eight other comics writers who are going to realize what I've done. I like to show my might and power, so that they may grovel before me. At the same time, there is a scientific element in it. I remember looking at some of the marvelous work of Frank King on *Gasoline Alley* that was done in the American newspaper strips around the turn of the century, and for my money, some of the most experimental and farsighted comic-strip work was done by the giants of the American newspaper strip during that period. I remember looking at one particular Frank King page, and the whole page was divided up into maybe nine panels. It was one of his *Gasoline Alley* Sunday pages.

It was a view looking down upon the alleyways, so that the whole page, all nine panels, was one single picture. In each square of this down-shot of the alleyway, in each panel, there was some little gag going on, a little gag that was complete and of itself. Now, I looked at that and thought how impressive it was, but at the same time I thought, "Well, there are no moving elements in it. Why hasn't he got, say, a moving element that wanders all through the panels?" And I thought, "Well, this is because once you get across to the right of the first tier of panels, your eye is then going to move down to the extreme left of the second tier of panels, and you can't really have a character making that jump." It's tricky. Is there a way that you could have a full-page picture divided into numerous panels, where it all was understandable as one picture, yet there was a moving element in it? You could trace trajectories of people moving in a logical way from panel to panel over the whole page, and in *Big Numbers*, which was an aborted series that I was doing in the late eighties, I did one page with a family around a breakfast table, and it worked like a dream. You've got the mother scraping food from a plate into a pedal bin, moving to the right, starting to wash that dish, moving to the right a little bit further, and drying it up, moving to the right a bit further to place it in the cupboard. Meanwhile, you've got the other characters moving, sometimes in different ways, counterclockwise around the table rather than clockwise, but it all works. Now, I know that there were a lot of readers who were impressed with it. I think that Neil Gaiman and perhaps one other writer actually phoned up to congratulate me on pulling it off. I was immensely satisfied. I'd proven scientifically that something could be done. I'd managed to show off to other writers and impress the audience. It doesn't get a lot better than that, really.

O: There are probably fairly few people in the comics world who are not wondering if you will, someday, manage to revive *Big Numbers*.
AM: Probably not gonna happen. After you've had two separate artists run screaming into the night, you start to think, "Is it me?" Having tried to revive the project, to get the project going twice . . . The first time it happened, it more or less wiped me out financially. Not a terribly pleasant period of my professional career, that one. I got through it all right, but it was pretty tough. But, emotionally, it was very draining to have this project which was intended to be a kind of magnum opus, for which I'd written about five issues. There is some possibility. I know that Alex Usborne of Picture Palace Productions, the film company that made the film adaptation of Irvine Welsh's book, *The Acid House*, optioned *Big Numbers* for television. I've got the whole of *Big Numbers*

plotted. I'd got this enormous A1 sheet of paper the size of a tablecloth that had been divided into forty rows down the side, and twelve columns along the top. One column for each of the twelve issues, forty rows for each of the forty characters. And then, in this grid in tiny, incomprehensibly small biro writing which looks like the work of a mental patient, and which gives you a migraine just to look at it, there is what happens to each of the forty characters in every one of the twelve issues. It's this map of the entire plot. I've never done it with any other work, because it is kind of an insane thing to do. I've kind of got all that stuff in my head anyway, so the only real reason for writing it down on paper is just to impress and frighten. But because I'd still got the plot, we were able to reconstruct the basis of a twelve-episode TV drama series. Whether it'll ever make it to TV or not, no idea. I'm largely leaving that to Alex. There's not very much chance, however, of it ever materializing as a comic book again.

O: In an old interview with the *Comics Journal*, you were asked what kind of research you did into plant biology for *Swamp Thing*. You said, "I have a spine-tingling terror of doing anything that remotely approximates hard work, such as research." Obviously, the things you're writing now must require a tremendous amount of research . . .
AM: Did I really say that?

O: The *Comics Journal* certainly thinks you did.
AM: Yeah, well, I guess I really did say it, then. I must have overcome my fear. I suppose what it was, was *From Hell*. No, no. It was the *Brought to Light* book that I did for the Christic Institute. Joyce Brabner asked me if I wanted to do that, and I kind of leapt at the opportunity, because it sounded important, and because I was interested in those areas myself, and because the Christic Institute sounded like a fundamentally decent bunch of people, as indeed they proved to be when I did go over there and visit them. But with that, they gave me their affidavit, which was a telephone-directory-sized legal document. They recommended all these various books on Iran-Contra, on the Cuba situation, on the heroin smuggling going on through the Golden Triangle, cross-referencing all the names. They said, "Right, this is the entire history of the CIA since the close of WWII. Get it into thirty pages." So that was a demanding job, to sift through all these books and condense the information and condense it further, and try and not condense it past the point where it would suddenly become confusing. But I think that it probably left me with a taste for the thrill of talking about the real world. There's a real buzz to talking

about events that really happened, which I think was probably what led me to *From Hell*. And by that time, clearly in a kind of morbid, grumpy way, I'm kind of enjoying the research. Because the research on both *Brought to Light* and *From Hell*, in some ways, was very miserable work, in that it's pretty grim stuff to have to wade through. But on the other hand, filling in a picture a bit at a time does have a certain intellectual excitement behind it.

O: With research-heavy books like *Promethea* and *From Hell*, do you start out with an area of interest and do the research and then decide to do a book, or do you decide to do a book and then start doing your research?

AM: With *From Hell*, I think the original idea was that I thought I'd like to do a comic strip about a murder. That was the idea. I thought a murder seemed like a complex and interesting human event which thankfully doesn't happen to many of us. But when murders do happen, they are so intense that it's the human condition in some sort of extreme. It struck me that maybe by looking at it, it might say something about the human condition in more general terms. But at first, I couldn't think of a murder that had ramifications that went far enough to actually talk about the kind of things that I wanted to talk about. Then, because it was the centenary of the actual murders in 1988, there was a lot of Ripper material about. I'd originally not even considered Jack the Ripper, because it seemed too played-out. It had been done so many times before, but I came across Stephen Knight's book, and a couple of other pieces, and thought that actually, there is an interesting way that you could tell this story that hasn't been done before, which I realized was going to take an awful lot of research. I was going to have to read nearly every book that had ever been written on Jack the Ripper, because in some ways I'd be writing about the story as much as I'd be writing about Jack the Ripper. It's the way that the myth has grown that is important. With *Promethea*, when I was coming up with the initial titles for ABC Comics, I thought, well, I want a comic with a strong female character. I'd also like to have a comic where I can release some of the steam of my magical researches. With *From Hell*, I came up with the idea, then did the research. *Promethea* grew out of research that I was doing anyway, something that I was already interested in, and which I suddenly realized that I could probably apply effectively to comics. It depends upon the work, really.

The Craft: An Interview with Alan Moore

DANIEL WHISTON, DAVID RUSSELL, AND ANDY FRUISH / 2002

Zarjaz 3 & 4 (2002–2003). Interview conducted on September 9 and October 29, 2002. Reprinted by permission of Daniel Whiston. Only part one is reprinted here.

PART ONE: SEPTEMBER 9, 2002

Having been graciously invited to his Northampton abode by the World's Greatest Comics Writer, myself (Daniel Whiston), along with David Russell and Andy Fruish had a long and fascinating meeting with the Enlightened One, surrounded as we were by shelves groaning under the weight of books and comics, walls covered with mystic paraphernalia from throughout the ages, and a constant fug of smoke. Having introduced ourselves (and established that the Dictaphone was indeed working), an intense two-hour introduction to Alan's methods, opinions and writing approach followed . . .

DW: I feel quite awkward doing this 'cos I've never really interviewed anyone before . . .
AM: Well, I'm a doddle for interviewing 'cos I'm completely infatuated with the sound of me own voice. You just have to say a few basic words, and I'll talk for the next hour or two. You prod me if you want me to stop or change to a different subject.

DW: The selfish motivation for me doing this is that I'm starting to try and write myself and would be really interested to get the benefit of your experience. So from that point of view, I'd be really interested in talking about the mechanics of the craft, and then maybe go on to talk about the higher-level creative aspects in a little bit.
AM: OK.

DW: So maybe we could start off with the nuts and bolts. What's your approach to plotting, for example?

AM: My approach to most things has been in a state of flux and has been developing over the last twenty-five years that I've been working at this. With regard to plotting for example, when I started out with this, I was living in a state of such terror that I would get to the end of a story and not have an ending for it, or would not have at least a satisfactory ending for it, that I would plot my stories out almost to the finest detail. If I was plotting a twenty-four-page *Swamp Thing* story I would have a kind of rough idea of where I wanted the story to go in my head. I would have perhaps vague ideas of what would make a good opening scene, a good closing scene, perhaps a few muddy bits in the middle. I'd then write the numbers 1 to 24 down the side of the page, and I would put down a one-line description of what was happening on that page. This kind of developed to the point of mania with *Big Numbers*.

When I plotted *Big Numbers*, I plotted the entire projected twelve-issue series on one sheet of A1 paper—which was just frightening. A1 is scary—it's the largest size. I divided it along the top into twelve columns and along the side into something like forty-eight different rows across which had got the names of all the characters, so the whole thing became a grid where I could tell what each of the characters was doing in each issue. It was all filled with tiny biro writing, which looked like the work of a mental patient. It was like migraine made visible. It was really scary.

I mainly did it to frighten other writers. Neil Gaiman nearly shat. The colour drained from his face when he saw this towering work of madness. I've still got it somewhere. I just don't look at it very often. It doesn't make me feel good. It's sort of: "Where was I?"

So, I used to plot meticulously, but I started to get the feeling that plot—if you're doing something that is very heavily plot-driven: If you're doing a crime story, if you're doing a whodunit or something like that where a plot is a very, very necessary thing—but some stories where there's nothing but plot, it does sound like someone walking through a bog, you know: "Plot plot plot plot plot plot plot plot . . ." "Yeah, yeah, your plot made sense, but I wasn't interested in it. I was not interested in any of these characters. Your plot hung together, but there was no real story." So I try not to get quite so obsessed with plot.

With the America's Best Comics that I've been doing along with most of the stuff I've been doing lately of any stripe, I'm much more liable to just come up with—it's not even a half-arsed it's a quarter-arsed idea at best—but it'll do it for the first couple of pages. "Yeah, that'll be good, let's have some three-eyed cowboys. I've got no idea what they're going to do in the story, but this issue's all about three-eyed cowboys. I mean, you might think of a story that's got three-eyed cowboys in it and hope it comes to some sort of resolution, but it always does.

I've been working for twenty-five years now, and I can probably bring near enough any story to a satisfactory resolution, just because I've been doing this every day for twenty-five years. You get more confident in your ability to bring a story home. So, you can ride bareback and take more risks. That is something I have a great deal of fun with. I mean, when I wrote *Voice of the Fire*, I knew that the last chapter being narrated by me would have to be something that was true, and that had really happened, and yet it would also have to tie up all of the themes and motifs of the novel. So, it took me five years to write that, and I knew that not only would the last chapter have to really happen, it would have to really happen during the month that I was writing that chapter.

So if it happened that nothing happened that month, and nothing happened that provided me with things like severed heads, you know, black dogs, all of the other motifs, then I would have wasted pretty much five years, because the novel wouldn't have an ending. I mean that is really high-stakes gambling, but the thrill, when it comes off, is really something. But it always comes off. If you've got the nerve, if you can sort of do it without flinching or worrying, then it always somehow kind of comes off, if you just follow the process. I mean, that's probably something—these days—when I started off, I was all technique. I was obsessed with technique, and I would approach every part of that technique meticulously, trying to think about it, how it might fit together, how it might be changed or modified, what effect you might be able to get by sort of twisting this a degree to the left, this a degree to the right.

These days I tend to find that I kind of improvise with a lot of confidence, and find that the material is often much better, much fresher . . .

DW: Maybe that's because you had a technique to start with . . .
AM: . . . and then you can go beyond it. I mean perhaps it's true to say that to actually get a grounding in the techniques . . . Once you know how all this stuff works, then you can throw away the rulebook. You can throw away the manual and then sort of, just do it. You know, improv . . .

DW: To someone starting off in my position, what would you say were the elements of that toolkit?

AM: The first thing is: think about what you are doing. Think about every aspect of it. Brian Eno was somebody whose thinking really influenced me when I was starting out. Now, he was a musician, and I was moving into comics, but his thinking was generalised enough that it applied to a whole variety of fields. One of the things that he said was that some creative people seem to be governed by a kind of superstitious fear about examining their own creative processes. It's almost like riding a bicycle, where if they stop to think about how they're doing it, they'll fall off.

Whereas my attitude is, if you're going to be making your living out of this stuff—It's like if you're making your living as a driver, you'd at least want to know what happens if the car grinds to a halt, what all that stuff under the hood actually does and is—actually understand your own creative process. Think about everything. Think about what you're doing.

If you're talking about comics writing, then many of the same things apply as with writing in general, but there is a whole couple of other layers to the possibilities because you've got an image track as well, and a kind of "over grammar," as I think I once heard it described as, where you've got the interaction, neither words nor pictures, but the interaction of both of them.

DW: Scott McCloud talks about that quite a bit . . .
AM: Yeah, Scott, he's a clever lad. I'm not sure about his new: "all comics are gonna be online." I think he's talking bollocks there . . .

DW: I think I agree in some ways . . .
AM: It's academic. He's pushing it with this second book. There's a lot of stuff in there, which isn't actually accurate thinking, but his first book's impeccable.

DW: Maybe that comes from being more of an analyst and less of a practitioner . . . He hasn't written as much as he's thought . . .
AM: I think he's become more "evangelist," is the word you're looking for. He's got very, very into this idea of: "everything would be better if it's on computers," without actually thinking about any of the practicalities of it . . .

DW: Like scrolling over the pages of a comic that's twenty metres wide . . .
AM: You could, and I believe he has actually done a strip especially for that format that can be read in all sorts of different ways. It sounds really cute, a really interesting experiment. I'm sure I'd love to do that once. The thing is, with *Promethea* #12, looked at materially, it's exactly the same technology as

Promethea #12, pages 22–23, by Alan Moore and J. H. Williams, III. Copyright © 2001 America's Best Comics, LLC, used by permission of DC Comics. All Rights Reserved.

Action Comics #1. It's a number of sheets of paper with like images and words printed on them and a staple in the middle.

However, *Promethea* #12 is a complete history of the universe broken down into the twenty-two Tarot cards, with a commentary in verse, a frieze. The whole thing is one panel, where if you duplicated it and got two copies of it and stuck it all together, yes, it could be put up as a frieze. The ends of the frieze join together so it runs forever. There's a flipbook worked into the sides of the pages. We've got this joke by Aleister Crowley running all the way along the bottom. We've got perfect anagrams of the word "Promethea"—twenty-two of them [laughter]—that fit in perfectly with both the Tarot cards and the era of history we are applying that Tarot card to. Now, that is a higher technology.

To me, the basic technology is the word. I mean, that's not technology. That is a fruit of technology. The clue with technology is the "logy" bit—technology means writing about a body of knowledge. The word is the mother technology. All technologies are based upon the word. The word is the primal technology. Dealing with language, dealing with being a writer, you're gonna be dealing with language. If it's comics, then that will involve a pictorial element, but a lot of the basic things are the same. If you want to learn how to write, be analytical, and that probably means when you're starting, be reductionist. It's too big a problem to grasp the whole thing at once, at least at the start of your career. Break it down. Start thinking about the different components of a story.

What things should a story have? It should have a plot, although this doesn't have to be the most important thing. The plot is the skeleton. Sometimes a beautiful and elegant plot is what a whole story's about, and that's great, but sometimes a plot need only be a string of events that takes you from point A to point B or D or whatever.

Now, there should also be what the story is about, which is not the same thing as the plot. What the story is about. What are you trying to say? What kind of shape or impression are you hoping to leave upon the reader? In a sense, the story, or poem or verse or whatever it is you're writing, you can kind of think of it as a kind of projectile. Imagine it is a kind of projectile which has been specially shaped to be aerodynamic, and that your target is the soft grey putty of the reader's brain. What kind of shape, what kind of indentation, what kind of lasting scar do you want to leave upon your reader? You design the missile accordingly. What are you trying to convey to them? It's going to be some kind of information—now that can be factual information, emotional information, psychological information. It's gonna be some sort of information. It might be nonlinear. It might be more like noise than information . . . sort of like James Joyce, because actually it's the noise that holds the most information.

Pure signal is like *Janet and John*. Yes, you can understand everything on the page, but there's nothing much there worth understanding. Noise—or something approaching noise—is like a page of James Joyce, a page of Ian Sinclair—where there is such a density of information that it almost becomes incoherent, but it is full of information. So, it's the ways of getting that information across. Plot, the story, has to be about something. It has to have a purpose. It has to have a shape. It has to have a structure. If you're going to be really clever, you can maybe get the structure, the plot, and the theme all to reflect each other in some way—but that's just being clever.

Watchmen was kind of clever. I was going through one of my clever periods—probably emotional insecurity. I thought: "People will laugh at me 'cos I'm doing superhero comics. I'd better make 'em really clever, then no-one will laugh" [laughter]. So, we've got all this sort of thing with the metaphor of the clock face, and yes it is a kind of clockwork-like construction—a swiss watch construction—where you can see all the works of it. Different areas where the text reflects itself, different levels—I was showing off.

But you'll need all of those elements. They don't all have to be tied up as fussily as that. In fact, I kind of decided after *Watchmen* that there was no point ever doing anything like that ever again, because having done it once, it would have been silly to have taken it further and done something more complex, when it's already this sort of elaborate wedding cake of a comic book. You don't want any more icing on the top.

DW: I remember at the time you were worried that DC might do *Kid Rorschach* or something . . .

AM: Well, it was always possible, you never know what DC might do: *Blot the Dog* [laughter]. So you need these things. Then, what you want to do—you're going to need a world for the story to happen in. It might be the real one. It might be an imaginary one. It doesn't matter. You're going to have to make it up in either sense, because there isn't a real world here. There's not an objective real world, at least I don't know anyone who's ever seen one. There's a lot of subjective worlds, like in *Voice of the Fire*, where I wrote about this area. You have to be as fantastic in your description, in your imagining, of the place as you would be writing about some alien world or some exotic landscape like the swamps of Louisiana or whatever. You have to wring the poetry out of the place—make it real.

Whether it's real or not, make it real. Give it an emotional reality. Give it the reality of writing, so when people read it, it will conjure a sense of location, of place, of situation. Remember that you've got more than one sense. Don't just tell them what everything looks like. Tell 'em what it smells like. Tell 'em what it feels like. Tell 'em what it tastes like. That can give a much more wraparound sense of reality. Now, characters are the most interesting and mysterious and wonderful part of the writer's craft in my opinion. Structure is dazzling. You can feel like a real big scientist when you're doing structure, but characters—they're strange because you'll think up some facts, some fragment of a character—It might be a name. It might be a personality. It might be a face, something like that, and once you've got that fragment, you think: "What does this suggest? If this is the name, what do they look like?" You put it together like a sort of broken vase, asking: "Now what goes next to this?" So eventually . . .

To pluck an example out of thin air, *Lost Girls*, the thing we've got coming out next year, me and Melinda Gebbie. It's probably quite a good way to describe the writing process, to talk about how that came about, on all the different levels. We decided that we wanted to do something that was erotic. Why did we want to do that? Well, we decided that there was a need for it, that most erotica—or pornography (and the distinction seems to be largely in the income bracket of the person buying it)—most of it is shit, sadly. It's ugly on all sorts of levels—aesthetically ugly, physically ugly, politically ugly, morally . . . on all sorts of levels . . . and there's no reason why that should be. When you can get people beautifying violence in the cinema . . .

DW: Any subject can be beautiful.

AM: Yeah, so why, with very few exceptions, has there never been any great pornographic art? Why has there never been any great pornographic writing that has actually tried to do all the same things that ordinary novels do . . .

DW: I think that's because people think that it should be ugly, and it should be dirty . . .

AM: Yeah, there's something wrong there. We identified a problem there. So, why not do absolutely brilliant pornography that was really horny, really clever, really beautiful, had characters and a story and all the things a regular novel should have. So ok, we cast around for ideas as to how we would do this and that took a long time, because there were lots of wrong ways of doing it that we considered and thought—"No, that's wrong"—and that's gotta be instinct, sort of pick up an idea and try and follow it through in your mind and see where it goes, and if it goes somewhere you're not interested in, put it down. Pick up another one. With this idea me and Melinda had, I had an earlier idea that I'd put to one side and shelved, that you could maybe treat *Peter Pan* as a kind of coded erotic story. I think I'd been thinking about the Freudian notion of flying as a dream metaphor for sex, and I was thinking: "So, Peter Pan, he teaches Wendy how to fly, there's the island of the Lost Boys." I could see that that would have had a lot of sexual shadows to it, but I never really thought of what I could do with it other than . . .

AF: What about Hook? [laughter]

AM: Oh well, we've got very good stuff with Hook. I didn't know what to do with that other than do a rude version of *Peter Pan*, where you could say: "Ah yes, this is going to be sexy . . ." and that didn't really seem to be enough, to sexualise a children's story, but Melinda was saying that she'd written a couple of stories she'd enjoyed that had had three women characters . . . that for some reason, she just liked to do stories about three women characters. That was just random input. But when I kind of connected that idea up with the Peter Pan idea, I suddenly thought: "Alright, what if Wendy, from *Peter Pan*, is one of the characters?"—and then immediately, I thought of Alice and Dorothy. I thought, all right, that's three different female characters from three different children's books. What if you had those women meet up at a hotel, or somewhere, and tell each other their stories, and their stories are sexually decoded versions of the stories that they are famous for.

So that sounded like it was going somewhere. It wasn't there yet, but it was going somewhere. So, then I started to look at the dates those stories were written and try and work out the relative ages of the three women, and what period they could have met, and what ages they would all have been. And I kind of worked it out that round about 1913, 1914, Alice would have been about sixty. Dorothy would probably be about twenty, nineteen, something like that. Wendy would probably be middle-aged, sort of thirty, thirty-five, something like that.

AF: Middle aged?!?!? [laughter]

AM: Later youth. She'd probably be in later youth, certainly not nearly dead. And I suddenly thought: "Ok, they can meet in this hotel in 1913," and then I thought: "1913, that was when the war was kicking off and there was that Stravinsky performance in Paris of *Rite of Spring*, when there were all the riots," and I thought: "Wouldn't it be interesting if this whole story was going on against a backdrop . . . if we had this story happening in a beautiful place, this sort of art nouveau hotel, where everything is perfect and lovely. It's erotic. Everyone's fucking, you know . . . It's a pornotopia, and then as a counterpoint, in the background, we have the riots at the Stravinsky concert, which to a certain degree show the emotional pitch Europe was at, at that time. Then we'll sort of take that on. We'll show the assassination of Franz Ferdinand. We'll show everything sort of careening towards war, and pretty much the destruction of European culture, or at least a massive blow to it. All the pretty things get burned."

And I was thinking: "There's something epic about this. There's something really stark about sexuality and war, because most of the people who get sent to die in wars are young men who've got a lot of energy and would probably rather, in a better world, be putting that energy into copulation rather than going over there and blowing some other young man's guts out."

It's a perversion. War is a perversion of sex. Also, you only have to look at things like the language of war, any of these excitable young American pilots coming back from bombing Libya, and they're saying: "Yeah, we shot our missiles right up their back door." Homoerotic. They will also, just before they attack somewhere, generally launch a sort of propaganda campaign saying the enemy is a homosexual. They have to make him into a woman. The Ayatollah Khomeini: "Oh yeah, he likes little boys." That's what we were saying just before we bombed the shit out of Iran, or were going to, or, "That Colonel Qadaffi, he dresses up as a woman." This was the CIA rumour put around just before we bombed Tripoli. There's a lot of connections between war and eroticism. So, it struck me that there was a story here where, yes, we could do our original thing of bringing weight and importance to pornography, and there seemed to be a plot there. The three women tell their stories and the First World War happens, and you put those two in juxtaposition against each other.

So, all right, then we had to come up with the characters. Now, you might say that the characters were already there, but the characters were already there as little girls whereas we wanted them as women. So, we looked at Lewis Carroll's Alice. What sort of sixty-year old woman would she be? She's obviously the most intellectual of the three girls. She's also the oddest. She's the most eccentric.

DW: Did you see *Dreamchild*?

AM: Yeah, I did. It was a nice take, but then Dennis Potter was a good writer . . . So what we came up with was this aristocratic lesbian with a laudanum habit, with a very active imagination, who's kind of lost. Something happened to her as a child. She kind of went through the looking glass and never came back. There's a sort of glass screen—probably something to do with the opium—between her and herself. And we did the same thing with Wendy. Wendy's very middle class, very maternal, very prim, almost insufferable, priggish, you know. So, she'd have got married to a man who was older than her, somebody who worked in the shipping industry and is really boring, who doesn't represent any kind of sexual threat at all, because she had something happen to her, and her response was to shy away from sex and to see it as something shadowy.

[Phone rings and then there is a tea break]

AM: We were talking about character, and there comes a point, when you've done all these things, when you've tried to imagine about the character, then you try to imagine a little scene with him or her, and you try and imagine how they move. You try and imagine what their body language is. One of the things I used to do was to actually act things out in front of a mirror, to actually try and get the body language right and see what it felt like to be that person. I can do all that in my head now, so I don't bother, but when you're starting out, it's not a bad idea.

DR: Is acting something you used to do when you were younger?

AM: You couldn't really call it acting. I used to appear in sketches with the Northampton Arts Lab, which was a sort of experimental kind of arts collective that used to be around back in the sixties. They were very popular. Being a method actor, there's tips you can pick up. Both you and an actor are going to have to create a character that is believable. You're going to have to know the way they talk, the sound of their voice, even if the reader will never be able to hear that because it's in word balloons or whatever. You wanna know what the sound of their voice is like. You want to know what their phraseology is like. Try and write a few words, see if you get a voice that sounds kind of natural. When you've got all these things, you find there comes a point with the character—probably sooner rather than later—where (this is a cliché, that all writers spout)—where the character comes to life. And that's not quite it. That doesn't quite describe the phenomena, although that's partly it. It's where the characters first start doing things that surprise you. It's sort of when . . .

DW: Sorry to interrupt. I've only just started writing myself, but I've experienced that myself on a couple of occasions, and it's rather—odd . . .

AM: It's the sort of thing that leads you to become a magician at the age of forty [laughter], because you can't come up with any rational explanation for it, because it's like the comic writer Alvin Schwartz, who used to write *Superman* in the fifties for DC—I think he wrote the Superman newspaper strip in the fifties?—He also wrote a book called *An Unlikely Prophet*, which is completely mad, but is really interesting, because what he says is, you sit round with the other writers, tossing around ideas for Superman stories, and somebody would come up with an idea: "What if Superman does this, this and this?"—and unanimously, the rest of the group would say: "Superman wouldn't do that." And he said that this had happened so many times that he'd thought: "Hang on, Superman isn't real. What do we mean 'Superman wouldn't do that?'" He started to come to the conclusion that there did exist somewhere, some sort of Platonic space, where there was—

DW: Ideational space?

AM: Idea Space is what I'd call it.

DW: My background is political philosophy, where I've heard a lot of that talked about—totally different discipline, but say aspects of globalisation . . .

AM: Something like Karl Popper, with his "World Three," or something like that? A space in which concepts exist . . .

DW: I think so, but it wasn't quite as philosophical as that, more of a Marxist school of thinking, in that the important things about globalisation are not what actually happens in the economy. I mean, that's important, but the actual essence of it is nothing to do with that . . .

AM: It's the immaterial structures and things like that that are the important things?

DW: And extensions of those into the world are what we observe, but that isn't what's causing it . . .

AM: Of course, Marxism is an example of what Karl Popper would have called a "World Three" structure, in that it's got immense power as an idea, but you couldn't actually hold up anything in the world and say: "This is Marxism." You couldn't even hold up *Kapital* and say: "This is Marxism." It's a book. Anyway, what he was saying was that there seemed to be some level—or he and the writers seemed to be behaving as if there was some level, some Platonic level, on which these archetypal sort of idea-forms actually existed, where there was a Superman, or some sort of proto-Superman, some sort of ür-Superman, who sort of, if a writer came up with a bad idea and he didn't like it, he'd just say: "No, I wouldn't do that."

Now, that is kind of stupid, but it's kind of true. I've worked on Superman, just using that character. If you're a conscientious writer, you can't help but feel the weight of myth and history that is connected . . . It's like if you were writing Sherlock Holmes. Sherlock Holmes is a massive figure in people's minds, more massive than a lot of real historical characters. These figures have real weight. They might be just made out of words and paper, but their effect in the world can be massive, if they've got the right kind of mass, the right kind of gravity and momentum.

So yes, there does come this point when characters start talking to you. They'll start telling you what they want to do. You'll know what they would say and what they wouldn't say. I mean when I started writing *Watchmen*, I'd got no idea that Rorschach was gonna be dead by the end of it. It was just by about issue three, I started to know the character and I thought: "He's got a death wish. He's so self-destructive. He's clearly . . . He wants out. There's no way that he's gonna live through this. He wouldn't be able to live with any sort of moral compromises, so he'll have to die. But it was the character himself who told me that, after two or three issues. I'd got no idea when I started it.

So OK, you'll have to go through all of these areas—characterization. They're all big. You could probably fill a massive book with your thoughts on all of them. Sooner or later you get down past—like I say this is reductionist thinking. You'll break it down into areas like characterisation, plot, ambience, place, location (location, location) . . . all these things. Sooner or later, you're going to get down into the molecules: the molecules and the atoms. This is down to words. An awful lot of my writing—why it reads well is because I've read it before I wrote it. I have read it to make sure that there are no clunky syllables, so that there's a nice sort of bumdabumdabumdabum. There's a nice sort of rhythm. There's no sudden three-syllable words, where there should have been a two-syllable word, on which the mental voice of the reader will trip. Rhythms—that was something I learned from performance, with the Arts Lab. If you're talking in the right rhythm, people don't even give a shit what you're saying. The rhythm alone will get everybody hypnotized. And that's true of written work. Not so much of written work—you have to rely upon the reader reading it in the right way and getting the right rhythm—, but you can write so that you can at least guide the reader towards certain rhythms.

If I ever write a book on writing, it will probably be called *Real Men Don't Use Thesauri*, because no, don't touch 'em. I think they're cheating. What's wrong with having an enormous vocabulary? What's wrong with thinking: "Oh, there should be a word that means this or that, could it be this, could it be . . ."—making up a word and checking in the dictionary and seeing if there is such a word and if it meant what you thought it did. That's better, and alright you can waste an hour trying to get the exact right word that's got the right kind of sound, the right flavour, the right colour . . . that fits just perfectly.

DR: Associations as well are important . . .
AM: Yeah, because a word sometimes will have completely illogical associations, just because they sound like another word . . .

AF: There's a sort of synesthesia going on there . . .
AM: There's an awful lot of synesthesia. I mean one of the greatest writers—a lot of the greatest writers—, one of my favourites, Vladimir Nabokov, he was a synesthetic. To him, the letter "O" was white, the word "Moscow" was green flecked with gold . . . olive green, flecked with gold. I can see that. And it's a

good thing to try and develop. Synesthesia is a great literary tool. You'll be able to come up with perfect metaphors that are really striking and strange, because they maybe jump from one sense to another. Try describing a smell in musical terms.

Actually, it can be quite easy. Also, it's how we tend to do things anyway. They've just proven that. You know when Jilly Goolden gets on a roll on *The Food Programme* [Jilly Goolden was on BBC 2's *Food and Drink*—*EB*], and she's talking about: "It's a kind of buttery, composty, tractory—I'm getting peat, I'm getting burning tyres . . ." Now they've done tests. Those people who describe the flavour and bouquet of wine, they're not describing the flavour or the bouquet at all. They are synesthetically describing the colour. They're taking visual cues. They did things where they'd put an odourless and tasteless colour agent into white wine to make it look like red wine, and then they'd note the kind of language the wine-tasters were using. When it was white wine, they were using: ". . . buttery, new-mown hay" . . . you know. Yellow, basically, was what they were saying. Whereas, when it was red wine, they were saying: "It's wonderfully fruity, blackcurrant" . . . talking about red things. It's synesthesia. It's how a lot of our senses . . . I think synesthesia is probably a lot more common than the sensory aberration that it's made out to be, and there's probably a key there, somewhere, to how we sense everything. Synesthesia. There's something there. But yeah, it's when you get down to the words themselves. I mean, I've got some books here that are incredibly valuable. I've got Bibles that are older than America. I've got signed books by Aleister Crowley. I've got some incredible shit. These are all Golden Dawn magic wands. That's Austin Osman Spare's original. These are Dr Dee's tables. The thing I'd grab if there was a fire is my *Random House Dictionary*, which is an etymological dictionary, which tells you where the words come from so you actually know what you're talking about. If you use a word like "fascism," you can actually have a look and see: "Now where does that word come from? What does it actually mean?" That'll save you a lot of embarrassment. It's also got a great encyclopedia function. It's a biographical dictionary. It's got all famous names and obscure names and dates. It's fantastic. And that is my best Grimoire, if you like, my best magic book, because it's got all the words in the English language, and where they come from, and what they mean.

If you're gonna be a writer, you'll cover all this territory, from the broadest categories down to, like I say, the subatomic detail of words and syllables . . .

AF: And when they get down to quarks and things as well, they talk about them in weird terms like "strangeness" and . . .

AM: "Charm." I think that "quark," as a matter of fact, is from James Joyce, a word from James Joyce . . .

DR: *Finnegan's Wake . . .*

AM: What's the actual quote? "A quark . . ." I've forgotten, or it might even have some associations with Lewis Carroll, *The Hunting of the Snark*. Yeah, you know, this is literally magical territory. Eventually, to learn all this technique, you can amass an incredible vocabulary, which will . . . you'll get cleverer. The more . . . as far as I understand it, consciousness is predicated upon language. Language comes first. It's not that language grows out of consciousness. If you haven't got language, you can't be conscious. You need words for things. You need words before you know what they are, before you can store any information. You need concepts, which are verbal. You need a concept of "I" to start with, and then all the rest. So much of this stuff is made up of language. So much of our reality, our consciousness, everything, is made up of language, that you can study it in so much of its fine details. You can learn all about the techniques.

And remember, when you're learning the techniques, remember what you're actually doing. Don't kid yourself. If you think there's a huge amount of difference between you and Paul Joseph Goebbels, you're kidding yourself. Any form of art is propaganda. It is propaganda for a state of mind rather than a nation-state, but it is propaganda nonetheless, and it's best if you accept that and understand what you're doing and be honest about it. You are trying to change the mind of your target audience. You are trying to change their perceptions. You are trying to stop them from seeing things how they see things and start them seeing things the way you see things. The ethics of that we could debate all night [laughter] but basically, the thing is, I can, so I will. I'm aware of how words can change people's minds, can change the way people think. So are all of the advertisers, so are all of the politicians, so are all of the people who run our lives. They're not pulling any punches. I would say that it is beholden unto any writer to equally not pull any punches on the other side. If you believe something, if you believe something is right or something is wrong then yeah, try and convince other people. Spread the idea around like a designer virus. Make it so that other people will repeat it. This is partly what you're doing. And you'll probably have to consider all these aspects of writing . . .

DR: It's like some of Richard Dawkins's ideas about memes.
AM: Yeah memes, interesting idea. You're probably going to have to consider

all of these ideas—and eventually you're gonna come up against: the mystery. I mean, because there is an essential mystery in writing. It's like you were saying [to DW] about the first time that characters you've created start doing things other than what you'd intended them to. Why do they do that? What do you actually mean when you say that? These and other things will start to impinge upon you. You will start to notice that, you'll maybe write some stories and you won't know where they came from. They were powerful. They were heartfelt, but they didn't seem to come from anywhere. And then a year later, the events will happen that make perfect sense of those stories if the stories had been written after the events rather than before them. You get enough things like that, and you start to—in my case anyway—you start to—technique, craft, these things have their limitations.

DW: A couple of questions come to mind—I had one initially but another one just popped in. A couple of creative people, one a musician, the other a writer—Stephen King and Shane MacGowan—have both made very similar comments about the fact that they discover what they do rather than create it from within themselves, necessarily. I think Stephen King's talked about writing as archaeology, finding things together and dusting them down. Shane MacGowan's talked about: "Songs are floating in the air, and it's my duty to grab them before some cunt like Paul Simon does."

AM: Ha-ha, good point, Shane. R. A. Lafferty, when I asked him: "Where do you get ideas from?" and he said: "Ideas are like pumpkins, they just float through the air, and hit people on the head." It's a similar idea. I've noticed—and this is an experiment that perhaps a lot of other writers could try—start writing upon a subject upon which you don't know very much, or about which you have no opinions. Start writing. You will find that you've not got something perfectly planned in your head, and you're writing it down. You'll find that the words are forming practically at your fingertips, on the keys of the typewriter. The ideas are forming, ideas that you never had before. Juxtapositions are occurring to you. Your mind goes into a very different state. If you actually notice this, you can write certain different types of prose, which can leave your mind in a state every bit as altered as, say, psychedelic drugs.

Because our entire universe is made up of consciousness, we never really experience the universe directly. We just experience our consciousness of the universe, our perception of it. So right, our only universe is perception. All of our perceptions are made up of words. You alter the words, you alter the perception, you alter the universe, and if you actually look back, you come, as I did, to a point where craft no longer really cuts it, where you want something more than craft. Yes, you know skilful ways of persuading people to your argument or things like that, but that's not good enough. That is when you come up against a point like I did where I started to look at the archaic notions of writing. Not writing theory as it is now. Let's look at what writing used to be, and of course, if you start looking at it, after a while it's obvious that writing must have had its origins in magic, in that anyone who'd got command of written language would have had supernatural powers.

AF: So, in those early times, anyone who had that bigger grasp of language, which was in its early stages, looked like they were doing something incredible, which is why these days . . .
AM: They were doing something incredible.

AF: Yes, they were. They were, but we look back . . .
AM: The thing is, imagine, the person who first came up with the idea of representative marks, to actually make that huge jump of saying: "Right, there's a hut—we haven't got a word for it yet, but—'hut.' That'll be 'hut.' That's what we'll call it—'hut.' So that sound means that thing over there, and if I draw this little thing, these lines on the wall—ah—the 'hut.' In some way they represent; they stand for it." That is a massive leap of consciousness, from which the whole of the rest of human consciousness springs from that point. That is what distinguishes us from the animals, written language. There's not much else we do that they can't, but written language does seem to be a very important point. So, you imagine someone who'd got written language. You could pass your thoughts at a distance. You could remember things. You could fix time. You could remember that: "Hang on, I did this yesterday and that the day before and that the day before . . ." You could suddenly start to build a consciousness for yourself, because you'd have words. So yeah, you'd be big time magic.

Now, you see this carried on into the bardic tradition of the Welsh bards, things like that. Now, as I understand it, the bards were feared. They were respected, but more than that, they were feared. If you were just some magician, if you'd pissed off some witch, then what's she gonna do? She's gonna put a curse on you, and what's gonna happen? Your hens are gonna lay funny. Your milk's gonna go sour. Maybe one of your kids is gonna get a hare-lip or something like that. No big deal. You piss off a bard, and forget about putting a curse on you. He might put a satire on you. And if he was a skilful bard, he puts a satire on you, it destroys you in the eyes of your community. It shows you up as ridiculous, lame, pathetic, worthless, in the eyes of your community, in the eyes of your family, in the eyes of your children, in the eyes of yourself, and if it's a particularly good bard, and he's written a particularly good satire, then three hundred years after you're dead, people are still gonna be laughing at what a twat you were.

[break in tape]

AM: I'll give a brief recap in case we feel we missed anything. Magic and language are practically the same thing. They would at least have been regarded as such in our distant past. I think it is wisest and safest to treat them as if they are the same thing. This stuff that you are dealing with—words, language, writing—this is dangerous. It is magical. Treat it as if it was radioactive. Don't doubt that for a moment. As far as I know, the last figures I heard quoted, nine out of every ten writers will have mental problems at some point during their life. Sixty percent of that ninety percent—which I think works out at roughly fifty percent of all writers—will have their lives altered and affected—seriously affected—by those mental problems. I think what that translates to is—nine out of ten crack up, five out of ten go mad. It's like, miners get black lung, writers go bonkers. This is a real occupational hazard. There's plenty of ways to go bonkers, some of them a lot quieter, some more insidious than others—drink, heroin. There's lots of other sorts of things, but this is dangerous. We're dealing with the unreal. You're dealing right on the borderline of fact and fiction, which is where our entire world happens. We're living in a world of fact, and we've got our heads full of fiction, the characters that we've invented for ourselves. We're all writers. We all invent characters for ourselves, roles in this little play that we're running in our head that we call our lives. With a writer, you're dealing with the actual stuff of existence. You're playing the God game. All the things that you will have to consider before you write a story are exactly the things God had to consider before he created the universe—plot, characters [laughter], and what's it mean. "What's it about? What's the theme here . . . motifs. A lot of them suns, they'll do. We'll put them everywhere. Hey, snakes! These are easy . . ." [laughter].

So you're dealing with dangerous stuff. You're in dangerous territory. It can . . . you can start to forget, for example . . . There's a great thing in a Jack Trevor Story book, and he's a brilliant writer, Jack Trevor Story. He was, just before he died. There's one bit where he's talking to this woman, and she's telling him about events that have happened, and she says: "Wait a minute, did that happen, or did that happen in my story?" And she suddenly starts to look terrified, and he's a writer himself so he knows what to do. He walks up, slaps her round the face and says: "What's your name?" and she sort of, so he slaps her again and says: "What's your name?" and she gives him a name, and he says, "Right, what's just happened to you is that you have for the first time confused your real life with your fiction. Don't worry about this. This is going to happen quite a lot. It's just important that you remember that you're a real person. This is your name. That other stuff was stuff that you wrote. Keep the line there."

But it's difficult to do, especially if you start messing around and writing self-referential things, like writing a novel about your hometown in which you are the final character.

AF: Alan World.
AM: Alan World. Well, actually, that was a complete mistake. Well, not a mistake—

AF: Well, it shows! [laughter]
AM: It was. I just looked through the phone book. All the names from *Big Numbers*, I got from the phone book, and I found A. World and I thought, "That's good," and I thought, "Alan." I could have thought, "Andrew," but I didn't. That's just the breaks.

So, it's a difficult job. It's a dangerous job. You're probably not gonna make any money out of it. Most writers don't. You go down to W. H. Smith's or Waterstone's, most of those writers on the shelves, that is not their only job. Yeah, alright, Stephen King and Catherine Cookson, Jeffrey Archer . . . Well, other than convict and embezzler, most of them have got another source of income. It's difficult. It's dangerous. It's not necessarily good for your mind. I mean the rewards of it are fantastic. I wouldn't do anything else. To me, it is the ultimate job, and yes, it has made me more intelligent, because it's like George Orwell. If you want to make people less intelligent, limit their vocabulary. Limit their language. Give them a sort of "Newspeak," that's like . . .

AF: . . . text-messaging.
AM: . . . text-messaging or *The Sun*. These are perfect Orwellian ways of limiting the vocabulary and thus limiting the consciousness. So the corollary of that holds true as well. If you want to expand people's consciousness, give them better language, wider language, new words. Learn to love words. Learn to delight over a new word that you've found. I mean, looking through *New Scientist*—the "amygdala."

DR: Oh yes, the part of the brain to do with fear isn't it?

AM: Emotion. All emotion is put through this tiny little bit called the "amygdala," or perhaps the 'Amidgda-luh.' I'm not exactly sure how it's pronounced, but it's great either way. A phrase I read once in a book—"the anneliden ancestor,"—and I thought: "Anneliden, what's that?" and I looked it up in a book, and I couldn't find a word "anneliden," and for about two years I thought: "I didn't dream that. That must be real, 'the annelidden ancestor.'" Eventually, I realised it's a word that's been kind of coined, based upon "annelid," which is a type of worm. So, "the anneliden ancestor" is kind of like Pichia, one of those flatworms in the Burgess Shale that have got the rudiments of a spine, and thus is an ancestor to anything that's got a spine. Yeah, words, they're lovely.

AF: "Simulacra," I like.

AM: I'm probably a bit dyslexic. I always pronounce it "sim-ul-ac-ra."

DR: Do you ever pick up the dictionary and start leafing through it?

AM: Oh yeah, sometimes I sort of . . . "Look up how many words do begin with 'N'? There's not many. I could probably get through that in half an hour," but you find words like "Xanthic," which means "yellowish." It's lovely. You've gotta love language, love writing right from the molecular level of words, or even letters. The letter "A" originally had wings.

DW: Aerosmith's logo's gone back to that.

AM: Yeah, well, they've always been ahead of the curve [laughter] or a long way behind it. And the letter "C" was the other way round and was supposed to represent the crescent moon. Language itself is such a fantastic phenomenon with it's own fantastic history. You can get involved in writing to whatever depth you want, but the thing is that really you have to kind of remember the best way to do it, with all this that I've said about the dangers of madness, treat writing the way that you would treat a god. If you believed in such things, if you were going to devote yourself to a particular god, then that's the best way to treat it. Treat it as if it's not just some abstract idea of a god. Treat it as if it was a real god that will maybe, if you do right by the god, will maybe grant all your wishes, will maybe lavish nothing but success and wonder upon you and, if you don't do right by the god, will begin to fuck with you in ways you cannot even begin to imagine. Treat it like that, and you won't go far wrong. In effect, that's what you're doing.

Writing will consume your life, because so much of writing happens in your head. You don't need to be "at work." You don't even need to be awake. You're not gonna get a respite from writing when your head hits the pillow. You're not gonna get a respite from writing when you go on a holiday caravan to Great Yarmouth, or anywhere—the moon. You can't get away from it. It's in your head. And if it's working properly, it's probably obsessive. If you've got a story on the boil, and if you're a writer you probably will have, you're probably thinking about problems with that story, good things about it that you wanna enhance and make even better, and you're probably thinking that all the time. You might be thinking that when you're having sex. You might be thinking that when you're eating dinner. You might be thinking that on public transport. This is something that will take over your life. Surrender. Surrender to it right from word one. Don't fight. It's bigger than you are. It's more important than you are. Just do what it says. Even if that seems to be completely ruining your life, do what it says. Even if it tells you to do something stupid—if it tells you to jump off a cliff—do it [laughter].

This is my experience. I mean, when I was twenty-five, I'd got a baby on the way, or my wife had at least. We were living up Blackthorn. It was really shitty, but I had got a job. I was working down the gas board, and it was a regular job. It wasn't a great job, but with a baby on the way . . . At which point, writing told me to quit my job, with a baby on the way.

AF: That must have been a tough decision at the time . . .

AM: But really, it wasn't. I hadn't really got much of a choice by that point, because I was kind of aware what the alternative would be, and I couldn't stand that. That frightened me. That frightened me more than dooming my wife and baby, which frightened me considerably. It would have just doomed me to something different, if I'd stayed with that gas board job. So yeah, if it says jump off a cliff, do it. It knows what it's talking about. It's more intelligent than you are. It knows more about you than you do. Treat it like that. Treat it like a god, and you probably won't go far wrong. And always try to do your best for the deity that you swore yourself to, and it might reward you. You shouldn't go into it expecting it to reward you. You just do this for the glory of writing itself. You want to do this for Thoth and for Hermes. You wanna write something that is just that good, just for the glory of writing. And like I say, that's a completely irrational attitude, but I think at the end of the day, that's the best one. That's got me through twenty-five years.

What was your second question? [laughter]

DW: I feel a bit anally retentive. We've talked about writing a lot, but what about in terms of writing for comics, about writing in collaboration with another creative person, rather than by yourself?

AM: *[Gets up and walks away to desk to fetch something and comes back with it.]* Now this is something that won't come over on the tape, but you can perhaps reconstruct for your audience.

DW: Using glove-puppets . . .

AM: Or give them a brief verbal description. Now, somewhere in here . . . *[Alan has fetched a battered blue hardback notebook of lined A4 paper. Falling apart at the seams, it looks like a family heirloom: Grandfather's old schoolbook brought down from the attic. He opens it out on the living room floor, and Alan and Dan crouch over it, Alan pointing things out to Dan.]*

DW: At this point, Mr. Moore reveals his Grimoire . . .

[The book has tiny sketched-out panels [stick figures basically], laid out quite precisely to form a rough outline of a page from a Promethea *script (the scene has two characters in conversation walking down a beach, with a boat on shore in the foreground in some panels). Each panel has a line drawn from it to handwritten dialogue that is accompanied by two reference numbers—one for the page number and one for the panel number.]*

AM: Horrible, tatty book, but what this has got in it is lots of crappy little drawings that are indecipherable to anybody else but me, but which are basically all I need for anything re: writing comics. They will give me a breakdown. They'll just be sort of these pages. These are bits of *Promethea*. I will break down the page area into a number of panels. Now, I've got a simple, mathematical mindless formula that I follow that is—I mean if you look at these little bits of dialogue that go in each of the panels, you'll see that they have little numbers written after each of the lines and what this is, is the number of words.

Now, this is basically something that I took from Mort Weisinger, who was the harshest and most brutal—

DW: DC editor?

AM: —of the DC editors during the sixties.

DW: Bit of a tyrant from what I hear.

AM: Oh Christ, he was a monster. I remember Julie Schwartz telling me—who was a lovely man. He told me about Mort Weisinger's funeral—and this was probably just an old Jewish joke that he'd adapted for Mort Weisinger—, but he said that apparently during Jewish funerals there's a part where people can stand up and spontaneously will say a few words about the departed—personal tributes, things like that. So, it's Mort Weisinger's funeral, and it gets to this bit in the funeral, and there's absolute dead silence, and the silence just goes on and on and on and nobody gets up and says anything and eventually this guy at the back of the synagogue gets up and says: "His brother was worse!" [laughter]

But anyway, Mort Weisinger, because he was the toughest of the editors, I thought: "Alright, I'll take his standard as the strictest." What he said was: "If you've got six panels on a page, then the maximum number of words that you should have in each panel, is thirty-five. No more." That's the maximum: thirty-five words per panel. Also, if a balloon has more than twenty or twenty-five words in it, it's gonna look too big. Twenty-five words is the absolute maximum for balloon size. Right, once you've taken on board those two simple rules, laying out comics pages—it gives you somewhere to start. You sort of know: "OK, so six panels, thirty-five words a panel, that means about 210 words per page maximum."

DW: And if you've got one panel you'd have 210 . . .

AM: And if you've got two panels, you'd have 105 each. If you've got nine panels, it's about twenty-three, twenty-four words. That'll be about the right balance of words and pictures. So that is why I obsessively count all the words, to make sure that I'm not gonna overwhelm the pictures, that I'm not gonna make—Oh, I've seen some terrible comic writing where the balloons are huge, cover the entire of the background—

DW: Doesn't that tend to often happen when you've got what's called the American plot style of scripting, which is where the writer basically gives a very broad breakdown—

AM: I've never really got on with that. I can't see . . . That just looks sloppy to me. I mean, I remember once Archie Goodwin, who I greatly respected, saying it does allow for serendipity. Yeah, I can see that, but I should imagine that as a reward that is probably outweighed by the fact that all the characters, the artist has to give them neutral expressions because he doesn't know what they're gonna be saying, or thinking, in those panels, so he has to make them look kind of neutral, a bit constipated, and everything gets sort of blanded out. Whereas, I can control this. I can make sure that everything works. At least in my little crappy drawings, I can make sure there's not too many words for any panel.

DW: So, this number refers to the page and the panel within the page?
AM: Er, yeah. Well, this is a spread, so it's 18 and 19 . . . 5, 18, and 19—

DW: Oh right, with the staple line in the middle?
AM: Yeah, that's it. It's a nice way to get to grips with a page. As to how you lay the page out in your suggestions to the artist, that will depend. How much room have you got? What's the pacing like? One thing to remember in comics—and this is an interesting axiom—space equals time. To convey time in a comic, it's spatial. I remember, when I was doing *From Hell*—I think it's the epilogue?—No, the prologue, the prologue, where I've got the prologue with just the two old guys on the beach, and I'd been doing that in just little panels because I thought, "That's good, keeps it intimate." These little panels just— one of them says this, the other one says that, the next one just sits down and takes a breather—and then I thought, "Alright, I'll have one of them say: 'It's getting cold. Shall we be getting back?'" And then I thought, "Right, they're right down by the tide line there, and actually it would take them quite a long while to walk back up the beach, and I don't just wanna suddenly jump to them on the seafront, and I don't wanna caption saying, 'Meanwhile, shortly later . . .'" So, I thought, "Alright, I'll just put a big wide panel taking up the whole tier—big picture of the beach at night—and there's these two little men, walking up the beach and the width of the panel will convey, "It took a long while to do this." Alright, it will take the reader three seconds—two seconds—to actually look at the picture and take it in,—there's no words in it—but it will convey time.

DW: There's some scenes in *Dark Knight* [*Batman: The Dark Knight Returns*], where Frank Miller really chops it up, in terms of one scene—
AM: —where you splinter the action. That is, all of a sudden, it's all happening. It's happening in slow motion. You see something that would take two seconds, and you do it in ten panels—

DW: —a drop of water falling while something happens.
AM: Yeah, yeah, that's it. I think most of what Frank based his stuff upon— on which any aspiring comic writer would do very well to go back to—is Will Eisner, Harvey Kurtzman. They're the best. Of their period. They came up with a lot of the devices, a lot of the ideas, that Frank and people elaborated

upon. You look through Eisner, and you can come up with so many brilliant ideas that he just throws away. Or probably even better, look back at the early American newspaper strips of the turn of the century.

DW: *Dragon Lady* and stuff like that?
AM: No, no, before that. *Steve Canyon* was sort of forties. *Terry and the Pirates*, that was all sort of forties. You go back to 1902. You look at Winsor McCay.

DW: *Little Nemo in Slumberland*?
AM: *Little Nemo in Slumberland*, *Dream of the Rarebit Fiend*. You look at Frank King, *Gasoline Alley*, a sort of deceptively mundane strip, but then you got the Sunday colour supplements, which were pieces of art that would stagger you if you came across them in the latest issue of *Raw* or something like that. So forward-thinking, so brilliant. I mean there was a thing that I did in *Big Numbers* #2, which was a thing that I did just for the pleasure of two or three—or the discomfort of two or three—other comic writers who'd be able to see what I'd done. And what this was, was that I'd looked at some of the early Frank King *Gasoline Alley* pages where, for the sake of variety, he'd used the whole page as one big image. You're looking down upon this warren of alleys, and he breaks this down into panels and in each of the panels there is basically a one-off sight-gag, or a one-off verbal gag, that are all happening at the same moment, in this alley. And I thought: "That's charming. There's something lovely about that. Wouldn't it be great if you could have a moving element that was moving between the panels," but I thought: "Yeah, I can see his problem here. As soon as you get to the right-hand side of the top row, then the action's gotta suddenly go to the middle left-hand side—"

DW: I guess you could spiral, couldn't you?
AM: Well, there are different possibilities, yeah, but with a spiral you're gonna end up in the middle, rather than the bottom left-hand corner, which is where you wanna end up. So when I did *Big Numbers* #2, I came up with this brilliant idea of how you could have a family arguing around a breakfast table, and you could have everyone moving logically in different directions. Panel 1, the Mum is, I think she's, now hang on a minute, I think she's taking a dish off the table. Panel 2, she's scraping it into a peddle-bin, which is just next to the sink, where she's washing it up, and then panel 4, she's putting it in the dish-rack, and she's starting to come down the right-hand side of the kitchen into panel 8.

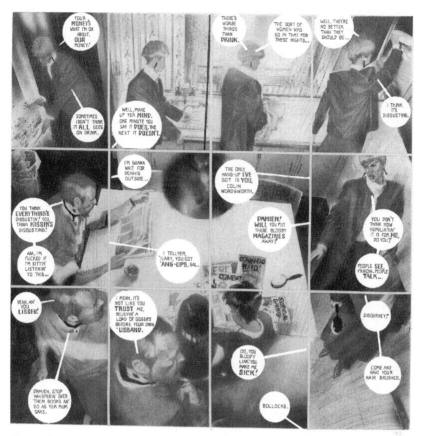

Big Numbers #2, page 7, by Alan Moore and Bill Sienkiewicz. Copyright © 1990 Alan Moore and Bill Sienkiewicz, used by permission.

Meanwhile, you've got her husband sitting at the table—there's the children at the table as well. They're having this conversation. It all works perfectly—, and he gets pissed off with her and storms out down into panel 9 and then walks out of the door into panel 12, where he storms out of the kitchen leaving his wife to come down through panels 4, 8, and 12, leaving the family looking after him. It's a brilliant little whirlpool of a scene.

It was all inspired by Frank King. I thought: "If only I could do what he'd done, but make it a bit cleverer and have moving elements in." I've done the same in *Lost Girls*. I've got a couple where that problem of having to have the zig-zag line—That's fine if you've got sort of a down view of a path that winds like that or a staircase that will double back on itself—so that that will do the right thing. Yeah, you can do it, but there's other variations.

DW: Do you think you could do that in any other medium?
AM: No. Which says that comics is a very versatile medium that's got possibilities that people have not even begun to touch.

DW: Underlying that, what do you think it says about the technique?
AM: Why does it work? Why do comics work? Well, you'd have to get into mad theory, but if you want more mad theory, I'd say that the reason comics work—and work they do—I mean, when I was researching *Brought to Light*, I found out that the Pentagon had done tests to see what was the means by which information could be most easily taken in and could be most easily retained—They'd tried straight text. They'd tried text with photographs. They'd tried illustrations with captions, photographs with captions, and they'd tried comics. Comics were best.

Now, why should that be? Why are comics so brilliant at fixing ideas in people's minds, getting them across? I would say it's because the verbal parts of our brains—what used to be called "left-brain" activities, before we found out that they're actually kind of all over the place—You might say that the "currency" if you like—for what used to be called our left brain—You might say that that was the word. Now, our pre-verbal minds—what used to be called the "right brain"—, you might say that the currency for that side of the brain—the pre-verbal part—would be the image. Now, comics might therefore be one of the only forms of art that calls upon you to actually have a kind of integrated experience. Because some people who have trouble reading comics—and there are a lot of people—well, they'll say: "Do you look at the pictures first or do you read the words?" Whereas if you read comics, you know that you kinda do both at once. You're taking in the picture peripherally while you're reading the words, and your eyes will sort of zig around, and you kind of absorb them both at once. And I think—

DW: That synesthesic thing is the same kind of thing . . .
AM: It's utilising both lobes of the brain, if you like, or what used to be called both lobes of the brain. And it might be that because it's the only control . . . Alright, films have an image track and they have a sound track, but, big problems: You can't synchronise. With a film, you're being dragged through the experience at twenty-four frames a second—that's a given. Even in the most complex films you couldn't—the reader—even if you've got someone saying

this line of dialogue just as something happens in the background or something that makes a really ironic connection, then it's gonna flash by. People aren't gonna see it. If it's in a Dave Gibbons-drawn comics page where they can sit and look at and absorb it at their own pace, then you can get layer upon layer of meaning and reference.

DW: Partly because it's self-paced.

AM: Yeah, because the reader is in complete control of the experience. It is a medium which not only combines the verbal and visual parts of our minds, but one where we are in complete control of the experience and where because it is so reader-friendly—You wanna check out this panel there to see if there's any connection, you can just flick back. You don't have to rewind the video and then pause it. You just flick back. Easy. And so it enables the comic book writer, the inventive writer, to utilize all those advantages and come up with really clever structures that would be lost in a film, but when they're frozen on the page where everyone can see how clever you are for all time, it works perfectly.

[The interview then abruptly ended with Dan and Dave madly scrambling into Andy's car in an (ultimately successful) attempt to make the last train back to London. However, Alan graciously invited us back for a second visit as we were still in full flow.]

Alan Moore Interview

JESS NEVINS / 2004

A Blazing World. Austin, TX: Monkeybrain Books, 2004. 243–86. Reprinted by permission of John Nevins.

Jess Nevins is the author of a series of books that annotate Moore and Kevin O'Neill's *League of Extraordinary Gentlemen*. In addition to the annotations, the books normally include several essays by Nevins about historical or thematic elements of the League and their nineteenth-century milieu and an interview with Moore. The following interview is an excerpt from the one published in the second book of annotations, *A Blazing World*, which covers volume 2 of *The League*. EB

JN: A lot of fans were disconcerted that the League were, in their eyes, too passive in reacting to the Martian invasion. I know that you wanted to remain faithful to the timeline and events of *War of the Worlds*. Were you also in some ways trying to subvert the cliché, which these fans expected, of the heroes sort of singlehandedly fighting off invasion with guns blazing.

AM: Yeah. That probably plays well in Hollywood, but if people want that, then they've got the film and they can go and see. That's not what the books are about. The books are a much more literary experience. I know that in most Hollywood films, this is what happens at the end, that the heroes will drive off the invaders—there'll be a big shootout. There'll be a High Noon. There'll be a big, obvious, physical climax that will solve everything, because this is how Hollywood does its movies, which is why I don't watch many of them. Everyone's entitled to their tastes. I think that that is kind of moronic. That's not being snooty or elitist. That's just my feelings. Other people are quite entitled to feel that that big, obvious, physical climax is required by every story, because it is required by every Hollywood story. But the world of literature is a richer, deeper place than that, and I don't really see why I needed to have the League or John Carter or Gullivar Jones suddenly turning up in a big spaceship and blasting all the aliens. What would that have done? I might as well have had Will Smith suddenly turn up through a time warp and sort the problem out. That might have been the most satisfying dramatic solution for some of my audience, but I would like to think, I would like to hope, that the majority of my audience would probably have preferred me to do something a bit more unexpected, like the stuff that I actually did do. It's so unsatisfying. It's what everybody does. It's these big, stupid clashes between good and evil, our guys and the other guys. I haven't been to see the *Lord of the Rings* films. I didn't think it was that good a book. It's kind of obvious, and I'm sure that will probably terribly offend lots of Tolkien readers or fans of the films, but it's not to my taste. And there's plenty of other stuff that will do that everywhere. It's not that I was deliberately trying to subvert the expectations of those fans, I just wasn't thinking about them very much. It just seemed to me that the best way to tell this story was the way that we told it, where you've got this use of biological weapons that is kind of shocking, given the time period that it's happening in. And you end the story on this downbeat note, with Allan just sitting there in the park, with all of those beautiful Kevin O'Neill and Ben Dimagmaliw autumn colors all around him. I think that we give our readers plenty of conflict and adventure, and, I mean—for God's sake, we actually have got Mr. Hyde physically fighting one of the Tripods at the end! I would have thought that that was satisfying enough for any of the readers. I mean, what, did they want to have Mr. Hyde fighting one of the Tripods while Mina's fighting one of the other Tripods with her vampire powers!

JN: Well, I think a lot of readers, the ones who e-mail me about this, are preconditioned by other superhero comics, and so they expect a climax in *The League* that's similar to a climax in the average story of *Justice League* or *Avengers* or *Legion of Superheroes*, where everybody pitches in. It was disconcerting to them.

AM: The idea of disconcerting comic readers is obviously a horrific one to me. If any future *League* stuff comes out, I'd hate to be going into it under false pretenses. It probably would be as well to tell everybody now that if they really do like those conventional *Avengers/Justice League/Legion of Superheroes* superteam books, then they're probably best sticking with them, because that's not really what the League is about. *The League* is this complex literary joke that is probably about a lot of books that they haven't read and would never be interested in reading, and I certainly wouldn't want to be leading the readership on under false pretenses or expectations that we're suddenly going to be doing stuff that's like a conventional superteam book.

JN: In fairness to them, they love the series. They just have minor cavils.

AM: Well, everyone's entitled to their own opinions. It's just that—there are similarities. It's a group of unusual, extraordinary people, which in the comic market, that is a generally pretty strong selling idea. But that is where it parts company with the superhero comic. It's not even my intention to tell a good adventure story every time, necessarily. There's nothing to stop me from suddenly deciding that I might want to tell a love story using this world of fictional characters. I'm not saying that I have got any ideas for that. There'll probably always be an element of rip-roaring pulp adventure in *The League*. Probably. But I wouldn't rule out that at some point I might want to use the characters to tell a completely different sort of story. The fun that I'm having with *The League* is not in doing a new sort of superhero group. The fun that I'm having with *The League* is being allowed to run amok through the entirety of fiction, in the past, the present, and the future. Copyright laws cannot stop us. We can play an elaborate, complicated, literary game, which I know is not everybody's cup of tea, but it is mine. I love it. It's such fun. And I don't want to play it to the point where we're ignoring the fact that we have to tell an interesting story. The interesting story has always got to be the most important thing. But that won't necessarily be an interesting story in the terms that superhero team books kind of—the fairly limited options for an interesting story that are presented by conventional superhero team books. It probably won't be that kind of interesting story. And probably *The League*, whatever happens to it in the future, it's going to get more extreme. If there's stuff that people don't like about it now, they're going to hate it by a couple of volumes down the road, because we feel incredibly liberated by this, me and Kevin. We're having the time of our lives. We hadn't even realized that it was possible to do stuff like this before. And we're going to take it as far as we possibly can. We're almost certainly going to take it too far. You wouldn't want to think that you'd held back, would you? That would be cheating the readers. I'd like to think that my readers expect me to occasionally gather them all in my arms and jump over a cliff. I think that that's part of the excitement. [Laughs] Of course, I might be completely wrong, and they might be horrified and hate that part of my writing, but, nah, I think that most of the people who like *The League*, they're probably sniggering at the same parts that me and Kevin are, and they're probably getting excited by the same parts. One of the things that I like best about *The League*, and this is something that no superhero comic book team book could ever do, is the fact that within the space of a few pages, because *The League* is not restricted to the same fairly narrow channels that most superhero team books are restricted to, we can do anything. One of the things that I was most pleased with in the second volume was the scene that starts off with Allan and Mina on the morning after they've had sex for the first time, and Allan is desperately trying to explain to Mina his reaction to her inadvertently glimpsed scars. It starts off with this very fraught emotional atmosphere. They're very angry with each other. Then, when Allan explains that his first wife had had scars around her neck—which, incidentally, how cool was that?

JN: I'm sure that when you read that in the Haggard book, you were pleased no end.

AM: Kevin told me about it, and I thought, "This is supernaturally perfect. This is one of those things that . . ."—well, you were saying earlier about readers wondering whether I'd had everything planned out in minute detail from the beginning. Well, when you read something like that, I can see how they'd get that impression, because it looks so incredibly clever! But, no, it just happened by accident. I'd got no idea that his first wife had got a scarred throat when I originally decided to give Mina one. Anyway, back to that scene in the forest, where he's explaining about his first wife, and talking about how that was the reason he reacted the way he did, not revulsion. And then it becomes incredibly tender between them, it's quite emotional, and from there it moves quietly to the bit where she's showing her scars to him, where he's taking her scarf off, and then he's kissing the scars. It moves very easily to the erotic. And then, when they're having sex against the tree and you suddenly see her catching sight of something over her shoulder, and you turn over the page and there's that awful bear creature shambling toward them, then it is both ridiculous, to my mind at least very funny, and also completely horrifying. In the space of that one scene, I was very pleased with the way that we moved from emotional difficulty to deep emotional compassion to eroticism to a mingling of comical absurdity and horror. You shouldn't really be able to put all those flavors next to each other. But something about the way *The League* is set up means that it's possible for us to be simultaneously deadly serious, horrifying, ridiculous—the death of Mr. Griffin is probably a scene that in the audience would have elicited mixed reactions, I would have thought. They would probably have been laughing and shuddering in about the same measure, because—partly it's really funny that the only character you could have that happen to in a comic is an invisible man. It was so perfect. When I thought of it, I was laughing. When I explained it to Scott Dunbier, I was laughing, because Scott was very worried about the scene, and me and Kevin were saying, "No, no, Scott, don't worry, you won't be able to see anything!"

From *The League of Extraordinary Gentlemen*, vol. 2, #5, page 6 (partial), by Alan Moore and Kevin O'Neill. Copyright © 2003 America's Best Comics, LLC, used by permission of DC Comics. All Rights Reserved.

That, to me, is the beauty of *The League*, the fact that there aren't really any expectations. It could be very sexual, it could be very funny, it could be very thrilling, or it could be completely horrific, or perhaps intellectually stimulating, all in the same couple of pages. I can't think of many books that have the same easy versatility.

JN: One of the things that people have been most struck by is the portrayal of Hyde. Some people have said that he's really the central character in the story. Was that your intention all along, or did he sort of seize control?

AM: I guess that you could fairly say that Mr. Hyde is a very central character in that second book. Yeah, to some degree it surprised me as much as anybody. That first meeting between him and Mina, just the conversation in the room. When that dialogue was writing itself, I found it very surprising the way it was coming out. It certainly wasn't anything that you could call tenderness upon Hyde's part. He's talking about beheading her, raping her, breaking her jaw, and you don't doubt him for a minute, that he could quite easily do these things if he was in the right mood. And he's talking about his own conflicted behavior when it comes to her, and her reaction to him, that, yeah, she's terrified of him, but on the other hand, this is a side of Hyde that nobody's ever seen before. It's fascinating and quite touching in a lot of ways. Hyde is never going to turn up and bring you a bunch of flowers or a box of chocolates. He's never going to ask you for an evening at the cinema. But to have him actually tell you that he doesn't actually hate you—that's probably as close to an admission of, not love, but as close as Hyde could ever get to it, and I found him an increasingly fascinating character, because when I started thinking about Stevenson's original concept, that Hyde was all of the evil, all of the dark side, of Jekyll, isolated into a different person, and I started thinking about what a stupid idea that had been and how it would obviously lead to disaster, and that led up to one of the sequences I'm proudest of, which is Hyde sitting there at the dinner table, explaining the difference between them, the reason why Jekyll is such a feeble wretch, and the reason why Hyde is about nine or ten feet tall and has got this huge body mass. It's because Jekyll has no drives without Hyde, and Hyde had no restraints without Jekyll. Which says something, I think, about the relationship between what we would conventionally call good and evil in the human being. Our demons and our angels, they are meant to work together. Separating them is ridiculous, and can only lead to the desperate extremes that are represented by Hyde. I found myself interested in him as a character and as a sort of symbol of the conflicted nature of human beings: terrified of their dark side and hating their dark side, wanting to be rid of it, and needing it so much. It's very often the right brain, that dark, unexplored territory, that most of our essential drives are contained in. That's where they come from: Hyde's territory rather than Jekyll's. Both halves of the personality, they have to work together in unison if you're going to have any sort of integrated and whole human being as a result. And I think that I saw something tragic in Jekyll and Hyde. Hyde's only urge can be to death. He would have to be—the pain of being Hyde, unmediated by any, I don't know, more contemplative or reflective or spiritual parts of the human personality. The idea of being a creature that had, by definition, no higher attributes, where the solace of those higher attributes was forever denied to it. Hyde's life would be just rage and hatred. There wouldn't be any other options available, except for perhaps enraged hatred. It's a kind of damned soul. The only thing that you could do if you were Hyde would be to get yourself killed. You would hate the universe that you were in. You would hate yourself. You'd hate everything. That lent a kind of tragedy and heroism—I really liked the scene with Hyde, like Horatio, defending the bridge. I thought that was great, because he never stops being Hyde for a minute. He's still as hateful and violent and psychotic. And yet I bet there weren't many dry eyes in the place. I bet everybody felt kind of moved by Hyde's sacrifice, even if, as he himself points out, he's not doing it to be noble. He's doing it because he really wants to kill something. Actually, the thing that he probably wants to kill is himself. But in either instance it's not nobility that's behind it. But Hyde almost achieves a nobility in spite of himself in that scene, which I thought was kind of touching. All of the characters go through some changes in the course of the series, but if the second volume of *The League* was centered upon anybody, then it was centered upon Hyde. He was just a character that suddenly, he'd been growing in importance throughout the first book, and he kind of blossomed during the second book, which I suppose must make it all that much more unfathomable to a lot of readers as to why we've killed or removed the three most visually interesting characters in *The League*, in this highly successful series, before the end of the twelfth issue. But, hell, that was just the way that it was going.

JN: It's interesting, the reaction I get between the traditional comics fans and the fans who are more familiar with literature than with comics. The fans who are coming at this from a literary base, they're not disconcerted or nonplused by Hyde's death or Griffin's death or the end of the 1898 League, whereas the comic book fans sort of expect that the status quo is always going to be maintained, that there's always going to be the same League, and they're wondering—

AM: Yeah, that obviously Hyde didn't really die, so, what did the Time Traveler take him way at the point of death, or—no, no he's dead. The only status quo in *The League* is—if people have been bothering to read the Almanac, they might notice that we've taken the precaution of making Allan and Mina immortals.

JN: The comics fans, they take the deaths as written, but they seem to be wondering why you're doing it. They're coming at it with a very different set of preconceptions.

AM: Why we're doing it is because, realistically, those characters, we couldn't just keep them all hanging around together for the next thirty, fifty, sixty, eighty years. For one thing, it's such an unstable group, made up of such unstable characters, that that's not likely to be how it develops. Also, as we take the characters out of their Victorian milieu, then characters like Hyde and Griffin will become less appropriate. And there are other characters, on the other hand, who become available. I see the League as having a very very long history that stretches for hundreds of years and that there has been a constantly changing membership. Hell, even the Justice League of America, over their relatively short history—what, about forty years?—they've done all sorts of things! There was that weird period when they had Gypsy and Vibe. [Laughs] This is just in forty years. I see the League of Extraordinary Gentlemen as extending over hundreds of years. So, surely, even to the mainstream

From *The League of Extraordinary Gentlemen*, vol. 2, #2, page 23 (partial), by Alan Moore and Kevin O'Neill. Copyright © 2002 America's Best Comics, LLC, used by permission of DC Comics. All Rights Reserved.

comics fans—the original gold-suited Iron Man is no longer in the Avengers. Things change, and in the world of literature, they change a bit more naturally than in the world of comic books. It's to be expected that some of these characters are not going to be around.

JN: It's more reflective of real life.

AM: It's more reflective of real life, and it's more reflective of literature. These characters—yes, all right, Conan Doyle brought Sherlock Holmes back when the demand was great enough. Yes, death is reversible in literature as well. But by and large people in literature are much more used to their heroes eventually dying, even if it's a series, or dying at the end of a book if it's a novel. It's a completely different set up, with different ground rules to comics. Publishing a book, yes, you can have all your characters die at the end of the book, if you want. Or, *Hamlet*, or something like that. If *Hamlet* had been a comic book series [laughs], then nobody would have died in it, because the writers would have been keeping the characters around in case somebody needed them.

JN: I don't suppose you ever saw the Arnold Schwartzenegger film, *The Last—*

AM: Actually, I know exactly what you're going to say. It's the only Arnold Schwartzenegger film that I've got the slightest shred of sympathy for. For a moment, there was the illusion that he actually had a sense of humor and was making fun of himself. Yeah, "Something is rotten in the state of Denmark, and Hamlet's taking out the trash." That was funny. "To be or not to be, that is the question." [Imitates Schwartzenegger] "Not to be." That shows the difference. Comics and Hollywood, you have to keep the hero alive, because it's a franchise. In literature, the characters are not regarded as franchises, so you are a lot more free. And actually I'd have thought the readers would have liked that, because genuinely in *The League of Extraordinary Gentlemen*, they can't take anything for granted. We could kill anybody.

JN: Well, as I said, some of the readers are coming at this from a comic-book background. They want their status quo. They want, basically, intellectual comfort food. And the ones who are coming at this from a literary background, they're more used to different fare, and so I think by and large most of the fans of *League* who—as far as I can tell, there are plenty of fans of *League* who are fans of comic books, but there are many more fans of *League* who are—

AM: We seem to be gathering—from the bookshop sales, I imagine—but we seem to be gathering a lot of people who don't usually read comic books, but who are interested in nineteenth-century literature or Rider Haggard or Conan Doyle or people like that. Which is very gratifying. This is not to despise the comic readership at all, and there are an awful lot of comic readers who also have a very solid and good literary grounding at the same time. I'm very happy to think that we're drawing readers of literature, people who are really familiar with these characters in their original literary form. To me, the test is, do they like what we're doing with it? The comic readers, yes, their point of view is important as well, but they've got no idea who Allan Quatermain is or whether we're handling him right, or anything, whereas, people who have read *King Solomon's Mines* or things like that, they're going to be much more critical, presumably, in that they are going to actually know the works of literature that we're referring to, and they're going to be able to see if we've travestied them. So far, I haven't had very many complaints. I think most people feel that we've been at least as faithful as anybody else has been, and more faithful than some, to the original sources of these characters. I think that even for the traditional comic book readers, I would think that *League* is quite refreshing because for one thing it takes place in what has got to be the best comic book or fiction universe of all time. The Marvel Universe, the DC Universe, how could they possibly be a patch upon the Fiction Universe? That is a universe crammed with fascinating characters, where you can afford to have a couple killed. You can afford to have hundreds killed, and there'll still be plenty to play around with. And it does restore some of that thrill that you can't usually get in comics. I remember what an incredible sense of special-ness there was back in the early sixties if I was reading a comic and a character actually died! I was incredibly shocked and moved and I thought it was a great story. Say, DC, it was obvious that their readers really liked stories in which, say, Superman died or got married or had some other continuity shattering experience. That was why they invented the "Imaginary Story," so they could allow for that without damaging their continuity. Actually, that whole thing of "this book is going to be coming out every month until the end of time or until it's canceled," that is something which damages a lot of comics. It's like when I took over on *Swamp Thing*. I identified one of the main problems with the character that it was based on a false premise. Officially, Alec, the Swamp Thing, was trying to find a way to regain his lost humanity and become Alec Holland again. But even the dimmest reader, the most uncritical, cliché-fed reader must have realized that that was never going to happen, because that would end the series. It's like *The Fugitive* or things like that: if the series ever fulfills its premise, the series ends. Which is so limiting. That's why I had to remodel *Swamp Thing*, to get past that, so that, no, that wasn't the premise anymore. The premise was something which allowed for all sorts or possibili-ties, so that the reader wouldn't know what to expect. I suppose that under-lines the difference between the kinds of comics I like to write and the kinds of comics I don't like to read. I'm not into reassuring my readership. I'm not into providing them with the same product every time. That might pass for consistency if you're a hamburger chain, that maybe your customers do have the right to expect exactly the same meal every time they go in, in exactly the same setting. But that's not how I operate, and I don't want to give the read-ers the cozy reassurance of another set of prepackaged concepts where they already know the structure, they already know that in the last few pages it's going to look like the villain's dead but then all of a sudden he's not really dead at all, and there's going to be a couple of shocking last minute blows traded before the villain's really dead, although they'll leave open the option that the villain's not really dead because there's a sequel to think about. That is how every adventure story is structured these days, and that's not something you go to for thrills. That's something you go to for reassurance. That's something that's become cozy and familiar to you. That's a thousand miles away, a million miles away, from anything that Art is supposed to be about. Art, and I do regard comics as Art, you might as well, they've got as much claim to be Art as anything else has, Art is not about reassuring people. We don't read Art to be reassured. We read Art to be challenged and to challenge our assumptions and to maybe extend our ideas in certain areas, which you can't really do without challenging them. So, that's probably my agenda with *League*. And anything we do in the future, it's probably going to be only more of the same. That agenda will probably get more militant as the series goes on.

JN: What do you think was going through Hyde's mind in his final scene with Mina, before he went out and marched to his death? Did he have some sort of epiphany, or was it the culmination—

AM: A cruel epiphany. He realized—he was torturing himself as much as anything with that. He just wanted to have it once and know what it was like, even though he'd already got a pretty good idea that what it would be like would be unbearable. There's no way you could consummate it. No future in it. It's never going to work. [Laughs] Even with the most optimistic, love-struck eyes in the world—and that's not a description of Hyde by any means—but even with the most optimistic and love-struck eyes in the world, it's never going to work for Hyde and Mina. So, yes, let's just kiss her once, to see what that's like, and touch her breast once. If I can manage to do that without suddenly going berserk and breaking her neck, just to see what that's like, and then suffer the incredible pain of knowing that that is the only time in your entire life that you will ever have a moment of tenderness, and then do what you gotta do. Take your jacket off, walk over the bridge, and settle these Martians. And sing a song as you do it. That seemed to be Hyde's style—immense pain, immense pain held in check by immense manic strength. I should imagine that's what was going through Hyde's mind. Almost torturing himself, almost cruelty. It would have been kinder just to walk across the bridge without even saying goodbye to Mina. It would have been kinder to him and to her. But he wanted to know it just once, even if it was painful. It confirms for himself that Heaven is a cruel place, because you can't stay there. It doesn't last. It's something else to be taken from you. In fact, that was probably one of the very few things in Hyde's life which actually caused him real pain. Physically getting hurt is not a big deal for Hyde. Emotionally, there's no way he can be hurt. He doesn't have normal emotions. So to inflict that pain on himself, by choice, yeah, it seemed appropriate for Hyde, who I was starting to see as a much bigger and wiser and more complex figure than I had originally. I'd never seen Hyde as stupid. But in that second book I began to see Hyde as wise, wise where Jekyll was foolish. Not stupid where Jekyll was intelligent, wise where Jekyll was foolish. Hyde's got a much better and clearer understanding of human nature than Jekyll ever had. It's perhaps a more brutal and stark and unflinching grasp of human nature, but it's wiser because it's truer, because it's more realistic than this hopeless, doomed idealism that prompts Jekyll to separate the two of them in the first place. I really did like that scene, and I'm sure that you would have noticed "You Should See Me Dance the Polka." You got the reference?

JN: Spencer Tracy.

AM: Yeah, my favorite film. That was the one with the nude girls harnessed to the coach. Was that the Fredric March version? No, I'm sure that was the Spencer Tracy version.

JN: I missed that completely.

AM: Isn't there a dream sequence where Hyde is setting on the box of a coach with a whip—

JN: Well, this is Texas. They probably don't show that sort of thing down here.

AM: Oh, it's really, it's the scene I remember. There are these sort of semi-naked—you probably can't see a nipple, but it was pretty racy for the time—these semi-naked girls harnessed to a coach with Mr. Hyde whipping them on, while "You Should See Me Dance the Polka" plays deliriously in the background. One of my favorite film sequences.

JN: Have you noticed a difference in reaction to the series from British and American fans?

AM: I don't really notice much reaction at all because I'm completely out of the loop. I don't go to conventions, I don't read the fan press, and I don't really have anything to do with the Internet. Have you noticed any difference in reaction between the Yanks and the Brits?

JN: What I've seen and what people have said to me is—it basically splits down the middle in terms of nationality. The American fans are a lot more squeamish and appalled by the violence and sex, and the British fans aren't.
AM: That probably sounds pretty reasonable. How did the sex go down? I thought that the sex scene at the end of number four, I thought that was lovely.

JN: I did, too, and a lot of the fans whose opinion I respect did, too, but there's always the Bible Belt wing of comic book fans in America who call it "pornography."
AM: Oh well. [Laughs] Oh, well. As long as it's the people in the Bible Belt that I'm offending. No offense, people in the Bible Belt, but they're going to be offended by almost anything. It was in the Bible Belt that the cops seized that Wonder Woman poster because that was pornography, wasn't it, a few years ago.

JN: Yeah, it was actually in the Bible Belt that they arrested a woman for selling a vibrator to a married couple. That was about fifty miles from where I live.
AM: Yeah, it was down South where I read about a couple going to prison because their little boy had mentioned to one of his friends that he'd seen daddy performing an act of oral love upon mommy, which was considered sodomy in that particular—the thing is, I can't make allowances for people like that. They're entitled to think that it's pornography, and they're entitled to think that it portrays abnormal sexuality. By the same token, I must be free to think that they are abnormal sexually. I think that that entire culture is. I'm afraid it's laughable. We don't have to deal with it over here so I can say this. There's no other country in the world but America where you'd put up with people like that or ideas like that. They're laughable. They're childish. That would be an embarrassment in any other country, those kind of ideas. That scene, I'm very proud of it. The quite honest, unabashed sexuality, and then that awful bit where her scarf comes unraveled, which is what it was building up to. It wasn't about the sex. It wasn't about the nakedness of her body. It was about the nakedness of her throat. All of a sudden we see a part of Mina we've not seen before. I don't mean her naked body. We see a part of Mina's psychology

that we haven't seen before, which for me overshadowed the quite ordinary sexual activity.

JM: She's suddenly vulnerable.

AM: You suddenly realize a whole lot about what she's been keeping to herself and how scarred her personality is. Not just her neck, but these are the sort of scars that go down a long way. To me that was much more important than the fact that they happened to have just had sex. Sex—we all got here because of sex. We all do it, if we're lucky. We've been doing it for millions of years. It's perhaps time we got over it and moved on. A couple of million years, that should be time for us to have gotten over our understandable panic at the idea of sexual reproduction.

JN: Did you have any trouble with ABC/Wildstorm about the sex and the violence?

AM: Nah. These are people who hired me, and they are familiar with my previous work. There's been plenty of sex and violence in my stuff right from the eighties. I'd like to think that it was handled in the best possible taste, but people pretty much know what they're getting with me by now. There was sex all the way through *Swamp Thing, Marvelman, V for Vendetta*. There was violence—all of these things. So, no, I think DC and Wildstorm understood. *League* is one of the best-selling comics, at least in book form. I think in bookshops it is probably the best-selling graphic novel.

JN: In pamphlet form, it outsells, I think, all the Superman books, all but one of the Batman books, and everything but *JLA*.

AM: In the book collections it does even better. Obviously, somebody likes it. Obviously, there are a number of people out there who aren't offended by it, or who could swallow their revulsion if they were really pushed. I've been completely open about the fact that that there'll probably be more sex in the future stuff—if that's appropriate. We're not just going to shovel it in for no reason at all, just for the sake of it. I quite like sex, myself. Call me crazy. But I think it's just as interesting to depict sex as it is to depict a couple of people trying to rip each other's windpipes out. It's part of human life, and it's an important part, and I should expect to find it turning up a lot more in *League of Extraordinary Gentlemen*. Because I want to normalize it. I want to get to a point where people don't think, "Ooh, it's a sex scene!" I'd like to get to a point where people could just think, "Yeah, this is just another part of the story. What are they telling us here," and not be distracted by all the boobs and buttocks.

JN: I think part of the fan reaction was that when you have Mina tell Allan to bite her neck, that gave fans a glimpse into more—I don't want to say "kinkier," but a more complex form of sexuality.

AM: Also, it's Mina's sexuality. Why would Mina tell Allan to bite her neck, to bite her shoulder? Doesn't that tell us something about what Mina's real take upon the events in Stoker's novel was? It's not so much hinting, "Oh, Mina's a bit kinky!" for any sort of titillation reasons, it's that I'm saying she's asking him to *bite her*. She obviously finds that sexually exciting. Why would Mina find that sexually exciting? Doesn't that suggest possibly a different take upon her feelings about Dracula? This is what I mean. We're getting over very important character information in a line of dialogue like that. It's not for titillation. It's not the kind of stuff you see in certain modern comics, Marvel Knights or Vertigo or whatever, where a reference to some sexual peccadillo is seen as spicy, spicing the story up. That's not what it was used for. It was trying to imply that there might be a certain degree of ambivalence to Mina's reaction to what happened to her in 1896 or 1897 or whenever it was. She might not have been entirely repulsed by the King of the Vampires. It might have been quite an experience. It might have left her, sexually, with a bad case of Stockholm Syndrome. These are speculations, but this is what I mean. A sex scene is a way of getting over very important character information, just as much as a fight scene is, and the reader really shouldn't be looking at it as, "Oh, this is purely thrown in for titillation." I don't really throw in anything in any of my stories just for this or just for that. There's generally some sort of story information being imparted as well, or character information. I love those scenes, but as a warning to the fainthearted there probably will be more of them in the future, so stop buying now.

JN: Why did Mina divorce Jonathan?

AM: I'm not sure who did divorce who. But . . . he's actually a profoundly dull little man. He's a state agent. He's not really a very interesting, or fascinating, or passionate man, and I figured that it would get very complicated between them after *Dracula*, because Mina's nearly fatal relationship with Dracula probably would have been the most passionate that she had ever had. It would certainly probably leave her relationship with Jonathan looking a little pallid. At the same time, I would imagine that Jonathan, like many men of the era, would feel that Mina was tainted, that—this is not just particularly limited to the Victorian era. I believe that it's a common response among the boyfriends and husbands of rape victims to completely turn against the victim right when she's most in need of support, because they blame her for it. "You could have resisted more. You could have resisted more. You could have done something to fight him off." This is I think what goes through the heads of a lot of men who've got no concept of what being raped is about. So, yes, she was probably getting very dissatisfied with him. He was probably suddenly afraid and revolted when he responded to Mina. She'd been dirtied in some way, and she was perhaps, perhaps she wanted it? Perhaps there was some kind of lust in her that he hadn't seen before, something frightening. I should imagine a combination of those factors is what led to the divorce. Partly it was her. Partly it was him. I'm not sure which one divorced the other one, or on what grounds. Maybe we'll at some point in the future return to that, if it ever seems fruitful.

JN: Was Griffin's death a response to the rape scenes in the first *League* series, a sort of balance—
AM: No, not really. I wasn't trying to appease, "Oh we've had a woman being nearly raped"—

JN: Well, we first see him as a rapist, and—
AM: Oh, yeah, well . . . I hadn't really thought of that. Yeah, if you want. It sort of provides a sort of symmetry for people who need that. But that wasn't what I thought. When I was thinking the scene through, I thought, "What would Hyde do if he got hold of Griffin?" And the answer was, "The worst possible thing." And then when he'd done that, he'd think of the next worst possible thing. And he would do all of them. And rape was obviously somewhere along the line of the spectrums of the very bad things to do to the Invisible Man. And it was something that would occur to Hyde. Hyde's a monster. And terrifying, brutalizing, murdering people, that's something which is kind of cozy to him, and so, yeah. And also, it struck me as kind of funny. I have to admit it, this probably says an awful lot about me which I shouldn't be admitting in public, but I thought it was just audacious and funny, to have Mr. Hyde raping the Invisible Man, because—one of the funny things about the Invisible Man in the girls' school—I thought it was funny having the Invisible Man having sex with the girls. I know technically it was rape. I still thought it was funny, just because—it's a funny idea, people floating in space with their

legs wrapped around nothing, gasping in rapture. That was funny, and so it was funny to have the Invisible Man on the receiving end, as it were, for the same reason. It's a good visual joke.

JN: Some of the fans also pointed out that Hyde's last words to Griffin in the first series were, "Bugger you, Griffin."

AM: I hadn't thought of it, but, again, they're probably attributing—the phrase, "Bugger you," in British, isn't really literal. So, there wasn't really any connection, but I suppose I could see why—it's an accidental connection. I hadn't really thought of it.

Moore: "We Wanted to Do Something Which Solved a Lot of the Abiding Problems That Pornography Has."

CHRIS MAUTNER / 2006

The Patriot-News (August 25, 2006): 15 pp. Reprinted by permission of Joan S. Clippinger, *The Patriot-News* (Harrisburg).

Patriot-News columnist Chris Mautner spent almost two hours interviewing *Lost Girls* author Alan Moore, from his home in Northampton, England.

Q: I'll start with the obvious question first. How did the book come to be? How did it get started?

A: Well, that is quite an obvious question. It's got a lengthy answer. I suppose that it originally started with me having done a number of mainstream comic books in which I felt that if the character was going to be completely rounded, even if that was a character like Swamp Thing, then there should be a sexual dimension to the character. So this was something that I had done in a number of my comic works where it was appropriate. And I found myself thinking that it might be possible to actually do a comic narrative that was about nothing but sexuality. I mean, it seemed to me that if most of the comics that were on the market at that time seemed to be about nothing other than fighting then it should be possible to do a lengthy work that was actually about nothing other than sex.

That was about as far as my thinking got for a number of years because it's more difficult than it looks to come up with something that is actually erotic or pornographic and which does all the things that that sort of material is supposed to do but at the same time is intelligent enough to interest me in actually working on it.

So, I had drawn a number of blanks. Then, sometime about 1989, there was a magazine proposed over here that was, I believe, going to be called *Lost Horizons of Shangri-La*. There's nothing of this since, so I presume it never came out, and it was "lost" somewhere.

They had asked me to do an eight-page story for them. It was an erotic anthology. They had asked me to write an eight-page story for them. Unbeknownst to me, they had also asked Melinda Gebbie, who was then working in London on the fringes of the comic industry, but she wasn't working in a day job as an artist.

I think Neil Gaiman had stumbled across her, and he told me this, and I had been an admirer of Melinda's work for a number of years since seeing her early California underground comics in the seventies and early eighties. So, I asked Neil if he could give her my phone number with an eye to collaborating with her upon this eight-page script for this proposed magazine.

So Melinda came up and visited for a few weekends. And we just talked about what we wanted to do with an erotic story and, most importantly, what we didn't want to do, which was that we didn't want to do anything that was like the pornography that was prevalent around us at that time. We wanted to do something which solved a lot of the abiding problems that pornography has, in that, generally, it's an ugly genre. Ugly in all sorts of ways. It can be aesthetically ugly; it can be morally ugly, politically ugly.

So we actually wanted to kind of rethink the genre to a certain extent. And it took us a while, thrashing it out: a couple of weeks. And then two half-formed ideas seemed to collide.

I'd had a vague idea that there might be some mileage in taking J. M. Barrie's *Peter Pan* and actually reworking it as a sexual narrative. I think this was based upon the fact that Sigmund Freud had made much of the fact that dreams of flying were dreams of sexual expression and there were, of course, a lot of flying scenes in *Peter Pan*. Which kind of sounds superficially clever but didn't really go very far. It was difficult to see how that idea could turn into anything other than a kind of smutty parody of *Peter Pan*, which was not really what we were after.

Melinda happened to mention that she always enjoyed in the past—when working on her own stories—working on narratives where there were three main women characters in some sort of dynamic balance.

And these two ideas kind of interbred, and I suppose that I started thinking, "Well, if Wendy from *Peter Pan* was one of the women in this three-women set-up, who would the other two be?" And immediately that led to thinking about Alice from *Alice in Wonderland* and Dorothy from *The Wizard of Oz*.

And once we'd got that basic idea, it was as if the light bulb switched on. It seemed like a really good idea, right from the start. Just having those three characters together in a single narrative.

And as we thought about it over the next couple of weeks, we realized just how good an idea it was, in that in the original stories that those characters come from, what they have in common, is that they're all about girls who are suddenly plucked out of the regular world that they had known and placed into a strange fantasy landscape where all the laws of logic and reality seemed to be overturned.

And it struck me and Melinda that that was a wonderful metaphor for the way that most of us enter into our first sexual experiences. That, to a certain degree, because sexual experience is one of the marker posts on the road between childhood and some kind of maturity, then it's one of the points of which we mark the end of childhood.

So, it seemed to us that perhaps these characters could stand as a metaphor for the way in which all of us—to a certain degree—when we first encounter sexuality, it is as if we've stepped into a world with unfamiliar rules, where all of the things that we've learned in our lives up to then no longer really apply. And where we're surrounded by strangely motivated, even grotesque, characters all of a sudden.

So it was very quick, the actual process of coming up with the whole story. I think that within a few weeks of having that initial idea, I'd pretty much got the whole story structure down, and by then it was very clear that this wasn't going to be an eight-page inclusion in an erotic anthology. We'd realized that this was going to take a little bit longer and was going to be quite a bit bigger.

Neither of us knew that it was going to take sixteen years, but if we had known, we would have still done it because we were convinced that this was a brilliant idea and would make for a brilliant book. That was our intention.

Q: Segueing into that, why did it take sixteen years? Why such a long gestation period?

A: Well, there were a number of reasons, like for one thing we had three different publishers, through no fault of their own, collapsing under. I must add, this was through no fault of *Lost Girls* either. It was just that the publishing industry in general in comics was going through a turbulent time during that period.

It also took us a long time to think this through and to make sure that we'd got it right. There were so many potentially wrong ways of handling everything. We wanted to be very careful to make sure that every image was saying what we wanted it to say.

This involved an awful lot of conversation between me and Melinda, where I would perhaps propose a scene, we'd discuss it, and we'd discuss what we did or didn't like about it. We'd revise it. We'd change images until we were both completely comfortable with it.

This was so that the book would stand a chance of being as appealing to women as it would be to men. I mean, actually writing pornography that will appeal to men is not a massive challenge, if truth be told. But understandably, women have not traditionally been attracted to the overwhelmingly male pornography that is available. And like I said, that's quite understandable.

So we wanted to make this something that would be inviting to both genders and to a broad range of sexualities as well. We wanted this to be kind of polymorphous, something that potentially could appeal to just about anybody.

That kind of process took us a long time. And also the actual artwork took a long time because of the meticulous way in which Melinda approached it, with these layers and layers of colors for every skin tone. There's a fair acreage of skin tones in *Lost Girls*. It wasn't just that she wore out six boxes of pink crayons. There were greens and purples and browns and all of these other colors worked in there too. Which is partly what gives *Lost Girls* part of its golden luster, but it was a very painstaking procedure, and it did take a long time.

There was also the settling into working together. I'd been used to working solely with men prior to that point, because, shamefully, there were not a great many female artists in the comics medium to collaborate with. That situation has improved. It's probably still far from ideal. I hadn't worked with a woman artist before, though that wasn't a big problem.

What was potentially a problem was that Melinda had never worked with a scriptwriter before, in that all of her early underground comics had been self-written and self-drawn, which was very much the custom amongst the undergrounds.

So there was Melinda getting these huge scripts which I'm notorious for. A script for an eight-page episode of *Lost Girls* might be twenty-four pages. I think that kind of crushed Melinda's spirit to a certain degree. She was just looking at these pages and pages of type, and she wasn't really used to decoding my panel descriptions.

So after a few episodes of this, we asked if there was a better way of doing it. And what we came up with was a way which is unique, at least in my experience of writing comics. It's certainly something that I've never done before, which was that I would do thumbnails for each of the pages.

Which is something that I've never done with any of my other collaborators because they live in other towns, cities, often other countries. So I can't sit by their side and explain to them that this deformed blob at the bottom right corner of a panel is actually meant to be the leading character's head, whereas, because Melinda was living here in Northampton, I could actually explain my thumbnails to her.

She could then go away and do the pages of finished artwork. And if she had added anything to my visuals—which she very often did do—then because I'd be doing the dialogue after the pictures were finished, I'd be able to fine-tune the dialogue to suit a character's facial expression or some element that Melinda might have felt like including. And so it was a much more seamless piece of work than a lot of my other collaborations have been. That said, it did take sixteen years.

At the same time, I can't think of a better time for it to come out than at the present moment.

Q: How so?
A: Well, if this had come out say seven or eight years ago, then it would have come out under a far more liberal Clinton administration. It would have come out during a period when the world, at least relatively speaking in comparison to today—was perhaps less war torn. It wasn't by any means a peaceful utopia back in the nineties, but compared to today it wasn't quite as bad as it is at present.

And I think that while *Lost Girls* might have received perhaps an easier reception, it would have been seen as much less controversial and perhaps even much less relevant.

The thing about *Lost Girls* is yes, it has a message that is very pro-sexuality and pro-sexual imagination, but just as strongly there is a very palpable antiwar message there as well. That sort of, we tend to put the two side by side, you know? The sexual imagination and war, which in many ways is a complete failure of the imagination. And which destroys so much of the culture that the imagination has struggled to create.

So yeah, these present times are, I think, ones which offer stark contrast. *Lost Girls* can't help but really be more resonant than [it] would be in slightly gentler times. It feels like this is a book that is coming out at exactly the right time even though we could never have predicted that obviously.

Q: Spinning off from that point, a lot of people who haven't read the book or who have concerns about it, a lot of stuff I'm seeing either in print or on the

Internet, are concerned with the pedophilia and teenage sexuality and the very notion, the very plot of the book is kind of offensive to them. What do you say to someone like that as a defense or to calm irrational fears?

A: Well, if the whole notion of people having sex under what is currently the legal age of consent in their country really disturbs them or any depictions of that, then probably they would be best not to buy *Lost Girls*.

But I would point out that I think this is a bit of a chimera really. It's a bit of a will-o'-the-wisp, when you actually consider that however we would like things to be, the actual reality is that very often people actually begin at least thinking about sex as soon as they are of an age where their bodies are starting to change and, with it, their emotions and sensations. Nature doesn't really pay much attention to whatever arbitrary age we have applied to this.

I mean in Victorian times, in the times when much of *Lost Girls* was set, I think that the age of consent was twelve. I mean, certainly there were twelve-year-old working-class children who were marrying and having children by then.

Now, I'm not saying that that's a good thing. Throughout the world, the sort of age by which we recognize someone as being mature varies wildly. I would point out that we are not actually talking about anything real here.

I have referred to *Lost Girls* as a pornography for a number of reasons. One is that I found it was less pretentious than calling it erotica. Another is that it means something very precise.

As I understand it, pornography means writings or drawings of wantonness. Now, that doesn't say anything about Polaroid pictures, or home movie footage, or shared files of wantonness. It's talking about drawings and writings, which seems to signal to me that this is taking place nowhere but in the imagination. No real men, women, children, or horses were harmed in the manufacture of *Lost Girls*.

So would it be OK, for example, to do a comic book in which children or young people were killed? I wonder if that would be more disturbing?

Q: It might be. I just got a book in the mail from a Japanese author called *The Drifting Classroom*, which has children dying in it, and it's very disturbing.

A: Although I'll bet that there'll be less outcry. I didn't see a huge amount of outcry over [the manga series] *Battle Royale*. In fact, I think that's become quite a teen favorite.

Q: Yes, it is.

A: But of course that was only children being blown to bits. It wasn't children in any way involved in sexual activity. There's something a little bit strange there I have to say. But you know, each to their own.

Q: Getting back to the issue of pornography, I could see someone saying, "Well, why be so adamant about calling it pornography?" Wouldn't it be politically smarter if you used a less charged term, like "erotica" or "adult fiction"? Because pornography has so much weight on it as a term and has such a view of it as being this nasty, ugly thing?

A: Well, the way that I think of it is, "Why wait for someone else?" I mean, I could have called it anything that I wanted. I could have called it "adult fiction." I could have called it "erotica" or "gentlemen's reading material." But that would have just been waiting for someone else to call it pornography.

And, like I say, I have no problem with the word "pornography" as I understand it, as its dictionary definition stands. Not that we were looking for a fight with this. It was just that I wanted to be honest.

I could have called it "erotica," but what that actually means is "pertaining to love." Now, I doubt that any of the pornography that either of us has ever seen would seem to be more about romance than it is about physical sexual activity.

Q: Nor most of the erotica for that matter.

A: That's it! It is more descriptive, it is more accurate, and, to some degree, it is preemptive. It is not waiting for someone else to come along and call this pornography. It is saying, "Fair enough, this is pornography."

But what we are trying to do is to reclaim the term pornography. We are hoping that through *Lost Girls*, we can show that it is possible to do an ambitious and lengthy work of pornography that has all of the things that one would expect from any piece of literature or work of art. That all of the objections to pornography that we considered—and we considered a great many of them—we have tried to answer and redeem in *Lost Girls*.

Now, arguments that come from the Religious Right we have not addressed, because those arguments are actually not coming from a standpoint that I can recognize as rational. It seems to me largely to be—and this is just purely my opinion, I hasten to add—but it seems to me largely to be unfalsifiable nonsense. And that is not a position that anyone can have a rational debate on, and one of the things about debate is that it does have to be rational.

So, we've not addressed any of those issues. We have, however, addressed most of the feminist arguments and critiques regarding pornography, because those, even though many of them I didn't actually agree with, they're at least rational. They are at least putting forward ideas that can be challenged and discussed. We've tried to make this something which does not do all of the things that pornography has traditionally done.

And when we talk about say, you know, sex with minors in *Lost Girls*, this has to be seen in a context of the fact that what we're doing is, we're exploring the whole of the human sexual imagination. Clearly the idea of sex with minors is a very big part of that.

We've got magazines like *Barely Legal* on both sides of the pond. And yes, we are told that these are all sort of just young-looking people who are in fact over the age of consent.

Whether that is true or not, I mean, we all remember Traci Lords. Most people, if they're told that these people are over the age of consent, that makes it all right, whereas the intention is obviously exactly the same as with anybody with pedophile inclinations.

This stuff has to be discussed. And I think that it's important that we come up with a form of pornography in which these ideas can be discussed openly because there seems to me to be a way in which pornography functions in societies, and it depends upon the relationship of those societies to their sexuality.

When you have countries like America and England . . . well, let's look at the other side of the coin first. You've got countries like Denmark, Holland, and Spain, where they have a very liberal attitude toward pornography, where quite hardcore pornography apparently is freely available in regular family bookstores and nobody pays it any attention, because it's so ubiquitous.

In these countries, they might have their houses wallpapered with pornography. What they don't have is anything like the amount of sex crime that we get here or in America. And certainly not the amount of sex crime against children. They look at countries like us and the U.S. with horror.

Now that suggests that there is some difference in the way we regard our own sexuality between sort of more liberal countries and countries like ours. I wonder if it might not be in our culture, pornography mainly functions as a control leash.

We live in very, very sexualized cultures. Every advertisement on television, whether it sells cars or perfume or pop noodles is liable to be slathered with sexual ideas, sexual imagery. Now this is not just selling cars and pop noodles. Sex is also selling itself. It is increasing the sexual temperature of the culture, if you like.

So, when you've got somebody who has been inflamed by the sheer amount of sexualized material around them, [they will seek some sort of release]. In

America, generally speaking, the moment that release has been obtained, there will be inevitable feelings of wretchedness, self-loathing, shame, guilt.

Now this is a bit like a kind of a really sinister Skinner rat experiment where you've got the rat so that they will respond to the stimulus by pressing the lever to get their reward. But these Skinner boxes are wired differently so that the moment they get their reward, they also get their punishment. They get this electric shock of guilt and shame.

And I suspect that rats actually kept in those conditions would probably go a bit crazy after awhile. And I suspect in healthy cultures, pornography might even be providing some sort of vital safety valve, as evidenced by the lower sex crime figures of those countries where they do have a liberal attitude towards pornography.

It strikes me that if there was a way to sever that instant connection between sex and guilt, then I think we might be healthier cultures because of that. I think that if we could actually own up to the sexual thoughts that may pass through our mind, realize that we are not monsters for having these thoughts, realize that these thoughts are in no way connected to reality, that it's perfectly OK within the confines of your mind to think whatever you want.

And if you are in a culture that tells you that is not so, that keeps that pressure cooker lid on, then the only possible kind of relief is an explosion. An explosion into actual real violence, of real abuse of real people in the real world.

So it strikes me that in some ways it is the very prudishness of our cultures and the shame-faced guilty way that we perceive sexual material that actually causes a lot of the sexual problems that we seem tormented by.

Q: Well, let me talk about that for a minute in the context of *Lost Girls*, because certainly the issue of fantasy versus reality seems to be one of the major themes of the book. And I think you go about it in a really fascinating way, which is to kind of flip back and forth between the erotic and the real life with the characters, starting with the sequence where Alice starts to tell her initial story where she's molested in the beginning, which is a haunting, very haunting, sequence.
A: It's not presented arousingly.

Q: No. It's quite disturbing.
A: It's one of the two examples of actual abuse in the book, of actual nonconsensual sex in the book. The other one is the rape of Tinkerbell, or the Tinkerbell-like character in the *Peter Pan* narrative.

This is presented as something which is appalling. And yes, with Alice, what we wanted to suggest was that this was something that is done to her and it shatters her psyche. It has a tremendous effect upon her and the rest of her life. And almost everything springs from that.

Now, I don't think that is—all right it's described in fantasy terms, but I don't think that that, in and of itself, is unrealistic.

In fact, one of the best reactions that we've had so far to *Lost Girls* was from this journalist over here, a friend of ours. She's very much involved with the sexual politics scene over here. And she had read one of the blotty, gray and white photocopy editions that I'm sure you squinted at as well.

And she was very impressed with it, and she was talking with a couple of friends of hers who were both women. She was talking to them independently. But they were both women who had been sexually abused as children. And she was talking to them about how the three protagonists in *Lost Girls* seemed to have taken elements of their early abuse or early sexual encounters and to have reworked them into a kind of distancing fantasy. And apparently both of these women independently said, "That's exactly what I did, and I shall really look forward to seeing this book."

Now, all right, everybody who is unfortunate enough to have been in those circumstances has got a different story, and they'll have a different reaction. And I'm sure that there might be a lot of people who would have a negative reaction to *Lost Girls*.

But in that instance, I felt to a certain degree vindicated. I felt that we had treated all of the material here as sensitively as we could and with as much compassion for the characters as we could.

In the scenes like the one you mention, it was important to us that we didn't make those scenes erotic, that there were scenes being not at all arousing about nonconsensual sex of any kind.

Q: It was a quite shocking sequence, actually, because I came upon it after I had been reading these erotic trysts, and then Alice starts telling her story. It was a 180-degree reversal. And when I kept reading the book and got to the sequence in the hotel, where the proprietor tells his story, and you have that marvelous sequence where you have the erotic story going on up top, and then he's telling his story on the bottom.

A: I think that one of the women present is commenting upon the erotic story that he is reading out and saying, "But isn't this wrong? This is people with children," and "This is a disgrace. This is horrific."

And he replies, "Well if these children were real, of course, you're right, it would be monstrous. This would be a terrible thing, but these children aren't real. They are purely in this pornography that I am reading to you."

What I was trying to say in my muddled, roundabout fashion was that of course the material that is purely in the mind, how can it be anything other than innocent? Especially when contrasted with the stuff that we're seeing on our televisions every day, of children being carried limp and bloody out of rubble. These are real children in a real world.

With *Lost Girls*, we hoped to have a sense of perspective on this. There is nothing as terrible as war. And whatever our current moral panics might say, even child molesting is not as terrible as war, and the imagery and the concept of child molesting is certainly not as terrible as war.

That is not to say the abuse of children is not terrible. Of course it is. The abuse of anybody is terrible. I don't know if sexual abuse is more terrible than any other kind or whether it's because we seem to apply a huge amount of power to the sexual realm, like the whole idea of rape as a fate worse than death.

I remember talking to Kathy Acker, the late, lamented Kathy Acker, about that issue. I remember her saying that she had been raped and she says, "You go home. You have a wash. You feel kind of messed up for awhile, but you're glad that you weren't killed." There is no fate worse than death.

What we wanted to do was actually raise these issues so that they can be discussed in an actual, rational way by adults. What does it mean when we have one part of our tabloid press howling for the blood of pedophiles or anyone who lives at the same address that a pedophile used to live at, which is what happened over here when they started publishing the addresses of pedophiles? Or anybody who is in a profession that perhaps sounds a bit like pedophile if you're really, really stupid, like pediatrician, one of whom was run out of town by an anti-pedophile mob in England after a tabloid newspaper campaign.

Now, on the one hand, we've got the tabloid press doing that, on the other hand we've got the tabloid press eagerly involved in the sexualization of children. Pictures of the fourteen-year-old Princess Eugenie and her younger sister on the beach in revealing swimwear. Gloating remarks about the swelling chest measurements of the then fifteen-year-old Charlotte Church on the same page as they were lambasting the brilliant and vitriolic comedian Chris Morris for his *Brass Eye Special*, which was a show lampooning the pedophile hysteria.

And, of course, with the Spice Girls, everybody liked Baby Spice. They all liked Britney Spears in her schoolgirl uniform.

Q: Well, over here you've got websites devoted to ticking down when Mary-Kate and Ashley Olsen will turn eighteen. Or take your pick of the teen pop starlets. There's a real unsavory atmosphere towards it.

A: Melinda and I have not created these ideas. What we're trying to do is talk about them, because we think it is important that they be talked about. And pornography is a wonderful vehicle in which to talk about those concepts.

As it stands at the moment, the only two possible arenas in which those ideas can be discussed are contemporary pornography, which is ugly and vile for the most part. Sort of seedy happenings on distressed looking sofas and strip lighting that looks like it's been set up for brain surgery.

That's on the one hand. On the other hand, you have the clinical and asexual sex manual. And I don't think that really either of those areas are ones that we traditionally think of if we're thinking about our own sex lives.

So, it struck us that pornography potentially could be a new form of pornography. A more liberated form of pornography could provide something that was invaluable in discussing these ideas and not giving them a chance to—because they are so hooked up with guilt and shame—just slink away into dark corners where they can fester and become something genuinely toxic on a personal and a social level.

Now, of course there are still a lot of people who will not like the idea of *Lost Girls*, and that is perfectly fine.

Q: Well, you were saying how it could open up discussion, but I can see a lot of people—and not even the idea that it's porn, but just that as soon as they hear that it's Alice, Dorothy, and Wendy, they're gonna go, "But those are children's books," and they'll shut down right there.

A: Well, there have been a couple of people who have said that when they first heard about the book, they imagined it was gonna contain distressing scenes of an eight-year-old "Alice in Wonderland" involved in sort of horrendous sexual activity. As anybody who has read the book will tell you, that is not the case.

All of the three main protagonists are teenagers who are sexually mature. Whether they might be under the age of consent today or probably over the age of consent for which those books were written, which those stories were set, is kind of immaterial. They are young women. They are not children.

And with regard to anybody who feels a love and attachment to those characters and fears that we may have degraded or debased them in *Lost Girls*, I would like to say that I doubt that there are any bigger admirers of those three books than me and Melinda.

Q: Yeah, I felt reading the book that you had a real admiration. In some ways the characters feel closer to Baum's work or Carroll's work than some of the Hollywood adaptations.

A: Well that was what we went for. We know those characters. We all know those characters. We read about them when we were very young and very impressionable. They're part of our childhood. They're part of us. So, we wanted our characters to be as faithful as they could to the originals, emotionally and intellectually.

Alice has still got that slightly dreamy, surrealistic turn of thought. Alice is also semi-addicted to laudanum. But again, that is, while there was no suggestion that Alice was addicted to drugs in Lewis Carroll's original, it is a rather drug-saturated text. Alice was certainly swigging down bottles labeled "Drink Me" and wolfing down cakes labeled "Eat Me" and sort of talking to hookah-smoking caterpillars as Jefferson Airplane remarked. It struck us that it didn't seem entirely out of the question for our portrayal of Alice.

We portrayed Dorothy as, she's probably the most adventurous and bold of the three and the most in charge of her own destiny. I mean, any problems with Dorothy, she'd probably strode boldly into them herself. She's very headstrong, and she's very adventurous, which I think is in keeping with Baum's original.

And Wendy is every bit the kind of prim little mother of Barrie's book in that she comes from a very middle class and repressed sort of Victorian world . . .

Q: And, of course, the three are at different stages of womanhood too.

A: This was very handy. When we first worked out that we were going to have these three characters in the narrative, we tried to work out a kind of spurious timeline for them, based upon publication dates of the original books. And we found that that gave us Alice as the oldest of the three and Dorothy as the youngest, Wendy somewhere in between.

To have a time period in which our main narrative would be set, in which Dorothy would not be too young, nor Alice too old, we found that gave us a time period around 1913, 1914, as the best possible window, which was very useful in terms of how we set the book and how the themes emerged from it.

It also gave us these three different ages of women. They're from three different social backgrounds. Alice is an aristocrat, Wendy is from the middle classes, and Dorothy is from a rural blue-collar farming background. They're three different body types as well for that matter.

And we wanted to do this because in most pornography, sex seems to be the domain of the under-twenty-fives only, and everybody has got to be buff and conform to the current standards of physical beauty. And that is not how real sex is. So we wanted to make *Lost Girls* something that was a bit more inclusive.

Q: Let's talk about the timeline for a minute. You bring in World War I, and *The Rite of Spring*, and those kind of cultural issues that are going around that period. What was the thinking bringing those issues in? You talked about war and how it's the opposite of imagination, of pornographic imagination.

A: Well, as I said, we wanted *Lost Girls* to be a pornography and yet at the same time to be able to do the same things that any work of literature or work of art would do. That meant that it would have to have characters, and a plot, and themes, and even fancy French-sounding things like motifs and metaphors. And it would have to have a meaning.

Now, when we started looking at the timeline for a period when these women could have met when, as I say, Dorothy wouldn't be too young nor Alice too old, and we started to see that it was around 1913, 1914.

And this was really suggestive because we realized that Stravinsky's *Rite of Spring* had caused riots at the Paris Opera in 1913, less than twelve months before the Archduke Franz Ferdinand was assassinated in Sarajevo, which, of course, led to the entire first World War.

With the benefit of hindsight, it looked to us very much as if *The Rite of Spring*, or the reaction to it, rather, was a kind of premonition of what was going to happen in Europe. It was an indication that Europe's heartstrings were at a very dangerous pitch. If something like Stravinsky's *Rite of Spring* could spark the reaction that it did, then it looked to us that it was almost prefiguring the kind of primal conflicts that would come.

When we realized that this was the kind of time period that *Lost Girls* was taking place against a backdrop of, we thought of the first World War, that pretty much set the tone for the remainder of that century and probably a great deal of this one. It's a blow that Europe has probably never completely recovered from.

It was sort of an apocalyptic time, and we thought, "What better backdrop to set this kind of delicate art nouveau erotic fantasy against?" What starker contrast could you hope for?

So, we decided to place it in an imaginary art nouveau folly of a hotel, in the Boden region, which is an actual region that is exactly on the borders of Austria, Germany, and Switzerland, with the borders of France about a short ride away.

So, that struck us as being right at the heart of Europe, at this point in time when everything was just about to explode, and we thought it would serve to make the human sexual activity and the human sexual imagination and the art and culture represented in the hotel, it would serve to make that seem much more fragile and much more precious and tender, and it would also serve to make the war look every bit as brutal and ultimately pointless as it genuinely was.

Like I say, we could not have asked for a starker contrast. It gave us, if you like, the message of the book, which we realized fairly recently was actually, "Make love, not war." And if we had gotten ourselves one of those badge-making machines sixteen years ago, we could have probably saved ourselves a great deal of time.

But in that sixteen years and 240 pages, we have perhaps unpacked that basic concept a little bit, and we've explained why you should make love, or think about making love, rather than thinking about making war.

Q: Just getting back to the themes, because I think the book is about more than that. Reading the book, it seems like the story is also about these three, and correct me if I'm wrong, women who've either been abused or who have had really awkward or painful early sexual experiences. And through meeting and telling each other their stories, are able to heal themselves.
A: Absolutely. As the title suggests, they've lost part of themselves, which is something that probably happens to all of us.

That when we eagerly enter into the jungles of adolescence lured on by the promises of all these wonderful new delights that are soon going to be available to us, we don't realize at the time that there's a kind of trade-off involved, that we will not be the same people at the other end of that process as we are going into it. And that perhaps our golden glowing childhood, that will end. We will have different information. We will have different agendas. We will not be those people that we were.

And in the cases of Dorothy, Wendy, and Alice, who have had pretty cataclysmic entries into the sexual world, it struck me that in the course of *Lost Girls*, it's by telling each other their stories, by actually talking to these other women, in a way that they've probably never been able to talk to anyone else, that enables them to kind of reintegrate with these lost parts of themselves, as you say, to heal themselves . . .

In Wendy's case, her entry into the world of sexuality, although she has been the strongest and most triumphant of the three women in how she dealt with her assailant, if you like, has been such a frightening experience for her that she pushes sexuality away into the shadows and launches into a fairly sexless marriage as a way of avoiding this dark, wild territory that she had stumbled into and had a very narrow escape when she was younger.

Yeah, a lot of us, for various reasons, we distance ourselves from our sexual imagination, through fear, through shame, through guilt. It probably is one of the most pleasurable parts of us, and in a world that is so beset with painful things, it strikes me that we would perhaps all be a little bit happier if we didn't make our sexuality one of those painful things with which to inflict harm upon ourselves.

Q: I want to talk really briefly about the layout of the book, 'cause it's one of the things I found the most fascinating, especially the way each character's stories are arranged differently, with Alice's stories being all ovals, and Dorothy's being rectangular, and Wendy's being these kind of stained-glass windows. What was the thinking behind that?
A: Well, the fact that they were from different social backgrounds, that they were different ages, different body types, and . . . we wanted to make each of them as distinct as possible.

We gave them different ways of talking, different attitudes, different ways of thinking. I know that Melinda, she gave them different skin tones. She gave them all different dress sense. And we were trying to distinguish between them, and we thought that one good way of doing that would be for each of their narrative strands to be approached differently.

So, Dorothy, born out there in the cornfields of Kansas, seemed to suggest wide panoramic vistas, so we went for those horizontal panels that typify Dorothy's story. I think that Melinda used pretty much exclusively colored crayons on the Dorothy section, which gave a certain look to the Dorothy narrative.

Wendy, we decided that upright panels would look more restricted in a way and more repressed. That would also echo the upright bars of the railings in the park. And we thought that the silhouette panels at the top of Wendy's pages, that worked well with the motif of shadows that we'd already established as part of Wendy's internal landscape.

The Alice pages, again, much of Alice's narrative seemed to be reflective. Having established the mirror as the main motif relating to Alice, we thought it would work well if we had these pool-shaped panels, often with some reflected or symmetrical element in the visuals to constantly be harping upon that kind of mirror world that Alice is inhabiting.

We wanted to think about every aspect of this, the design, the pacing. We didn't want to miss a trick. We wanted to do everything we could to treat these three characters as lovingly as possible and to express them as personalities as fully as possible.

That is one thing that is notably missing from almost any pornographic narratives: that the people in them are meat puppets, they're not actual genuine human beings.

Q: And character would be one of the things that could actually be an erotic feature in a story.

A: Absolutely. This goes back to what I was talking about at the start of the interview, about how, originally, I was doing characters such as Swamp Thing for the mainstream comic companies and, where appropriate, I would try to make them a rounded character by giving them a sexual dimension.

Now, the same thing in reverse applies to *Lost Girls*. These are characters in a pornography. But what we've tried to do is give them other parts to their personality as well that are not necessarily to do with sex. And to make them into more rounded human beings so that they'll seem real to the reader, or at least hopefully so.

If you were talking about sex in real life, it's the difference between an inflatable doll and a real person. That difference is the animation. It's the personality. It's the character of the person that you're involved with. Which, I'm sure for most of us, is every bit as important, if not more important, than what a person looks like. It seemed like those would be good values to import into pornography.

Q: Speaking of Alice, mirrors and reflection seem to be a recurring theme in the book, not just with Alice but in the sequences with Wendy and her husband, where they're both seduced, and it's laid out exactly the same way.

A: Well, there are kind of symmetries throughout the book. We open and close, for example, with the mirror, with the whole chapter reflected in the mirror. Which was something that I thought of early, because that would give us a neat set of bookends with which to frame the entire narrative and would give a nice sense of completion, especially if we built up the mirror throughout the whole book as a window into this fantasy world.

Then, I thought that seeing it shattered in the last chapter would probably be very visceral and perhaps quite upsetting, if you think about what that mirror has come to symbolize.

I suppose that was an element that just arose out of the Lewis Carroll

Lost Girls, chapter 16, page 2, by Alan Moore and Melinda Gebbie. Copyright © 2006, 2009 Alan Moore & Melinda Gebbie, used by permission.

narrative more than the others, but it struck me that in some ways fiction is a mirror of reality and the imagination, which was what we were talking about. All right, specifically the sexual imagination, but we were talking about imagination and art and culture in general.

It struck me that culture and art and imagination are in some ways a reflection of our practical, material human reality. One is the mirror image of the other. One is perhaps the way that we'd like to be or dream of being or that we fear being.

Q: Well, that's certainly true of pornography, which is kind of a fantasy world where nothing bad can ever happen.
A: Yeah, where we project our reflected images. That is another good point. The fact that you say that nothing bad could ever happen. I think that Neil Gaiman . . .

Q: That's who I stole that from.
A: In most pornography, it happens in a kind of pornotopia, where there are no consequences. Whereas in *Lost Girls*, there are obviously consequences, sometimes devastating ones.

Q: And that's what I found so fascinating about the book, the way you segue back and forth between these stories where real things happen and then into this fantasy world. It seemed like you were walking a real tightrope there at certain points in the book.
A: Also, it seemed kind of natural. I mean, we've got Alice, who is kind of cast adrift in this world of the Red Queen and her perverse circle.

Alice is sort of dragged into this because she's been destabilized and damaged to a degree by her early experiences. She's not protected. She's very vulnerable. She's drawn into this further and further. And, at the end, she has to undergo a period in a mental asylum.

I've known people who've followed that arc. It is one of the consequences that can sometimes occur.

And Wendy's sex games in the spinney get out of hand, and Dorothy's sexual exploration of the men that she has available to her on the farm gets out of hand.

All of these things have different consequences. Some of the consequences you'd expect, some are perhaps ones that you wouldn't necessarily expect but which kind of make sense. And these people have to deal with these narratives for the rest of their lives.

Until they've actually spoken them to other people, until they've sat down with the other women and told these stories, they do not know they are not alone, and this is something that we felt very strongly about with regards to the pornography that we were writing.

Generally art, real art, the purpose that it serves is that we look at and we see an idea that we perhaps have but have not expressed, and in doing so that might fulfill us alone. We feel that somebody else has had these ideas. Somebody else has had these thoughts.

Now, traditional pornography has had the exact opposite effect to art in that it makes us feel more alone and wretched and lonely. We wanted, in *Lost Girls*, to be able do a pornography that could be purchased and read without shame, without stigma. You can have it on your bookshelves, and it might even be quite hip, who knows? But certainly it wouldn't lead to social ostracization.

I don't know about Kansas and those states in the middle. It may lead to ostracization there. I'm not familiar with the territory.

If we could kind of do that, then people perhaps wouldn't feel so isolated as if they were the only one who had ever had this or that idea. Because I think that is the kind of thing that leads to the sort of isolation that I was talking about earlier, where people's sexual ideas can kind of curdle and go bad. Because of the isolation, because they're so alone in all of that.

Q: It seems almost as if you start confusing the fantasy with the reality. You can get lost, to bring that up again. It's the start of the problems.
A: That's it, and if you're on your own with no one that you can talk to, more importantly, if you could actually talk about these things with someone else then there wouldn't be so much chance of getting lost or of confusing borderlines between where fantasy ends and where reality begins.

Which is fairly plain for most of us I think. As the guy in the book says, it's mainly only psychopaths and magistrates that have a problem with the two.

Q: I see that all the time around here, where they're trying to legislate against violent video games saying they're going to cause all sorts of real crime.
A: I was hearing a lovely track by somebody called Todd Snider the other day. It was a track called "The Ballad of the Kingsmen," and it was talking about how . . . the Kingsmen clearly had got no idea of the order of the verses when they recorded their 1950s classic ["Louie, Louie"] and yet that was blamed for being an incitement to all of the 1950s juvenile delinquency at that time, just as Marilyn Manson, Eminem, and all the rest have been blamed.

You might think that in any halfway self-aware society people might, after a few of these dreadful things have happened, thought, is it something to do with society, rather than that disposable 45-rpm pop song?

Q: But that takes real work.
A: That does take work. It's easier to ban a record or a book than it is to actually deal with the problem, the real problems, that are at the root of all of these terrible things that happen from time to time.

Q: I was doing a story on a controversial video game that's coming out at the end of the year, and the one thing the PR rep said to me was, he never underestimates the cluelessness of the American politician.

So to bring that around to *Lost Girls*, are you prepared, are you worried or concerned at all about any kind of fight or controversy you may have to go through with this book? Or do you feel like it's not going to create that much of a ripple? When I talked to [publisher] Chris Staros, he seemed to feel as though everyone was behind the book.
A: That is pretty much the impression that I'm getting. I did, some months ago before the book had come out, say to Melinda that, in a worst-case scenario, if there was a slow news week, if England got knocked out of the World Cup too early, or there was nothing else to put in the newspapers, then we might be subjected to what is referred to over here as a "monstering," which is where you get members of the tabloid press turning up on your doorstep with flashbulbs and long lenses and a sensational barrage of questions, or a barrage of sensational questions if you like.

But actually what seems to have happened is that—all right, the book isn't officially out yet—but the response of the people who have actually read it has been so favorable that I'm starting to worry that we might get whatever the exact opposite of a monstering is. Where you get an "angeling" or something like that, where people smother you with praise.

Yes, there could always be any kind of backlash at any point. I know that at the moment over in America there is a case that the Comic Book Legal Defense Fund is fighting which concerns an image of Pablo Picasso painting naked. Which is historically accurate. If that sort of stuff can be attacked then, yeah, I guess anything can be attacked. I have heard of Wonder Woman posters being seized from some comic shops by enthusiastic law enforcement personnel who felt that a woman in a one-piece bathing suit was simply beyond the pale, that this was hardcore.

So because there aren't any functioning laws upon obscenity that actually define what it is, then I suppose it's feasible. Obviously, Chris has talked to lawyers, and they all assure us that *Lost Girls* would be defensible anywhere in America.

So we'll have to see, but the sense that I'm getting from the response so far is overwhelmingly positive. I get a real sense that actually there's a lot of people who have been waiting for something like this. I mean Melinda says that at the San Diego convention, where apparently Chris sold out of the initial five hundred monstrously expensive volumes that he had flown into the country, Melinda was the toast of the convention and was being carried around in a gold sedan and showered with tickertape, at least to hear her tell it.

There were people coming up to Melinda who'd actually bought the book . . . more women than men, including apparently one woman who'd come up the next day with tears in her eyes to thank Melinda for *Lost Girls*. That's a great reaction.

So, anything could happen. When we included *Rite of Spring* at the end of the first book, we did so purely because of its dramatic meaning and the dramatic way that it carried, but since then we've thought there actually are at least some parallels between the *Rite of Spring* and *Lost Girls*.

I'm not by any means associating *Lost Girls* in terms of quality with *Rite of Spring*, which was an absolute blinding masterpiece—at the same time, they're both productions that are largely about sex and death. These are very primal themes. They're both emerging at the beginning of their respective centuries. They're both emerging into worlds where there are very taut political tensions that could explode into horrific war at any moment.

In the original performance of *Rite of Spring*, you've got the audience going absolutely berserk and you had Najinsky—the great Najinsky climbed up onto his chair and was standing there amidst the seething mob and shouting, "You are all stupid!"

So, I suppose that I would hope people who might criticize *Lost Girls* will at least think about how this might look in the future. Do they want to be the prosecuting attorney at the *Lady Chatterly* trial who said, "Do you want your wives or servants reading this kind of book?" and who has been ridiculed ever since for the incredible pomposity of that statement. Would they like to be down in the foam-flecked baying audience of the Paris Opera, or would they like to be up there on the chair with Najinsky? It's a stark choice, you know.

Q: It seems to me like it might be a test for comics. Comics have changed so much in the time period from when you started *Lost Girls* to now. I wonder,

On stage, night had fallen, both acts merging in the time-divorced minds of the audience. Girls, starlit, stamped their circling path and curled their arms to rigid serpent hooks for dragging down the moon.

Ringed by a tide of moving womanhood, a girl was singled out, thus rendered naked; vulnerable; targeted by fate. There in that moment she was all of us, was every young girl plunged into the dark of that experience. She was Miss Dale, caught up in her tornado. Wide-eyed, she was Mrs. Potter, stricken by that primal glimpse between the old, dark trees. The awful knowledge in her eye was mine, led helpless to the looking-glass room by my father's friend.

The brass and percussion stab through the staccato; stab and stab in the rising tempo, stabbing space, stabbing time, stabbing, stabbing... Everyone was lost within the mirrorland of music. Anything could happen. My right hand mapped thunderstorms of static on the silk of Miss Dale's knee. My left was clasped by Mrs. Potter, wondering, to her breast. A rabbit pulse leaped there against the beat.

Lost Girls, chapter 10, page 5, by Alan Moore and Melinda Gebbie. Copyright © 2006, 2009 Alan Moore & Melinda Gebbie, used by permission.

if there isn't an outcry, doesn't that say something about how the American and British public regard graphic novels and comics? They're not this kind of lost, redheaded stepchild anymore.

A: I think that's definitely true, whatever the response to *Lost Girls* is. It's clear that whether they actually deserve to or not, graphic novels have come in from the cold. That's by no means an endorsement of everything that has appeared in the graphic novel format over the past fifteen years. I'd say that, perhaps if there was an outcry over this, perhaps that would indicate that comics are being taken more seriously. I don't know.

One thing that I would observe is that, considering that comics, when I got in them, were considered to be a children's medium, I would remark that it's been possible to do things in comics that I could not have done in any other medium, except, perhaps, possibly prose.

I mean, *From Hell*, the comic book, was something that it would have been impossible to duplicate as a film. The very flat approach to the violence, whereas it works very well in a kind of almost sort of autopsy sense in the comic book. An almost forensic approach to the violence.

If that had been filmed and in color it would have been unendurable. It would have meant something completely different. It would have meant to shock people with viscera, whereas the comic book medium allows you to do something different with it, just as it allows us to do something different with the sex in *Lost Girls*.

I think, perhaps, if people notice just the capabilities of the comics medium as expressed in *Lost Girls*, hopefully that might tempt people to try something a bit more ambitious.

Q: At the same time, in the culture at large and also in comics, I've seen attempts at creating these sex-positive, for want of a better term, works. I know Fantagraphics has published more art-flavored dirty books like *Dirty Stories* and *Small Favors*, and I even saw a book last year called *True Porn*, which was a bunch of people doing comics about their own sexual exploits.

A: Yeah, I think that there was a thing I can remember from a few years ago called *Real Sex*, which was by Dennis Eichhorn. And there have been some very interesting books in the past.

Obviously a huge hero to both me and Melinda is Robert Crumb, along with a lot of the other people who were around at that point, who were real pioneers of this kind of material and broke off a lot of the ground for us.

There are also some standout publications in the interim. I'm thinking of Guy Colwell's *Doll*, which was a miniseries from the mid-eighties, early nineties, that was intelligent and emotional in places. But I still don't think there's been actually anything that is quite as ambitious as *Lost Girls*.

Q: No, definitely not.

A: And I think that extends further than just the confines of the comics industry. I am quite familiar with the history of erotic art and erotic literature, or I have become so over the course of *Lost Girls*, and I don't think there's ever been anything as ambitious as this anywhere in erotica, in the broader field of erotica rather than just comic books. I can't think of anything else.

The Marquis de Sade, of course. Even if his work is quite unpleasant a lot of the time, he is a very important pornographic writer, because he was probably one of the first ones who tried to use it as a kind of social scalpel or something.

But even the Marquis de Sade, after I think fifteen days of Sodom, he threw in the towel. He was bored after fifteen days. After day fifteen, he was ready to pack it in. There's very few sustained and structured pieces of erotica on any kind of scale, let alone the scale of *Lost Girls*.

Someone was gonna do it eventually. Someone was going to attempt it eventually, to do this kind of sustained, ambitious piece of pornography and have it also be a piece of art. I'm just incredibly smug that it was me and Melinda.

We got a letter from Brian Eno a couple of days ago saying he'd seen the book and thought it was fantastic. If we never get another piece of good feedback on the book again I would die a happy man, knowing that one of my great heroes has enjoyed it.

Anybody who might object to it, they really should have done it earlier because we've done it now. If they'd objected at some point during the last fifteen years, during which there were earlier comic book versions that ran for a couple of issues . . .

Q: Yeah, I think I have the original Kitchen Sink issues.

A: Yeah? You're a lucky man. Few people have got that. This has been around for fifteen years, and if people had any serious objections, they perhaps should have raised them before. It's a bit after the fact now. I think this is one horse that has rather bolted. What culture's reaction to that is, that's up to culture.

We've done the best that we possibly can on this and people's reaction to it is entirely up to them, but I hope that they might give it a chance, and they might find it was a beneficial rather than a shocking and demoralizing experience.

Q: Are there any developments with the Ormond hospital?

A: I don't know much about that. They have expressed some sort of concern. Chris has been looking into that along with copyright lawyers. As far as I understand it, the *Peter Pan* book is in the public domain in the United States at the moment and will be in a year over here. And as far as I have understood it, J. M. Barrie only gifted the rights to the stage production to Great Ormond. I might be wrong about that.

I know that Chris and the legal people that he's got on retainer have been looking into all of this and probably Chris could give you a more coherent and lucid update on it than I could.

I don't think it's a major obstacle to me. I guess it might delay the distribution of *Lost Girls* in England, but England is a part of the world market, and it will only delay it. It won't stop it. I'm more or less just talking off the top of my head and don't really know what I'm talking about. You'd be better off getting an informed opinion from Chris or someone.

Q: I can ask him. I still have his phone number. What are you working on now? How do you follow up something like *Lost Girls*?

A: That is a bit of a puzzler isn't it? At the moment, and for the past eighteen months, and into the next eighteen months, I have decided to write another novel. It's going to be over half a million words long, which has gotta be pushing the upper limit of what you can actually get into one physical book.

How am I following up *Lost Girls*? The whole novel is a lucid, coherent, and, I hope, entirely satisfying answer to where do we go when we die? So, I've decided to solve the entire problem of life, death, and mortality in my forthcoming novel, *Jerusalem*.

It's completely mental. It's the most personal thing I've ever written. It's all about the place where I grew up, and a lot of it's about my family, with the names changed to protect the guilty.

It deals with a lot of issues of which life and death and human continuity are only one. It's talking about poverty. It's talking about race. It's talking about history. It's talking about Jerusalem. It's talking about William Blake and Charlie Chaplin and various other people who are connected to this area by some unusual threads.

It's gonna take me about another eighteen months just to finish the first draft. Then I'm gonna have to go through it. I've got my very good friend Steve Moore who is editing it brutally and covering it with red pen as I go through it. Just correcting my sloppy grammar and my freewheeling Marx

Brothers approach to dates and history and facts and things like that. By the time it's in the readers' hands, it will all make some sense.

Q: What kind of comics are you doing? Anything more with comics?
A: Well, I'm pretty much out of comics, with the exception of *The League of Extraordinary Gentlemen*. Kevin is just finishing *The Black Dossier*, which is the last piece of work that will be emerging from Wildstorm/ABC/DC comics.

That is an idea which incidentally grew out of *Lost Girls*. I'd such a good time working with previously established fictional characters in a pornography, I suddenly thought, "I wonder if this would work in an adventure story?" That was pretty much where *League of Extraordinary Gentlemen* came from.

Lost Girls is an idea that has got a certain length. Once the women have told their stories, that is the end of the book. Whereas *The League of Extraordinary Gentlemen*, it's limitless. And so, yes, we're finishing off the *Black Dossier*, which should be out by the end of the year. I finished it a while ago. Kevin's just doing the final sequences of it.

Then after that, probably through Top Shelf, we'll be doing Volume III of *The League of Extraordinary Gentlemen*, which will be structured a bit differently. It won't be six thirty-two-page comic books. It will perhaps be three seventy-two-page comic books, so that we'll be able to tell a complete story in each book so that it won't be too tantalizing a wait between issues for the reader. But so that the three books will eventually build up into an overarching story comprising the third volume.

And after that, there's plenty of other things that Kevin and me could do. I know that Melinda's working on an illustrated version of the William Blake piece that I did as a performance over here four or five years ago, a piece called "Angel Passage," which has been out on CD from Top Shelf, but which Melinda wanted to do an illustrated version of that.

I know that José Villarrubia is working upon an illuminated version of a passage from my first CD. It's a section of the CD which is called "The Book of Calculations." I know that José was doing an illustrated version of that that he's working on.

So, there'll be things coming out in all sorts of forms, I'm sure. Probably I will not be working in comics, certainly to the extent that I have been, again. That is the last of it for me. At the moment, it's mainly *The League of Extraordinary Gentlemen* that is the ongoing comics project.

But that's not to say that there won't be others that will occur to me down the line, but at least for the moment and for the next couple of years that's likely to be the main thing.

Q: Is it just that you want to focus on other things, like the book?

A: Yeah. It's partly that I am a bit fed up with the comics industry. I've had a hell of a time in those last couple of years with all that business over the *V for Vendetta* filming. It was an exhausting war of attrition. I'd rather be writing.

And also I think that the comics industry, really, if it wants to attract, if it wants to be talked about as a grown-up medium, then it ought to be a medium that will attract grown-ups, in terms of its right as an artist [sic].

It ought to be a grown-up medium. It ought to grow up in its business practices, rather than have them still rooted in the prohibition-era gangsterism of the 1930s. If it really wants to be an industry that's proud of itself, then it really shouldn't go around alienating the talent that has actually lifted it up out of the quagmire.

That is obviously something that is not in my control. It is purely in the industry's control. I think that having spent twenty-five years laboring within the comics industry, that has probably reflected better on the comics industry than it did on me. Probably the comics industry got more out of the association than I did.

While comics remains a medium that I love dearly and that I think has got immense ground yet to be broken within it, there are things that I would much rather be doing. You reach fifty and the math starts to add up a bit differently. Whichever way you shape it, you're certainly more than halfway through your life. So you have to think a bit more carefully about what it is you want to do and who it is you want to do it in association with.

And *Jerusalem*, I've been working at it every day. I'm probably working harder than before I retired, but a lot more joyfully. I'm getting up to the quarter-million-word mark and it's been a pleasure so far. I'm looking forward to getting it finished so everyone else can see what it is that I'm on about. It should be worth the wait I think.

Q: Two last questions and then I'll leave you alone. I just wanted to get back for a minute to your collaboration with Melinda. You mentioned that she liked stories where there are three women. Why is that?

A: It's just something that she found from her early self-penned work that she found that she had a facility for and that she enjoyed.

I remember one story called "My Three Swans" that I think was featured in *The Smithsonian Book of Comics [The New Smithsonian Book of Comic-Book Stories]*. But she had done a couple of other pieces as well that had just got three women characters in them, and I just thought that she'd like the dynamic. It just seemed to make stories live for her in some way. I don't know if there's anything very logical behind it.

As with my writing, or with any artist's work, we sometimes don't know exactly why a certain thing works for us and a certain thing doesn't. I think it was purely that in her own early work she had always been attracted to that kind of a story, that kind of a dynamic. You'd have to ask her about that, and I'm afraid that she's not here at the moment.

Q: You talked a little bit about how the collaboration was a very new experience for you, and I was just wondering if you could go into a little more detail. Was it a more enjoyable experience than say, writing something like *Watchmen* or *Swamp Thing*, where you had to do it all on your end first and then send the pages off?

A: Well, it was a much more intense experience than *Watchmen* or any of the other books, because of the nature of the work. Obviously, if you're doing a work of this nature, then you have to be completely frank about your ideas, your thoughts, in a way that probably other partners in relationships might not ever necessarily reach that point.

I mean, this was how we started our relationship, with that complete frankness. And I think that our relationship and the comic book both benefited each other. I don't think that there would have been the warmth that there is in *Lost Girls* if we hadn't been partners in an emotional sense, opposed to just a collaborative sense. I also think that probably our relationship has benefited from the amount of exploring of ideas and concepts and talking that we had to do about some raw emotional issues in the course of this book. I think that the two of them have benefited each other greatly.

That was the most striking thing about working on the book. Yes, the fact that technically I worked upon it very differently, that was unusual. But I have modified my work methods before.

If someone were to ask me, I would say that the secret to a strong relationship is to collaborate on a sprawling, epic work of pornography together.

The *Mustard* Interview: Alan Moore

ALEX MUSSON AND ANDREW O'NEILL / 2009

Mustard 2.4 (March 2009): 14–21, 28–34. Reprinted by permission of Alex Musson, editor, *Mustard Magazine*.

The below is nearly the complete *Mustard* interview, which spliced together a 2005 and a 2009 conversation. Edited out are some brief sidebars wherein Moore talks about some of his older work, mostly covered in greater detail elsewhere in this book. EB

Alan Moore sinks into a chair behind the coffee table in his home, an unassuming terraced house in Northampton. Bookshelves, tables, and parts of the floor overflow with impressive looking volumes and occult paraphernalia. Comparatively, the kitchen—into which we follow him, tape recorder in hand, at several points during the afternoon—is like any you would come across in Midlands suburbia. Moore himself is a similar contradiction. He cuts an imposing Rasputin-like figure, impressive of hair and beard, with snake walking cane and skull-ringed fingers, but his manner is extremely warm, and his Northampton accent belies a massive intellect. And boy, can he talk . . .

Q: Do you see humour primarily as a tool for developing character, as comic relief, or simply for its own sake?
A: I see it as an invaluable tool, as all of them are. It's one of the notes on the piano that I've got to play on. If you've had a really horrific scene, then to strike a note of humour at exactly the right point without diffusing the horror can give it an entirely new contrast. I mean, some things I like to do just for their own sake. Just because I think they're funny.

Jack B. Quick is the thing which, since *Bojeffries*, made me laugh the most when I was writing it. There's a story called, "I, Robert" where he comes up with an artificial intelligence which is just a scarecrow, a tape-recorder, and some junk in a wheelbarrow. But it passes the Turing test authentically. So these things are mass-produced all over the world and eventually take over. Even though they're just a scarecrow. So, eventually Jack comes up with the solution as to how to overthrow the robots—the "Roberts"—which is: "If we just stop pushing the wheelbarrows . . . they'll be helpless." When I wrote it, I thought, "Actually, I've just said something profound there." Probably the answer to all mankind's technological problems. If we just stop pushing the wheelbarrows, they'll be helpless.

In some instances, I just want to do comedy for its own sake, but comedy that makes people think about ideas in a different way. But most things benefit from a little touch of comedy here and there. Except perhaps funerals. Wait, no! I went and did the reading at my great friend Tom Hall's funeral. One of the finest musicians Northampton's ever produced. The best funeral I've ever been to, and I got some great jokes into my reading. There was another guy I knew that ran a local heating company, The Dimmer Brothers. At the end of his funeral, his brother said, "Trevor chose this piece of music because he wanted to be remembered for his contributions to the plumbing and heating industry." And, as they went out of the church, they were playing *Rawhide*, because he was a cowboy. Everybody was walking out of the church laughing and weeping. That's gotta work. Everything benefits from a bit of humour. I mean, this is probably a bad thing to say to someone from a comedy magazine, but I don't like genre. I think that genre was something made up by some spotty clerk in W. H. Smith's in the 1920s to make his worthless fucking job a little bit easier for him. "It'd be easier if these books said what they were about on the spine." My experience of life is that it is not divided up into genres. It's a horrifying, romantic, tragic, comical, science-fiction, cowboy, detective novel. You know, with a bit of pornography if you're lucky.

In the novel I'm writing, *Jerusalem*, there's an awful lot of funny stuff, and there's supernatural stuff. There's stuff in the prologue that's as good as Stephen King, and it's just a description of walking through a block of flats. It's horror. And there's social history. There's political stuff. Why not mix it all together? Because that's what life is actually like. We laugh. We cry. You know, we buy the t-shirt.

Q: What can you tell us about the new *League of Extraordinary Gentlemen*?
A: This third book has been a very liberating experience because we're now working with Top Shelf, a publisher that we trust. We were quite surprised to find ourselves thinking in a different way to when doing a project for a mainstream comics publisher. There's a kind of "Boy's Adventure Comic" mindset that seems to settle over you when you've been working in that medium for a

few decades. You've absorbed the requirement that there should be a strong action-driven plot that will carry the reader through the narrative. The early volumes of *The League* were pretty much relentless action. Even *Black Dossier* had an extended chase sequence. But with this new volume we've taken a different approach.

We've also undoubtedly got a lot of rancour out of our system. Particularly in the first issue, which Kevin [O'Neill] was drawing just after he finished up all the last remaining bits and pieces for Wildstorm/DC. There's an awful lot of anger that we've channeled into the work! [laughs]

The third volume is called *Century*, because the story takes place in three eras during a hundred-year period. It's coming out in three seventy-two-page volumes, each of which is a self-contained story, so that readers won't have a cliffhanger between episodes. "Century" isn't a reference to how long it'll take us to do it. [laughs] Kevin's working really hard on it, and I don't want to rush him, because the end result will be so exquisite. So, if there is a delay between chapters, we're hoping that it won't be a nail-biting wait for the reader. We've made each chapter complete in itself, but they all build up to a fairly stunning climax.

There's a strand of narrative running through all three chapters that's based around the occult fiction that was coming out at around the turn of the century. It incorporates Aleister Crowley's *Moonchild*, which was set around the time of the First World War. We've got the same characters at a slightly earlier period. We've also got a pseudo-Crowley character. We've taken all the various fictional Crowleys, of which there have been a tremendous number, and tried to ingeniously work them together so that they can all be the same person. The real Crowley took on so many different pseudonyms and identities throughout his life that, actually, it's quite realistic.

The main one we're using is Oliver Haddo from Somerset Maugham's *The Magician*, who was trying to invent an artificial magical child in the form of a homunculus, which is coincidentally what the magicians in Crowley's *Moonchild* are trying to do. We've also worked in M. R. James's Carswell from *Casting the Runes*, Anthony Powell's Dr. Trelawney from *A Dance to the Music of Time*, Dr. Hjalmar Poelzig, the satanic architect from the Boris Karloff film, *The Black Cat*, Adrian Marcato, a figure based on Crowley who's mentioned in [Roman Polanski's film] *Rosemary's Baby* and the similarly named Mocata, the black magician in [Terence Fisher's film, based on Dennis Wheatley's novel] *The Devil Rides Out*.

Also, when we get to the 1960s part of the action, there are minor figures from *The Avengers* episode "Warlock," which featured a bearded dark-haired figure called Cosmo Gallion who resembled a younger, mountaineering-period Crowley and went around saying, "Do what thou wilt." We've tied all these together with the details of Crowley's actual life to provide a continuing plot thread that runs through all three books, giving us the overarching storyline.

So, the first chapter is set in 1910, the whole Belle Époque era. As always, we've used elements from fictions that were created in or set around that period. The main inspiration is Berthold Brecht's *Threepenny Opera*, which was set at the coronation of King George in 1910, the year Halley's Comet was going over. From looking at the first German film versions, I believe it was originally set in London, and although Brecht was basing the story on John Gay's *Beggar's Opera*, about the highwayman MacHeath, he must have also been influenced by Jack the Ripper in his creation of Mac the Knife.

We've got Pirate Jenny and Mac the Knife as characters, and we've managed to conflate Mac with fictional versions of Jack the Ripper. It's not *From Hell*. I'm not dealing with the stories that were told in reality about Jack the Ripper. I'm dealing purely with the way he was treated in fiction. These include Frank Wedekind's *Earth Spirit*, made into the [Georg Wilhelm] Pabst film *Pandora's Box*, where, in the final scene, good-time girl Lulu takes home a customer that turns out to be Jack the Ripper—even though the setting of 1910 suggests its about twenty years too late. We've done something which makes sense of that, and we've also tied in the brilliant Peter O'Toole film, *The Ruling Class*—a hysterically funny, incisive picture of the British class system and its various madness—which has a coda that again connects with Jack the Ripper.

There's also a visit to an occult detectives club, where characters like Algernon Blackwood's John Silence and [Arthur Machen's] Mr. [Charles] Phillips are sitting around congratulating each other like a bunch of luvvies.

With the second book, we move on to the 1960s and a sequence set in 1969 in swinging London where we're dealing with a load of cult films of that era. Kevin's just started to pencil that one now, and he's having fun recreating the Soho of that period. It wasn't that long ago, but it's completely changed. Kevin didn't trust his memory that practically every shop was a sex shop, but looking back at the photos, it's true! It was as seedy and glamorous as we remember. He's having a lot of fun doing that.

The third part will be set in 2009, and I'm writing that at the moment. It will be bang up-to-date, using fictional characters from the present day. Obviously, we'll have to be quite delicate with some of them, given copyright laws, but the fictional present day is every bit as exotic as the fictional Victorian era. Me and Kevin are enjoying it immensely. It's looking tremendous. The colouring that Ben Dimagmaliw has done is wonderful. It gives it a completely different look. I can't wait to see what he does with the 1960s version, where we're going a bit psychedelic in some of the sequences.

Q: And there's a text story at the back as in the previous volumes?
A: Yes, it was a fairly last minute thing. Kevin said he'd had the preposterous idea of setting a League story on the Moon. No particular reason. He just fancied drawing the Moon. So I started thinking about all the fictional stories that relate to the Moon and realised there's an incredible wealth of material.

There's Lucian, the first person to describe being taken to the Moon by waterspout, and Baron Munchausen who copied him. There was a Northampton man in the 1600s called [Francis] Godwin, who entranced young ladies with his claims of a voyage to the Moon in a goose-pulled chariot. We're also referring to H. G. Wells's *The First Men in the Moon*, Jules Verne's *From the Earth to the Moon*, and the film *Amazon Women on the Moon* quite prominently.

We've worked out a history of the moon that actually makes sense. When our story opens there are various Earth settlements because, in the science fiction of the period, the Americans, Germans, Russians, and French were all writing about places on the Moon. And there's a war going on between the two native lunar species: Wells's giant insect Selenites, and the naked Amazonian women.

We've tied in lots of old pulp books. We've got some Clangers, the Soup Dragon [both from the BBC animated TV series *Clangers*], and a few black monoliths [from *2001: A Space Odyssey*] which we've used to explain why some areas of the Moon had oxygen for Lucian, Munchausen, and Godwin.

Q: So, it's prose with Kevin doing illustrations?
A: Yes, and this time we're pretending it's in a 1960s sci-fi magazine, based on Mike Moorcock's excellent *New Worlds*. Apparently, when *New Worlds* was going through all the trouble with W. H. Smith's, with all the outrage about its sexual content, Brian Aldiss suggested they change the title to *Lewd Worlds*. So, our story is *Minions of the Moon*, as serialised in *Lewd Worlds of Science Fiction*, edited by James Colvin, a Moorcock pseudonym who, he claimed in an editorial in the late sixties, had been killed under a filing cabinet filled with rejected manuscripts. And as the author, we've used "John Thomas," an old pseudonym of John Sladek, one of my favorite *New Worlds* authors.

It's intricate and demented fun. *The Black Dossier* was a bit of a gamble, something we really wanted to do, but we were a bit apprehensive that most of the audience might be enamoured of the Victorian material and might abandon us in droves if we moved it into the twentieth century. But it sold better than the preceding books, which suggests that there's an audience out there who are more interested in the century they grew up in. Hopefully that will be the case with this third volume.

[We now move on to Alan's novel *Jerusalem*—first here's a snippet from our interview with him in late 2005:]

Q: What can you tell us about *Jerusalem* at this point?

A: I decided that my first novel, *Voice of the Fire*, which was purely set in Northampton, was much too far-reaching and cosmopolitan, and I really ought to stick with what I know. So the next one, which is going to be a much bigger novel by the looks of it, is going to be about the few blocks that I grew up on. The novel after that is going to be about my living room, or this armchair [laughs].

Jerusalem all came to me in a rush. Having turned fifty, the odd thought of mortality does occur to you. Realistically, you've got about twenty-five years, you know? That's half what you've had already, and you know how quick that went. So, there's nothing to be scared of, I don't think, but it might do to examine some of these thoughts rather than shut them out. To say, okay, "What do I really think about life and death and all of this stuff that we seem to be involved in."

Einstein and Hawking seem to agree that this is a four-dimensional universe, with the fourth spatial dimension being what we *perceive* as time. So, it's not that the fourth dimension *is* time. It's more like time is the shadow of the fourth dimension, and it's only our perception that we're moving through it.

I realized I've touched upon this, seemingly, throughout my entire writing career. I've got stories about this sort of notion in *2000 AD*. There's Dr. Manhattan's view of time in *Watchmen* and all the stuff in *From Hell*.

C. Howard Hinton, one of the Victorian mathematicians who first proposed a mathematical fourth dimension said you'd have to suppose that it's only our *awareness* that we're moving through time. That nothing is actually changing. The universe is a four-dimensional solid, like a great big egg, with the Big Bang at one end, the Big Crunch at the other end, and every moment that has ever or will ever exist suspended, forever, in between.

So, if this is the case, you'd have to think of a human life as being a fourth-dimensional shape which is about 6 foot 3 foot by 2 foot deep, by about seventy years long. So, I imagine it'd look a bit like a centipede. Something like that, with [Eadweard] Muybridge arms, the multiple arms and legs. But these things would be little filaments in the giant egg of space-time, and they'd be suspended there forever.

So, your birth and your death are no more meaningful than the soles of your shoes and the top of your head. I don't exist 6 foot 4 above sea level. That is not a great cause for concern to me. If you start to see birth and death as things in a physical geography where time is ignored, then, does that mean that—forget reincarnation and heaven and everything like that—we just have our lives over and over and over again? That this is not the first time we've been here having this conversation? That in some senses we've already been dead for centuries, and in another sense our most remote ancestors have not yet been born?

It would also mean that we don't have free will and would explain things like déjà vu and premonitions. It would also suggest that we are already outside the third dimension. We're reading this, reviewing it. If you think of our lives as a book, a narrative, when you finish the last page of the book, "The End," and close it, the book doesn't self-destruct. It's still there, all the characters and the events of their lives are still there, in one entity, in one thing. And I wonder if it might be something like that.

[Finishing the tea he's been making:] Now, what was the sugars arrangement again? Help yourself to the milk.

So, Schopenhauer said that it wasn't just space that exploded out of the primal particle—it was space-time. He said God does not create the universe in the transitive sense but in the immanent sense, which means that God didn't create the universe ten billion years ago and then just walk off and do something else, but God, or this notion of "God," creates the universe nanosecond by nanosecond. Every instant. Which is a lovely, mind-boggling idea.

Anyway, this thinking was just for the purposes of fiction. I don't know if that really is what happens, but since I've had the idea, it's been eerily difficult to disprove.

So, for *Jerusalem*, my idea was, "What if we were already dead and our third dimensional lives were almost like a book or a drama that we could review from outside time, in whatever existence we may have there—that this life might just be a third-dimensional facet of a fourth-dimensional structure?" We might be like little barnacles or something, growing on the outside of space-time.

And if this is true, then everything is fourth-dimensional: me, everybody I know. This matchbox has a fourth-dimensional equivalent that I can't

perceive. This room, this house, this street, this neighbourhood, every neighbourhood, every town—are there fourth-dimensional towns unfolded above
these? Sort of timeless, where everything is there forever?

So, I began to think of this in light of the few miserable blocks where I grew
up, "The Boroughs," a square mile of dirt, a horrible area. It's the red light
district. There's a prostitute who gets beaten and raped—it's reported every
month. It happens every week. There was a Somali guy threatening to kill
himself under armed police siege. My sister-in-law's cousin strangled his wife
in a block of flats there. It's been the poorest area of the town for the last few
hundred years, and it's a fucking hellhole. Nothing good ever happens there.

If you start looking back beyond the 1500s, that area was the whole town.
It was Northampton, which means Shakespeare's *King John* opens at the end
of our street, where he had his castle. This was where three of the Crusades
were raised by Richard the Lionheart; where the first ever poll tax was raised,
which led to Wat Tyler's revolt in the 1380s; where the first ever parliament in
the world was raised.

And now, it's the station where the sex workers arrive from Milton Keynes
and Rugby. There's an overnight truck park at the other end of Andrews Road,
rich pickings for the vice girls. So, you've got these crack-head prostitutes in
the area where Thomas à Becket was condemned. He ducked out, got on a
horse, rode down Andrews Road and eventually got to France for the next
three years, before returning and getting killed in the Abbey.

Charlie Chaplin did his first ever stage performance at the New Variety
theatre on the corner of the Boroughs, the junction with Horseshoe Street
and Gold Street. Y'know, this starts to get a bit suspicious. Philip Doddridge
was the man who basically introduced nonconformism into English religion
and totally changed the face of the Church of England. He did it all from the
Castle Hill Ministry, which is right in this square mile of dirt.

Oliver Cromwell rode out with Fairfax from the Boroughs, from Marefair,
just up from the station, when he went to finish the English Civil War up at
Naseby. The War of the Roses concluded in Cow Meadow, just at the fringe
of the Boroughs. That was where the king was captured. Henry the Sixth, I
think. This is a tiny insignificant area. It's worse than insignificant. It's a black
hole. It's ASBO [Anti-Social Behavioral Order] land, you know? One of the
chapters of *Jerusalem* is going to be called "ASBO's of Desire."

And I also thought, my family came from this place for about three genera-
tions. Let's have a look at my family history. Of course, once you open those
kinds of closets . . . there's not just skeletons. I've got entire ossuaries. You
could reassemble tyrannosauruses from what I've got in my closet. We found

madness, incest . . . deep, tragic things that, if they'd happened to kings or queens in antiquity, would have been the subject of classic tragedy. But they didn't. They happened to working-class scumbags in this forgotten area that nobody cared about. And this is the way it goes with history. We only ever get the history of Church and State. Because none of the rest of us matter. Yet there is this fantastic history, the history in people's families, in people's neighbourhoods.

So, all of these ideas kind of churned up together and blossomed into this book that's got hold of me called *Jerusalem*. I've written the first chapter in ten days. It's thirty pages, something like that. The first chapter of *Voice of the Fire* was sixty pages long and took me six months. This is just pouring out.

I don't usually rewrite. The only think I rewrote with *Voice of the Fire* was the last chapter, because I'd written it in a bit of a hurry as I thought the deadline was looming sooner than it was. Then it turned out that I'd got an extra couple of months. So I rewrote it, and it was much better. With this one, I've written it and printed it out, and now I'm going back and painstakingly polishing it. I figure that's how I'll do it: write each chapter in a rush and polish it before moving on to the next one. It's got a building feeling to it. Each chapter is like a little brick, and I've got this three-part architectural construction that I'm starting to plan out, and if I make each of the bricks perfect, then it will be a real cathedral of a book.

[Pulling tobacco and papers from his pocket] Sorry, is it all right if I smoke by the way? I'm having a little bit of tobacco withdrawal.

[Okay, now back to 2009]

Q: So, how's *Jerusalem* been coming on since we spoke three-and-a-bit years ago?

A: *Jerusalem* is the biggest project I'm doing, the one that obsesses me the most. Immediately after I last spoke to you, I decided it was insane to work on the cover of what was going to be a thirty-five-chapter book, so I'd better stop. I'm really glad that I did, because a cover for what the book was going to be about then wouldn't have been appropriate to what the book has developed into. I've still got that partially drawn cover, and I'm waiting until the book's finished, at least the first draft. Then I'll go back and finish it.

The idea of carefully polishing each chapter as soon as I finished it also went out the window. I got into the momentum of the novel and started turning out chapters, planning to go back and check them later. Round about this time, I started to employ my great friend and mentor Steve Moore as an editor. I was determined not to have a publishing house editor near this book, but I wanted someone to pick up my spelling errors or the bits where I'd been unclear or done something stylistically embarrassing. On that level, Steve's one of the best editors in the business. He learned how to edit old school through the various children's comics he worked on in the sixties. I had Steve editing the various chapters of the first book—*Jerusalem* divides into three parts. There are eleven chapters in each part, a prologue, and an epilogue. When I got to the end of the first book, I went back and revised the previous twelve chapters according to Steve's revisions, but as the book has progressed, and I've realised what a huge and complex thing it is, I've told him to hold off until I've got the whole thing finished. We'll have to do a huge editing job and a final revision before it's ready for publication.

As for the actual writing of the book, I'm on chapter twenty-six of thirty-five, exactly at the three-quarter mark. I'm only just starting to realise the scale of the thing and how it's all going to come together. I've had the blueprint of how to do it from the very beginning. When I spoke to you, I had about thirty-five chapter titles—smartarse titles like "ASBO's of Desire." I'd written a couple of lines of notes under each title suggesting what they might be about and arranged them into sensible order, into three books, three parts of the same narrative. Not like *Lord of the Rings*. It's not a trilogy. It's one book of enormous length.

I realised when I was a few chapters in that if I kept on at that sort of rate, the finished novel would be somewhere between half and three-quarters of a million words, which is the biggest thing I've ever written. When I got to the opening chapters of this third and final part of *Jerusalem*, I was starting to feel the burn and realise what an enormous task I set myself. I also thought, "I don't have to do this." It was arbitrary. I just came up with thirty-five titles. If I hadn't made the book this long, I wouldn't have hit this initially worrying stretch, when I thought, "Can I keep up the energy for these last ten or so chapters?" And the answer is: "It's up to me." The way to sustain a narrative over that incredible length is pretty obviously to crank up the energy. So, I'm making these final chapters the most sparkly and experimental in the book.

The one I'm doing at the moment is based upon Lucia Joyce, James Joyce's daughter who spent the last thirty years of her life in St. Andrew's Hospital, the mental institution next door to the school I used to attend. I've got this story about Lucia wandering through the madhouse grounds. She's also coming unstuck in space and time a little bit. She's wandering in her own mind. I decided to write this in an approximation of her dad's language.

It was doing that, and being quite pleased with how it turned out, that made me resolve that each of the final chapters of this book should be just as ambitious. One will be in the form of a Samuel Beckett play, which is relevant because Beckett used to come to Northampton to visit Lucia. He was very fond of her, even if he didn't love her like she wanted him to. They were certainly close friends, and I believe he used to come and visit her grave after she died. And he once played cricket against Northampton. He's got an entry in *Wisden [Cricketers' Almanac]*. That night his cricketing colleagues went out drinking and whoring, and he went out on a church crawl. He went round all these gothic churches he'd heard about in Northampton. So that chapter is partly about Samuel Beckett on his church crawl, written in Beckett's style.

I hope these final chapters will be experimental enough to push this novel over the finishing line, to resolve the multitude of themes and ideas that have developed in the course of this book. It's turning into a huge beast, but I'm really excited about it.

Q: There seems to be recurring elements. *Jerusalem* and *Century* both come in three parts and feature chapters written in different genre styles. *Century* features Jack the Ripper, as did *From Hell* . . .
A: He also turns up in the section I'm writing for *Jerusalem* right now! It's part of Lucia Joyce's wander in the madhouse woods. She's just had an encounter with John Clare and has now bumped into the unpleasant shade of J. K. Stephen, who was a misogynist poet (not a very good one) and, briefly, a Ripper suspect. He died in St. Andrew's Hospital, as did John Clare. I've just been in Joycean language writing the exchange between him and Lucia, in which I've managed to encode, into this casual conversation, the names of all five canonical Ripper victims, in order, and the addresses where they met their end. I'm having a lot of fun with it.

There are also references to *Alice in Wonderland*, almost like a reprise to *Lost Girls*. But that's because James Joyce identified his daughter with Lewis Carroll's Alice. "Lucia" is almost an anagram of "Alice."

There are certainly scenes that have been recurring in my work since the earliest days. Things in some of those early 2000 AD *Future Shocks* are connected with things I'm doing in *Jerusalem*. We all have obsessions that haunt us and that recur, that we're probably trying to figure out, in one form or another, all the way through our careers or our lives. *Jerusalem* looks to be the most ambitious thing I've ever attempted, and, at the moment, I feel it's probably the best thing I've ever done. This is the work I'll want to be remembered for—just because it's something I'm doing completely on my own, unlike the things I've done before, which have mostly been collaborations. I'm very proud of *Voice of the Fire*, but this is more ambitious, although inevitably it picks up on a few of the same themes, as it's set in a smaller version of the same area.

It's very exciting. The whole middle section of the book is like a demented children's story. It's a completely different style to the chapters of the first part of *Jerusalem*. We're suddenly following a gang of dead children as they tunnel about through time in a kind of fourth-dimensional afterlife, where they watch a couple of angels having a punch-up, or visit Oliver Cromwell sleeping restlessly in Northampton just after the Battle of Naseby. All of these things, real or mythical, are a part of the landscape of the book. And the third part is different again. It's several books in one, but I hope it fits together in an ingenious fashion, so it won't be too much of a disorienting experience for the reader. This is the only chapter that's in a made-up language, and it's not the first one, like it was in *Voice of the Fire*. So, people will have a chance to get used to the book before hitting the hard chapter.

I'd say, other than this final section, it's probably more accessible writing than I can remember doing before. There are a number of interwoven difficult concepts, and I decided that I should express this stuff in as clear a language as possible, so it was accessible to the readers and wouldn't put them off. I'm having a bit of a lapse with this James Joyce chapter [laughs], but by and large it is a very accessible book.

It's been a fantastic experience, and I'm learning a lot about myself as a writer. In about a year, I hope to get it finished, at least the first draft. Maybe in another couple of years, it'll be ready for publication. That's the plan. I think it'll be worth the wait.

Q: Which of your works do you actually have the rights to?
A: Kevin O'Neill and I own *League*, which is why I was able to take it away from DC with such a flourish when they offended me over the *V for Vendetta* film. For the other ABC titles, we still get royalties, but we don't own them, because when I made that non-creator-owned deal, it was with Jim Lee, who's an officer and a gentleman. And then Jim got bought out by DC.

There's a brilliant book that I'd advise you to get called *Men of Tomorrow* by Gerard Jones. Rick Veitch turned me on to it, saying, "This explains why everybody at DC acted so fucking weird when we worked there in the mid-eighties." I'd always known that Harry Donenfeld, the man who put DC together, was a confederate and a close associate of gangsters. But *which* gangsters was a surprise, because it was Meyer Lansky, Lucky Luciano, and Bugsy Siegel!

You know, I love the comic medium. It is one that I shall never abandon. But the industry—in fact, increasingly all forms of industry—it's dark satanic mills. And in all my experience of them, these people are gangsters by any other name. They might not be Meyer Lansky or Bugsy Siegel, but they are gangsters, and I don't see why we put up with them, why we don't just take them out and shoot them. Is that a bit extreme?

Q: Several of your books have been dumbed-down for movie versions. There seems to be a kind of dumb feedback loop in cinema. Most films have so little depth that people lose the ability to watch anything more complex . . .

A: I agree, except that I would probably have a bleaker view—that it has already been going on for a couple of decades, and is now so entrenched that there does not appear to be any possible hope of a cultural recovery. It's an extreme view. It's cranky, and it is kind of born of my recent problems with the movie industry that led to me quitting DC Comics in a snit forever—which was great, very liberating and I feel fantastic about it—but which also really got me thinking about films.

Back at the start of my career, I met with Terry Gilliam to talk about the *Watchmen* film, and he said, "How would you make a film of *Watchmen*?" And I said, "Well, frankly, if anybody had bothered to consult me before this point, I would have said, 'I wouldn't.'" And I think he eventually came to agree.

I'd written *Watchmen* expressly because, on one level, I was a bit tired of this easy analogy between comics and movies that some of the most intelligent people in my medium still trot out without really thinking about. I mean, undoubtedly, someone who understands cinematic storytelling is going to be a better comic writer or artist than somebody who doesn't. Will Eisner went to see *Citizen Kane* thirty times. That's all fine.

The problem is that if comics are always seen in terms of cinema, then ultimately they can only be a film that doesn't move and doesn't have a soundtrack. With *Watchmen*, I wanted to find those things which were unfilmable, that could only be done in a comic. So, for example, we had split-level narratives with a little kid reading a comic book, a newsvendor going into a right-wing rant next to him, and something else going on in the background in captions, all at the same time and interrelated.

These are the things you can do in a comic, but not even the greatest director in the world could manage, not even if they cram the backgrounds with sight gags, like Terry Gilliam, who would in many ways have been the best director for *Watchmen*. It's not the same as reading a comic, where you can flip back a few pages and look at a detail that Dave Gibbons put into the background to see if it really connects up with that image that you remember from a chapter or so back.

Whenever I read a film review where the critic has exhausted their repertoire of things that are nasty to say about a film, they'll accuse it of having a "comic book plot," or "comic book dialogue," and I think, "By that, do you mean illiterate? Is that the subtext there?" Because you need to be quite literate to read most of the comics that I write, or that I'm interested in. Whereas, actually, you don't need to be literate to watch a film.

This is not to say that there haven't been wonderful films made. What was it that was on the other day? *Orphée*—one of my favorites, Jean Cocteau. Now *there's* special effects. He wants to have somebody walking into a mirror, so instead of throwing a million dollars at it to get a CGI effect, he fills a tray with mercury and turns the camera on its side. It must have cost him about five quid! That's fantastic. I adore that. That's magic, the magic of cinema.

So, I started to think about films and why don't I really enjoy very many of them. One thing is, I think that the medium has had certain flaws since its inception. Not the industry, the *medium*. Cinema is technologically, and therefore financially, intensive. So, inevitably, you end up with accountants making the decisions, rather than creators. Sure, occasionally a good film will slip through the net, but that still leaves you with a medium where 99 percent of the product—particularly in these Hollywood-governed times—is shit.

My daughter was saying the other day, "Yes, Dad, but 99 percent of everything is shit. It's Sturgeon's Law." And I quite agree. There are plenty of shit comic books, novels, and record albums—but they don't cost 100 million dollars to make. And when you're talking about sums like that, which is probably, what, the food or education budget for an emerging Third World nation? That's where it starts to cross over a line from being a little bit distasteful, to actually being evil.

I also don't like the immersive quality of film. In nearly every other medium, the audience is in control of the way in which they experience the work. At an art gallery, you can just glance at a painting, or stand there for a quarter of an hour, or come back to it. If you read a book and you're feeling a bit tired, you can put it to one side. You can read at your own pace. But with a film, you're dragged through the experience at an unvarying twenty-four frames a second.

Everything is being done for you. There's no space for the imagination. In a book, you have to create the smells, the sounds, the people's faces, their voices, the whole ambience, all from the code of printed words on a page. That's wonderful. You're having to do a little bit of work. And I think that the little bit of work is what most of us, in truth, genuinely enjoy about good art. But now we have this spoon-fed culture, which movies have got to take an awful lot of the blame for.

Q: Can I play devil's advocate and ask if there's any upside to the *Watchmen* movie?

A: Well, Warner Brothers have behaved, in my opinion, appallingly badly, even by their standards, by putting pressure on me indirectly via my friend Steve Moore, a man to whom I owe my entire career and who is currently coping with a terminally ill brother. They'd offered Steve the job of writing the *Watchmen* film novelisation. He'd done a great adaptation of *V for Vendetta*, and they knew he was the only person that I'd give the okay to. This looked like a ray of light in a very dark time for Steve, as he hasn't worked for several years.

Then they announced they were going to bring out *Tales of the Black Freighter* as a full comic, a facsimile of the one the kid reads in *Watchmen*. I didn't think it was a very good idea, as it's a bit like taking all the counterpoint out of Mozart and releasing it on its own record. But Dave Gibbons wanted to do it, and he's a lovely man who I have a lot of respect for, and I know he's got a completely different approach to this film than I have. So I said it was fine, and Dave said, "Yeah, DC Comics said you'd be quietly compliant." And I said, "Why did they say that? Have they forgotten who I am?" [laughs] He said he didn't know, that it was a cryptic comment to him.

I said it was fine, as long as my name's not on it. Dave said, "Don't worry. They're going to use the fictional author's name from the book." Then I thought, "Hang on. If nobody's name's on it, how will anyone know who wrote it?" I said to Dave, "Can they put a note on the inside cover saying, "Alan Moore is not participating in this project?" He said that sounded reasonable.

I heard shortly thereafter that it wouldn't be going ahead. Then Steve Moore heard out of the blue from Warner Brothers that they weren't going to do the novelisation. He wouldn't be getting the work, and I realised what they meant by "quietly compliant."

You can imagine, I was quite cross. I wouldn't put my name to their wretched little side project, so they took it out on my oldest and best friend.

At that point, I spoke to Dave Gibbons and said that, previously, I'd been quite prepared for this wretched film to come and go because they had at least taken my name off it. But in their treatment of Steve Moore, I feel that all bets are off, and I'm at liberty to say what I actually think about it.

It's a completely pointless idea, because *Watchmen*, at least in my mind, wasn't about a bunch of slightly dark superheroes in a slightly dark version of our modern world. It was about the storytelling techniques and the way that me and Dave were altering the range of what it was possible to do in comics; this new way that we'd stumbled upon of telling a comic book story.

The plot was more or less incidental. All of its elements were properly considered, but it's not the fact that *Watchmen* told a dark story about a few superheroes that makes it a book that is still read and remembered today. It's the fact that it was ingeniously told and made ingenious use of the comic strip medium.

From everything I've heard, the director belatedly realised that, no, he couldn't handle the *Black Freighter* narrative in the film, because that's an example of me doing something that can only be done in a comic. He also realised he couldn't include the back-up material. Apparently, they're releasing animations of *The Black Freighter* and *Under the Hood* separately. Now, I'm sure that's terribly clever, but I can't help think that me and Dave were able to make this as one coherent package twenty-five years ago, using eight sheets of folded paper and some ink. It was a completely thought through, coherent package in its most perfect realisable form.

Sure, I've heard it's great seeing Dave Gibbons's images reproduced on the big screen. "They're exactly the same as in the comic, but they're bigger, moving, and making noise!" Well, putting it cruelly, I guess it's good that there's a children's version for those who couldn't manage to follow a superhero comic from the 1980s.

It's the same with Will Eisner's *The Spirit*, surely one of the greatest comic strips of all time, which has been butchered and made into this ridiculous film by Frank Miller, where he's fallen back on similar visual techniques of *Sin City*, as if that's all he knows. He's produced a film about a character that doesn't look like the Spirit, doesn't occupy a world that's recognisable as Eisner's, has none of the charm of Eisner's story, and which seems to think the whole point is a story about a crimefighter who lives in a cemetery. The whole point of *The Spirit* was the way Eisner told the story in the comic book form.

So, when that business with Steve Moore happened, I cursed the film and pretty much everything to do with it. And I use the word "curse" in a very professional sense.

About a week later, I heard about the lawsuit between 20th Century Fox and Warner Brothers over the rights to make the film. On Christmas Eve, as a special present just to me, the judge awarded the case to Fox and now

Warners will have to give them a chunk of the money. Apparently, it will now have to do as well as *The Dark Knight* [the 2008 Batman film] for Warners just to break even on it.

And the ruling has also suddenly opened up the whole chain of ownership issue. Comic creators who had their work made into film or TV series may well bring lawsuits against the film makers and comic companies. And it serves them right. They've all been making money out of the work of people who weren't credited and who never got more than their page rate for creating these characters. Comic book films are based upon a theft. Hollywood may regret basing such a lucrative industry on such a shaky premise.

In a nutshell, that's how I feel about the *Watchmen* movie. I don't think any good will come of it. I wouldn't like to claim that my curse brought any of this about, but it gives one a warm glow to think my diabolical powers may have triumphed. [chuckles]

Q: What effect have drugs had on your writing?
A: I started smoking dope around the age of fifteen and acid around sixteen. Had a b-i-i-i-g year of taking acid a couple of times each week. I'd done about a hundred trips, and this was when acid was acid, let me tell you. This was 500 mics, 1000 mics a tab. I've never really taken acid since. I've confined myself to an enormous amount of hash, which I do 24/7. It doesn't seem to turn me into a shambling pothead, either. I use it to work, always have done. It gives me kind of an edge.

There was a physicist who was accepting the Nobel Prize for Physics some years ago—think it was for molecular biology. During his acceptance speech he thanked Mum, Dad, all the rest, but also said: "I feel that I should mention the enormous contribution that psilocybin has made to my research. I'd be sitting down there on molecules, watching the particles go by and understanding the way that they fitted together. And psilocybin gave me that ability." I've also heard another scientist comment that "caffeine science is very different from marijuana science."

So, yeah, I still take mushrooms. I haven't done so for a couple of years now, and always as part of a magic ritual these days. I don't take anything purely for entertainment's sake, which I think is perhaps my saving grace. We are certainly not the first culture to use drugs, but we may well be one of the first to have a drug problem. I think there is a place for drugs in society, but it's a shamanic space that we don't really have anymore.

Robert Graves noted that a lot of cultures' names for mushrooms are "snots" or "shits," things like that. He says it's like telling a child "kaka"—"poison," sort of dirty, because the mushroom is taboo, which is not the same as just being dirty. Taboo is, yes, profane, but it's also sacred. The mushrooms were sacred at one point, which meant you weren't supposed to eat them unless you were properly initiated in a tradition, you'd done your Eleusinian Mysteries or whatever.

And that's part of the problem. In our current society, the only context we have to take drugs in is a leisure context, which a lot of time is disastrous. Something I noticed when I was about sixteen was the difference between drawings inspired by LSD and drawings attempted while under the effects of LSD.

With a lot of those *Promethea* issues, especially the kabbalistic run, I was doing magical rituals that often—not always, but often—involved drugs, in order to put myself in those spaces so I could write about them. I think it was issue #23—the one that was the second sphere of the Kabbalah, the grey, sort of pearly place. I'd had Steve Moore up. We'd had this incredible magical experience. Then he went home. I was still sitting down here, buzzing with the mushrooms, and I suddenly thought, "Right, *Promethea*. I know exactly how I'm going to do this next issue that I'm gonna start tomorrow. I know that the series is going to last until issue #32, because 32 is a good number. This has just been revealed to me. I know that the last issue is going to be some kind of incredibly weird comic book that somehow unfolds into a marvelous psychedelic poster, and great, well that's the rest of *Promethea* sorted out, so I'll go to bed now. The next day, I laid out the entirety of issue #23 in four hours, every page. It just came in this incredible burst of energy. It then took me fifteen hours to write, lay out, dialogue, and type the entire issue. And then, two years later, I finally got around to issue #32 with the giant poster thing.

So, yeah, those are instances where I didn't try writing anything in the surge of the drug rush, but the next day I'd got all the information there. It's important to have a channel, I think. If I was just taking this stuff purely for entertainment, then I wouldn't have anything to do with that energy. And it is an energy, which I can direct. I can ground it in this huge variety of works that I'm doing at any one time.

It works great for me. I think I've probably been more creative—my output's certainly been higher—since I formally took up magic. And that was one of the big proving points of it. I'd said to people, "If I become less productive, or if the work turns to shit, then pull me out, because I might not know." But that hasn't happened, in fact generally quite the opposite.

Mushrooms are the only psychedelic drugs that I take, and I don't take them very often. But I would trust them. Once you've done them a few times, it's very easy to feel a sense of entity. You can feel that there is a characteristic in this level of consciousness, which almost seems . . . playful? Or aware, or sometimes a bit spooky. I know that is probably something which I am imposing, or that other people have imposed upon the experience, but you get the impression that they're probably called magic mushrooms for a reason. And given that these have been the shamanic drug of preference since Neolithic times, Paleolithic times, then we've got quite a good history of a relationship with mushrooms that goes back quite a long way, and they seem to treat us alright.

Q: Have you ever considered a work detailing your insights into drug use?
A: Well, probably not, because I actually tend to think of drugs as an implement and a tool, rather than a thing that is interesting in itself. I'm reminded of that wonderful Spacemen 3 song: "Taking Drugs to Make Music to Take Drugs To," which is a pretty good description of my working methods. I'm kind of taking drugs to write comics to take drugs to. Most of the psychedelia, I want it to be there on the page in the writing. I want my work to be acting like a drug as near as I can manage. I'd like to think that if you put the words in the right order with the pictures, you can create a psychedelic state, a fugue state.

With my performances, I have a dense monologue going on: complicated music at the same time as a film show, or fire breather, or ballet dancer, so that you're overloading the audience. It's a technique people have used since time immemorial. The Catholic Church has its stained glass window light show, incense, incantations, sonorous music, beautiful architecture—trying to push people into this peak aesthetic experience, which I think is very close to the psychedelic state, which is very close to the magical state.

One of the best letters from a fan I ever got—which I lost and wish that I could write back, so if she's reading this, get in touch!—was about what *Watchmen* had meant to her when she'd read it at thirteen. She said she was just coming to the conclusion that the world wasn't as straightforward and linear as she'd been told, when she'd discovered *Watchmen*.

She was with a load of girls playing softball, in New York in the late eighties. She'd been sent as an outfielder, where you don't get much to do, right at the edge of the park, near a little old guy on a bench watching them play. She glanced over at him and realised he was masturbating, watching all the thirteen-year-old girls playing softball. She was standing there thinking, "What!?!" when he looked up with a wretched expression and said, "Fuck off and leave me alone! Everybody's been here before me!" and at that moment the softball hit her on the back of the head.

And I thought . . . "Everybody's been here before me." It's like, "Everybody's been a lonely old man masturbating on a bench at a softball game. You've all been me—stop pretending that I'm outside the human circle." Something like that.

Q: Are you still using drugs in your work?

A: I haven't done any of the hardcore ritual stuff for some years now. I had one experience early on with my magic stuff where, just for a few seconds, I was a boy of about seventeen, and I was dying in a trench just outside Ypres. It was the small hours of the morning—that grey bit just before dawn when the birds are singing. I was lying on my left side up against the side of the trench because my right foot was infected with maggots. It didn't hurt, but it itched. Unbelievably. And there were other kids, teenagers, slumped up against the other side of the trench and some of them were asleep, I knew, and some of them weren't. And I'd never had sex with a woman in my life. The woman I had the closest relationship with emotionally was my sister—I don't really have a sister—who I was missing profoundly and wishing I could see her one more time.

Me and Melinda [Gebbie] were working together, both on drugs. She'd seen me lay back and close my eyes and noticed that my eye sockets were full of cobwebs and there was blood and worms in my hair. And she thought, "Eurgh, that's horrible. I wonder if I should wake him up and tell him? No, I don't want to impose my bad vision." At that point I sat up, said "Jesus Christ!" and burst into tears. I'm normally not terribly emotional, but I couldn't get myself under control for about three-quarters of an hour. I couldn't stop crying, because I'd just suddenly realised that the First World War had happened.

And my immediate feeling was, "Was that me? Was that a previous life I'd had, like Shirley MacLaine tells us?" And I thought, "No, I'm not convinced of that. The feeling that I have is more, 'Was everybody *everybody*?'" which again ties back to, "Everybody's sat here before me." Is there some huge commonality? Are we all the same person? Is this all God talking to himself?

Q: What was the reaction to *From Hell* in occult circles?

A: Foolishly, I'd gone to some kind of occult forum. I'm interested in the subject but not the scene. Some of those people creep me out. This guy came over and said, "I've psychically confirmed that the things you said in *From Hell* were what happened," and I said, "Well that's lovely, but I made it up."

I've had people ask me if the pentacle over London is real. Well, you know, those points are in those places, and you can draw lines through them to make this kind of wonky pentacle. But then, with a city that has a concentration of historical stuff like London, a small enough map and a thick enough magic marker, any three points are in a line. You know, you shouldn't get fixated on all the *DaVinci Code* stuff. It's easy to make meaningful patterns from a field of noise. It's one our greatest human talents that we can look at a Rorschach blot, and we can see something in it. But don't mistake that sort of tendency for genuine insight.

Q: The *Birth Caul* performance is your only autobiographical work. How did you decide on this subject?

A: David J, from Bauhaus and Love and Rockets, and Tim Perkins came over, and we did some magic mushrooms. We asked, "What should our next performance be about?" Which is one of the great uses for magic. You don't even have to think up the ideas yourself. And we then had an experience where for the whole evening, instead of talking about angels and demons and all that stuff that had been on the previous CD, we found ourselves talking about our childhoods—me, in particular, I was just spewing out all of this stuff. So, we thought, "Right. So this is about childhood." Then me Mum died and, going through her effects, we found the birth caul, which I've still got over there somewhere.

We were trying to set up the performance in Newcastle. They said, "Where do you want to put this event on?" And I said, "How about an old Infants' School?" They couldn't find one, but they did have a lovely old Victorian magistrate's building, which we loved as a venue, even if it hadn't got anything to do with our subject.

So, I wrote the whole thing, and we did the event. Then afterwards, I found out that it wasn't only sailors that used to prize the birth caul, it was lawyers as well. In fact, it's the origin of the barrister's wig. They used to wear a birth caul on their head to denote wisdom. On the first page of *David Copperfield*, his birth caul is advertised for sale, and it's bought by a solicitor. So, when we'd done the performance in the courtroom, it'd been perfect all the time.

[Back in our 2005 interview, we asked:]

Q: What advice would you give to someone starting off in magic?

A: Hrrrrrmm . . . alright. Fill your head with any old shit that you come across, and then rely upon developing a sense of discrimination, so that eventually you'll be able to sort out the stuff that is rubbish—which is a lot of it—from the stuff that makes some sort of sense to you.

Look at the lives of people like Aleister Crowley and Austin Spare. Read two or three biographies of these people. Especially Crowley. Opinions tend to vary. Ask yourself if you really think there is anything in all this. Ask yourself how you think it works.

I approach magic the same way that I approach writing. No one taught me how to do it. I just thought, "Let's take a look at this from outside, see if I can figure it out and come up with my own approach from there." Y'know magic is an art, so I approached it the same way I would any art.

I mean, for me, the whole turning point in my thinking about magic was when I realised that the only place this has to happen is inside your head. And that doesn't mean it isn't real. I think we have a problem in that we live in a materialist society. I don't mean, "Everybody's a bread-head man." I mean that we believe that the material world is the only one that exists. Despite the fact that believing requires *thinking*, and science can't actually explain how we think. It's the ghost in the machine, forever outside the province of science. You can't reproduce a thought in an empirical laboratory experiment, so you cannot properly talk about thought. Thought is a supernatural event, which we all experience every minute of the day.

The world of ideas is much more important than the material one. I mean, what's more important, the reality of a chair, or the *idea* of a chair? I'd say it looks like the physical world is actually predicated upon the intangible world of ideas and the mind. It looks like that's the more important territory. Okay, so let's treat it literally as a territory. There might be ways to explore it, ways since time immemorial that people have used to explore it. Drugs. Meditation. Some unpleasant ones like scourging and fasting, which never sound like much fun to me. Lots of ways that people have found over the years to get themselves deeper into this mental space.

There's also books written by people who have been there before you. Kabbalah could be seen as one of the maps of this imaginary posited space that you can explore with your mind, and which does appear to be inhabited. The Enochian system of John Dee is another map of an imaginary space, one that has some correspondence with the Kabbalah but seems to be a completely different universe.

And then the best way is experiment. Carefully. Realise that most magicians end up mad, or dead, or worse in some way. That doesn't mean that all of them *have* to. It means that most of them *do*. Ask yourself how much you really want to know. It sounds very good, doesn't it, conjuring demons, or stuff like that? It sounds kind of cool, a bit like *X-Files* and very romantic. Do you really want that? Make up your mind before you go in the door, because that's the thing about magic being something to do with language. You have to be very careful what you say. All words are magic words, and you can find them coming back to haunt you. And in my experience, magic always gives you exactly what you ask for.

In practical terms, I'd say my chosen methods, obviously, are drugs, and creative work itself. If it's drugs, it should be a drug that you're comfortable with, that's not addictive, and that won't send you mad. Something like psilocybin. In whatever dose you're comfortable with, and then something to focus your mind, a ritual. Make it up yourself, or borrow it from a book. Doesn't really matter, but frame your intention in a little ritual. Burn a certain sort of incense that you associate with the subject of your enquiry. Have a certain colour around that you can associate with it. This is where Kabbalah is quite useful, because it's a huge chart of correspondences, so you can theme your rituals with a nice book on Kabbalah.

And may I please stress that when I say the word "Kabbalah," it means something very, very different to when Guy Ritchie's ex-missus talks about it. You will notice I don't have any bits of fucking red string, and I just drink water out of the tap . . . It's good enough for me.

One of the books you're going to use the most is Aleister Crowley's 777, which has got tables. You don't have to read all the essays. You won't understand them, and he was slightly mad anyway. There are simple tables that tell you all you need to know about the Kabbalah. Get yourself a good tarot deck or some other divinatory tool—they're quite good as a way of getting into magic. I'd recommend the Thoth tarot deck. Other people prefer Waite. Whichever works best for you. And then try it out, play around with it, and you'll start to notice that it's changing the way you think. It's giving you a different language of symbols to work with. And having a different language is the same as having different consciousness. It's a linguistic phenomenon.

And the first time one of these things sits up and answers you, don't freak out. You're not going mad. They're not that scary, really. Respect them. Treat them as you would anybody. Don't go "Aaaaargh" when you see them, because that would offend anybody. Just treat them as you would any sort of imaginary entity from ancient Persia that you happen to find yourself talking to, and you'll be fine.

It doesn't matter if they are only some sort of externalized part of your own personality, as long as they give you accurate information. That is the key criterion. If they tell you all the stuff that they apparently tell David Icke, you should perhaps ask yourself whether this is a decent source of information.

If it seems to be morally and intellectually and emotionally true, then I'd say that, even if it is a hallucination, it's as good a source of information as any.

[And now back to 2009 again:]

Q: Okay, last question. What are your upcoming projects?

A: There's *Jerusalem*, the ongoing *League*, and there's *The Bumper Book of Magic*, which I'm writing with Steve Moore, and which is turning out marvelously. It's every different kind of grimoire all at once. A grimoire can be a history of magic, a book of practical magical instruction, theory, or even fiction if it has genuine occult knowledge in it. We're weaving these all together in the style of a glorious imaginary Victorian-to-1930s children's annual. There's a continuing text occult story that runs at intervals throughout the book and a series of one-page *Believe-It-Or-Not* style features called "Old Moore's Laws of the Great Enchanters" which tells the entire story of magic, something I don't think anyone's ever done before.

We found new information about Dr. John Dee, who we agree is the greatest magician of all time. In his Angel Language, he, or Edward Kelly [née Talbot], seemed to be influenced by Paracelsus, the father of modern medicine, who created the concept of the anesthetic and the idea that disease came from outside the body.

We've got a Kabbalah board game, in which the winner is the first to achieve enlightenment. As long as they don't make a big deal out of it.

There'll also be a set of "Moon Serpent" tarot cards, which I'm doing with José Villarrubia. Our criterion is that it has to be at least as good as Aleister Crowley's deck, or there's no point doing it. We're setting ourselves quite a high standard. They'll be included in the book and probably also made as a separate deck.

There's going to be a pop-up temple that Melinda will design for today's Magus on the move—a portable shrine. And a combination memory Renaissance theatre as well. There are rainy-day activity pages, suggesting practical experiments with magic. It will be beautifully illustrated by a whole range of wonderful artists, and we hope it's going to be a clear account of what magic is, how to use it, how not to use it. It's history, romance, colour, humour, and beauty. And occasional spookiness, but that's just life.

To my knowledge, it will be the first grimoire, created for mass public consumption rather than for occultists. We don't believe magic is about secrecy or hiding information. Hopefully, it will be a very transparent volume, where people can read it and make up their own minds about whether there's anything to it. We're being as fair and open as we can. It'll be a beautiful book.

It'll be a couple of years, but I'm in it for the long haul with all these projects. It will be worth the wait when they finally creep out into the daylight.

Index